I Dwell in Possibility

Of Chambers as the Cedars—
Impregnable of Eye—
And for an Everlasting Roof
The Gambrels of the Sky—

Of Visitors — the fairest—
For Occupation — This—
The Spreading wide my narrow Hands
To gather Paradise—

—Emily Dickinson

Gathering Paradise

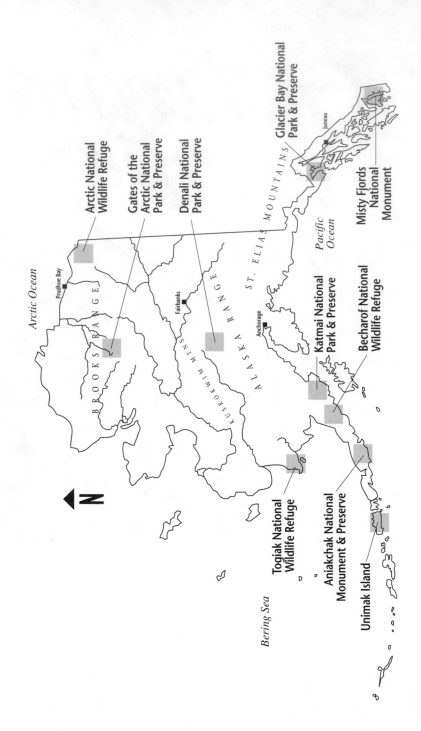

Gathering Paradise

Larry Rice

ALASKA WILDERNESS JOURNEYS

Fulcrum Publishing

Library of Congress Cataloging-in-Publication Data

Rice, Larry M., 1950–
    Gathering paradise : Alaska wilderness journeys / Larry M. Rice.
      p.   cm.
    Includes bibliographical references.
    ISBN 1-55591-057-2
    1. Alaska—Description and travel. 2. Wilderness areas—Alaska.
I. Title.
F910.5.R53   1990   89-29590
917.9804'5—dc20   CIP

Printed in the United States of America

10   9   8   7   6   5   4   3   2   1

Fulcrum Publishing
350 Indiana Street
Golden, CO 80401

To all those individuals and organizations who have striven to keep Alaska wild; and to *Ursus arctos*, the grizzly bear—the essence of Alaska's wilderness.

CONTENTS

FOREWORD

Come, dear reader. Find a quiet corner, a comfortable chair. Larry Rice is going to thrill you with ten Alaskas.

The dazzling item is that even when he has done this for you, there are still some other Alaskas to look forward to. It is indeed "The Great Land."

I have quoted many times Ella Higginson, writing in 1884: "I know not how the spell is wrought; nor have I ever met one who could put the miracle of its working into words. No writer has ever described Alaska; no one writer ever will, but each must do his share, according to the spell that the country casts upon him."

But in this true narrative Larry Rice gives us not only the physical descriptions, but also the sounds and sights and odors of all these places—birds, mammals, weather, winds, storms—plus his own delight in all of them.

Here you can struggle with the paddles, groan over the heavy packs, feel your almost frozen hands and feet. Real adventure you will find.

The rewards of all the misery? Here, vivid descriptions of every region visited, each in its own character—mountains, glaciers, volcanoes, perilous trekking through the unaltered natural world; sunrise, sunset, glorious blue skies, lowering fogs, flowers of every shade, on and on you will go with this eager explorer and his companions.

And of all the creatures encountered, who is the star of the show every time? Of course—the grizzly bear! Biologist Adolph Murie used to say that the ever-predictable thing about this actor was that he was unpredictable! And this is proven for us many times in this fascinating true story.

Read on; breathe deeply, and enjoy!

Margaret E. Murie
author of *Two in the Far North*
Moose, Wyoming

ACKNOWLEDGMENTS

I had absolutely no idea during my travels to Alaska that someday I would be distilling my experiences into a book. Thus, along the way, I have neglected to record the names of many people who have offered me assistance, information and sometimes a well-needed shower and a hot meal that didn't come out of a plastic bag. To all of you kind souls, wherever you are, my heartfelt thanks.

Some names, however, I do remember, and they belong in these acknowledgments. The following individuals gave me invaluable advice on their respective areas: David Manski and Clarence Summers of the National Park Service; John Sarvis, David Fisher, Lee Hotchkiss and Randall Wilk of the U.S. Fish and Wildlife Service; Ken Taylor of the Alaska Department of Fish and Game; and Jules V. Tileston of the Bureau of Land Management.

A work such as this would have been impossible without the services of bush pilots. Not only were these individuals a gold mine of information, in many cases they were our sole link with the outside world. I'd like to thank Tom Classen of Fairbanks, in particular—as good a pilot as there is.

A complex, lengthy chain of events led me to compile this manuscript. Two individuals were instrumental in encouraging my interest in the wilderness: my cousins, Ron and Bud Stackler. Ron came through in the clutch when I needed it, and Bud, by his example, let me know it was possible for a city kid to make a life in the conservation field.

I can hear my parents waiting to be mentioned, so: Mom, Dad, thank you for your loving support no matter what path I followed. You never once discouraged me in my chosen field of wildlife biology, even though the rest of my friends were becoming doctors, lawyers and entrepreneurs. Your encouragement of my other line of work—writing—has helped make the valleys less forbidding and the peaks more rewarding.

An author is an orphan without an editor and a publisher, and to this end I am indebted to Betsy Armstrong, Darby Junkin and Bob Baron of Fulcrum Publishing for their belief in this project from the very start, and for giving me the opportunity to tell my stories. Carmel Huestis deserves special thanks for her assistance during final editing. Appreciation is also extended to the folks at *Canoe, Backpacker* and *Alaska* magazines for finding room over the years for my articles, and keeping me busy at the writing craft.

Charlie Roger, Clyde Vicary and Mike Peyton deserve special mention for putting up with me for days on end in the bush. Next to the grizzly bear, they are some of the key players in the episodes I describe.

Finally, there's Judy Bradford, my wife, trip companion, best friend and ruthless, live-in editor. From the very beginning, Judy helped make journeying to Alaska a reality. I can honestly say that without her involvement and support this book would have never been launched. My mother keeps telling me how lucky I am to have a wife like Judy. You know, Mom, you're right.

Gathering Paradise

INTRODUCTION

ALASKA!

Just the name—Alyeska, the Great Land, to the Aleuts—conjures up visions of glacier-hung mountains, Arctic tundra, abundant fish and wildlife and boundless wilderness. No visitor can doubt the power of the Alaskan landscape to inspire. John Muir, the outspoken, turn-of-the-century conservationist, declared that "no other part of the earth known to man surpasses Alaska in imposing and beautiful scenery." Henry Gannett, chief geographer for the United States Geological Survey in 1899, wrote: "For one Yosemite of California, Alaska has hundreds." And Sigurd Olson, a legend among canoeists for his reflective essays on nature and the outdoor experience, referred to the Alaska backcountry's "outrageous magnificence." But perhaps it is the bumper stickers around Anchorage that say it best: "After you've seen Alaska, everything else looks like Texas."

I first felt the desire to visit Alaska as a boy growing up on the outskirts of Chicago, Illinois. I remember staring at a map of the soon-to-be state, musing over a big green block in its far northeastern corner. I believe it was called the Arctic Range at the time, a simple name for a place I knew nothing about. There were no roads leading there, no towns for a hundred miles. It was a wonderful blank spot between the mountains and the sea. For an eight-year-old boy who dreamed of being a big game hunter and explorer but had never so much as slept on the ground, this was the epitome of wild frontier. I had been born too late to travel with Peary or Lewis and Clark, but here at least was country where a man could still get "ate" by a griz or have wolves prowl around camp at night.

I had been out of college for four years when I finally made it to Alaska. The Arctic Range was still beyond me, so I settled on a two-week backpack trip to what was then called Mount McKinley National Park; with me was the woman who was to become my wife. What an extraordinary experience that was. I had seen a bit of wilderness by then—had slept under the stars more nights than I could remember, but nothing I had seen or read prepared me for the realities of Alaska. The landscape swallowed us up with an enormity of superlatives: everything was on the grandest scale. We crossed paths with grizzly bear, moose, caribou and Dall sheep. Mount McKinley—Denali—loomed over us, a pyramid of snow and ice. And though it was the middle of August, we saw no other people once we left the park road. Almost every year since that journey, and sometimes twice a year, I have made it back to the Great Land. Those wilderness journeys are what this book is about: ten stories of one man's affair with America's last great wilderness.

This book is not intended as a guide—there are already many of those around. However, when exploring a new area, whether by foot, skis, paddle or the pages of a book, it is important first to learn a little about the lay of the land. This is especially true of Alaska, a place mythical in proportions, so immense that its size and the architecture of its landscape are difficult to comprehend. Speaking from personal experience, first-time visitors to the forty-ninth state aren't the only ones who are overwhelmed. About traveling in Alaska someone once said, "everything really is bigger and better, and a summer's day is 23 hours long." Hyperbole, perhaps, yet there is some truth to those words:

- Alaska is one-fifth the size of the continental United States, over twice the size of Texas and bigger than France, Switzerland, Norway and Sweden combined. If one explored a thousand acres a day, it would take over a thousand years to see it all.
- Alaska's coastline is longer than that of *all* the lower forty-eight

states combined—33,000 miles—and is washed by the North Pacific Ocean, Bering Sea, Chukchi Sea, Beaufort Sea and Arctic Ocean.

- More than 365,000 miles of rivers run through Alaska, ranging from whitewater torrents to meandering flatwater streams. Ten of these rivers are longer than 300 miles, including North America's third largest river, the Yukon, which rises in Canada and then flows 1,979 miles to empty into the Bering Sea on Alaska's western coast.

- Alaska has more than *three million* lakes; 119 million acres of forest; 1,800 named islands, rocks and reefs; nineteen mountains higher than 14,000 feet (including the highest mountain in North America, 20,320-foot Mount McKinley); and more than 5,000 glaciers—one of which, the Malaspina, is larger than the state of Rhode Island.

- Alaska has fewer than 500,000 inhabitants. Seventy-five percent of the residents live in urban areas, leaving over 90 percent of the state uninhabited. If the people were spread throughout the state, each person would claim about 1.5 square miles, forty times more elbow room than the average for the rest of the United States.

Fascinating facts, these, but they only set the stage for more important issues. In Muir's and Gannett's day Alaska's remoteness protected its grandeur against the erosions of modern civilization, but as illustrated by recent events, this is no longer true. When the *Exxon Valdez* ran aground in Prince William Sound on March 24, 1989, more than ten million gallons of crude oil were spilled into pristine waters. The drifting oil slick has fouled the beaches and shorelines halfway down the Alaska Peninsula, a distance of nearly 1,200 miles. If this disaster had happened off Cape Cod, the entire eastern coast of the United States south to the Outer Banks of North Carolina would have been oiled.

The effect of the spill on wildlife has been devastating. Thousands of seabirds, sea otters and bald eagles died as a result of oil contamination. The extent of damage to the Gulf of Alaska fisheries remains unclear but is expected to be significant. Alaska public lands affected by this tragedy include some of the locales I discuss in this book: the fjords and bays of Katmai and Aniakchak National Parks, and Becharof, Alaska Peninsula and Kodiak National Wildlife refuges have all been slimed with *Exxon Valdez* crude.

Pain and suffering from the tanker's rupture have not been

restricted to wildlife. Capturing the bulk of the media's attention was the plight of hundreds of Alaska fishermen whose livelihoods depend on the rich waters of the Gulf of Alaska for their catch, but the spill created an emotional distress for those connected to the environment that goes much deeper than lifestyles or jobs. To me this was driven home during a telephone call I received from a friend living in Alaska, someone you will meet later in these pages. After the disaster he volunteered to work at a hastily assembled sea otter rescue center in Seward. Scores of oil-covered animals were coming in daily, pathetic cases suffering from shock and hypothermia. Despite the efforts of the clean-up crews, only a fraction of the otters survived. My friend was despondent, disgusted and angry, very angry. For the first time since he was a child, he cried. He wasn't alone.

The oil spill, and my involvement with this book, have caused me to ponder about the last time I heard some really uplifting environmental news coming out of Alaska. Unbelievably, it was a decade ago. In 1980 the Alaska National Interest Lands Conservation Act was signed into law by Jimmy Carter in the closing days of his presidency. With a single stroke of the pen, approximately 104 million acres of Alaska's wilderness were added to our national parks, forests, wildlife refuges, and the Wild and Scenic Rivers System. Combined with previously set aside federal and state land, this brought the total protected land in Alaska to nearly 160 million acres, an area larger than the states of California, Indiana and Pennsylvania combined. By classifying 56 million acres of these lands as wilderness, the law tripled the size of the National Wilderness Preservation System.

Since passage of that bill, conservationists in Alaska have had little to cheer about. Alaska has become an ecologically embattled land. More parklands and refuges and wild and scenic rivers should have been created, but the last decade has been witness to a continual chipping away of protected areas by the federal government. A case in point is the repeated effort to introduce oil exploration and drilling in the North Slope of the Brooks Range within the Arctic National Wildlife Refuge, one of the most significant natural ecosystems remaining in the world—that blank spot between the mountains and the sea on my childhood map. What happens in the Arctic Refuge in the next few years is critical, but this is by no means the only brush fire to fight in Alaska. Other problems include offshore drilling in Bristol Bay, old-growth forest clearcutting in southeast Alaska, giant molybdenum mines in Misty

Fjords, and countless other conflicts with mineral, coal and oil and gas interests over public lands and waters.

Those who cherish Alaska's wilderness, its wildlife, its "outrageous magnificence," are the front line for its defense. But "how much wilderness?" is a question facing Alaskans, Americans and human society worldwide. Consider that in arctic latitudes more than 100 square miles are needed to sustain a single grizzly bear. Unless we want grizzly bears to go the way of their brethren in the lower forty-eight states, we need to keep what wilderness we have and ensure that other critical habitat is preserved. Wilderness and grizzly bears are as much American natural resources as oil and coal.

As naturalist-biologist Adolph Murie said in *Mammals of McKinley Park*, published in 1944, "We come to Alaska to watch; to catch a glimpse of the primeval. We come close to the tundra flowers, the lichens, and the animal life. Each of us will take some inspiration home: a touch of the tundra will enter our lives and deep inside make of us all poets and kindred spirits."[1]

Alaska is a long way from where most Americans live, but it touches us all. Its wilderness reminds us of what our entire continent used to be. Every visit to Alaska's backcountry presents fresh challenges and new horizons. They are what drew me there initially, and they are why I continue to return.

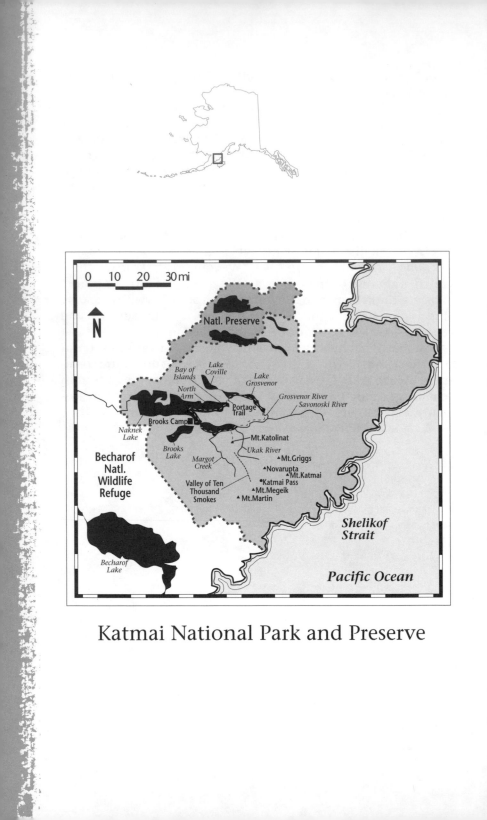

Katmai National Park and Preserve

Among the Kings of Katmai

"I HOPE YOU LIKE BEARS," the park service ranger said as he filled out our backcountry use permit. "You might see quite a few of them where you're going."

I do like grizzly bears—in fact, they're one of the reasons I wanted to return to Alaska after my first trip to the state. For me, no other land mammal in North America so embodies the essence of wilderness. Without them, the Alaska backcountry wouldn't have the same excitement or appeal, an edge that demands one's senses be razor sharp. While listening to the ranger's precautionary briefing, however, a small part of me questioned the wisdom of what we were about to do.

The ranger, a tall, blonde-haired man not much older than I, explained that the "park" portion of Katmai National Park and Preserve where we were headed harbors the largest population of unhunted brown bears in the world. "The bears are down from the mountains now and are congregated around the salmon-spawning streams that enter the lakes, but you might run into them about anywhere. Be careful on shore and keep a clean camp. Matter of fact, just this year one group had their folding kayak demolished—

clawed and slashed when they left it to go on a hike. Griz likes batting around those rubber hulls. Hiking is tough around the lakes. You don't want to walk back."

As he continued to jot down our names, home addresses, persons to notify in case of emergency and other bits of information, I glanced at Judy Bradford, my paddling partner for the next sixteen days. Her blue eyes showed apprehension, but on her face was a thin smile. I smiled back. No words were necessary, each of us knew what the other was thinking. During our three-year relationship we had been on a number of backpacking and canoeing trips together, some quite challenging, but this was different: for us, this was serious stuff.

I signed the permit, acknowledging that I had received and understood the warnings about hypothermia, river crossings and bears. Uncomfortably warm from the crackling wood stove (I was dressed for the cool and rainy temperatures outside), I was turning to leave when the ranger motioned us toward a large topographic park map on the wall. "One more thing. If you do run into trouble, don't expect any help for quite some time. Katmai is an awfully big place—over four million acres. Unfortunately, we don't get out on patrol that often, and it's unlikely you'll see anyone else where you're headed." He noted that we were only the fifth party this year undertaking the lake-river circuit, and since it was mid-August, we'd probably be the last.

We thanked him for his advice. I was embarrassed at how much I was sweating and wanted nothing more than to gulp in the brisk, sweet air outside and get our gear sorted.

A few steps brought us to the gravel- and pumice-lined shores of Naknek Lake. At the water's edge were two neatly packed green duffel bags containing our Klepper folding kayak and two backpacks bulging with food, our tent and other supplies necessary for the weeks ahead. There were so many things to do to get ready, I didn't know where to start. "Don't think of bears," I told myself. "Don't think of winds. There'll be plenty of time for that later when we're trying to sleep."

An hour earlier we had arrived at Katmai from King Salmon, a small community of mostly federal and state government employees located at the northern end of the Alaska Peninsula, about 300 air miles southwest of Anchorage. King Salmon borders the western boundary of the national park, but to reach Katmai's headquarters we and five other passengers boarded an amphibious Grumman Goose airplane for the thirty-five-mile flight. The 1937-vintage, twin-engine workhorse looked ready for retirement, but the young pilot, who wasn't even born when the plane was built, told me he flew it daily to Katmai during the summer months. An approved landing area for floatplanes near the park's summer headquarters provides the only convenient access to Katmai's interior.

Perhaps because of the rain, everyone aboard our flight had quickly disappeared into the rustic lodge, cabins and walk-in campground near the ranger station. Called Brooks Camp (it used to be a fishing camp), this complex of park buildings and visitor accommodations is the only human habitation in the national park except for a couple of small, privately owned lodges. From conversations with our fellow travelers, we learned that they would all be staying in Katmai for only three or four days and were primarily interested in fishing the nearby Brooks River for world-record rainbow trout or taking a twenty-three-mile-long van tour along the only road in the park. We weren't interested in fishing, but if we had the time we certainly would have enjoyed following the road to the Valley of Ten Thousand Smokes.

In June 1912, a cataclysmic volcanic eruption ten times more powerful than the 1980 blast of Mount Saint Helens quickly changed much of the Katmai area into a wasteland. Within minutes more than forty square miles of lush green land were buried under volcanic deposits as much as 700 feet deep. All living things in the scorched zone were destroyed. For several days ash, pumice and gas spewed forth, and a haze darkened the sky over most of the northern hemisphere. At nearby Kodiak, a person could not see a lantern held at arm's length. But out of the devastation came exquisite beauty: a lunar-like valley containing countless hissing steam vents, or fumaroles. Katmai's valley was considered even more astonishing than the geyser fields of Yellowstone, which at the time were considered to be dying.

The Katmai region remained deserted until 1915, when the National Geographic Society began a series of explorations there. The first to arrive were greeted with a never-before-seen sight. According to one of these early observers, within the ash-filled valley were "literally, tens of thousands of smokes curling up from its fissured floor." Dr. Robert Griggs and his associate, Lucius Folsom, named the place "The Valley of Ten Thousand Smokes."

Griggs and his colleagues were so impressed with the steaming valley that upon their return to Washington, D.C., they urged Congress to protect this geological wonderland in the shadow of the Aleutian Range. Their lobbying paid off. In 1918 the immediate area around the Valley of Ten Thousand Smokes was proclaimed a national monument. Later, as Katmai's other natural assets, primarily its diversity of habitats and wildlife populations, became known, the monument was reclassified as a national park and preserve and its boundaries were extended four times. Ironically, the early geologists who had predicted that Yellowstone's geysers would vanish and Katmai's would take their place in importance were mistaken. As it turned out, Katmai's columns of "smokes" have cooled while Yellowstone's remain active.

Backpacking in the Valley of Ten Thousand Smokes would be sensational. Although the smokes have died out, the valley is almost as desolate and forbidding as when it was first discovered. The volcanic desert of multihued ash has congealed into gorges, fluted cliffs and grotesquely shaped buttresses. Rivers plummeting down from the Aleutian Range to the coastal lowlands of Bristol Bay have eroded deep channels through the volcanic debris. The valley would be in stark contrast to the forests and grasslands we would find elsewhere in the park, but a trip there would have to wait. We had our own itinerary to follow, a trip by boat we had been planning for nearly a year.

The first order of business was putting together our touring kayak, a task we had practiced only a few times before. Except for short day outings on the backwater lakes of the Illinois River, where I manage a 6,000-acre fish and wildlife area for the Illinois Department of Conservation, we had not spent much time paddling the German-made Klepper. We had purchased it the previous winter specifically for this and future trips to Alaska. The disassembled boat and break-down kayak paddles fit into two duffel bags and are accepted by commercial and charter airlines as regular baggage, thus permitting us to reach normally inaccessible rivers, lakes and coastlines.

As we followed the German-language directions (which neither of us could understand, but there were pictures), the boat slowly materialized out of a bewildering assortment of ribs, rods, girders and a folding skin. Manufactured in West Germany since 1907, the Klepper folding kayak consists of a canvas-decked and rubber-hulled superstructure supported by a wooden skeleton frame. Beamy, rugged and extremely seaworthy (inflatable air chambers running the length of the boat make it virtually unsinkable), the Klepper has proven itself on expeditions worldwide, and people have even sailed it solo across the Atlantic Ocean and paddled it around Cape Horn.

While much easier to transport than a rigid canoe or kayak, the Klepper does have its faults. For one thing, it can be tough to pack. In trial sessions at home we had carefully planned exactly where everything would go, but it took an hour of pushing, shoving and rearranging to get the mountain of gear stowed. Finally, with everything crammed under the blue canvas deck (except for the two empty backpacks, which we lashed atop the stern), we positioned the boat near the water and prepared to take off.

With some difficulty, Judy slipped into the bow seat. "Good thing I'm not any taller," she grunted. Her compact, five-foot-three-inch frame was solidly wedged in between foam ground pads and waterproof gear bags. My half of the boat was equally jammed; at six-foot-two I wasn't sure how to squeeze my long legs inside.

I was contemplating what to do next when I heard voices behind us. Only then did I realize that while we were busily occupied in packing, a small crowd of people—tourists, rangers, the lodge kitchen staff—had formed on the porch of the ranger station and were enjoying watching us more than the stunning scenery. As any cocky twenty-seven-year-old would have done, I tried to pretend I knew precisely what I was doing. Those gawkers didn't need to know that this was our Klepper's maiden wilderness voyage.

"Okay, Judy, we're ready," I said softly, so no one could hear. "Brace yourself, I'm going to get in." I plopped into the kayak, wormed myself into the stern seat, tightened the sprayskirt around my waist, and found the rudder pedals with my feet. I felt as if I was sitting in the cockpit of a grossly overloaded, antique bi-plane. Muscle power was our only engine, and we stuck the paddle blades into the sand to shove off.

Umph!

"Oh Geez," Judy hissed. "We're stuck."

"Can't be," I said through clenched teeth. "We're in four inches of water. Push harder."

Ugh! The paddles bent; the boat remained where it was.

With a sigh of exasperation, I was about to unsnap the sprayskirt and extricate myself when I heard someone say, "Stay put, I'll push you off." A powerful heave broke us free of land, and we skimmed across the clear green water.

"Thanks," I mumbled, a bit ungraciously.

The ranger who had written our permit was standing at the water's edge trying to conceal a grin.

Under a steady drizzle and a freshening wind, we dipped the paddles into Naknek Lake and headed east. Ahead lay the wilder-

Larry Rice ready to launch the kayak on Naknek Lake. Mount Katolinat is in the background.

ness of Katmai National Park and the realm of the brown bear. After we had paddled awhile, I checked our bearings against the map. Our intended route would take us into the heart of the Katmai backcountry, a region of rivers, streams, marshes, ponds and elongated lakes formed in valleys left by retreating glacial ice. Many trips are possible here, but we had settled on paddling a ninety-mile loop through a chain of mountain-ringed lakes and rivers. Starting at the ranger station, we planned to follow a zig-zag course across Naknek Lake to reach the Bay of Islands on Naknek's North Arm. From there we would portage over to Grosvenor Lake, follow the Grosvenor River to the Savonoski River, and eventually end up on Naknek Lake's Iliuk Arm, which we would follow back to the park headquarters. Our loose schedule allowed ample time for side trips, even a three-day climb to a mile-high summit where alpine tundra and loose scree replace the subarctic coniferous forest below.

All our goals looked so obtainable while studying maps at home. Now that we were actually here, however, with bear warnings, a storm brewing behind us and waves building far out on the lake, I wasn't so sure we were ready for the test. It wasn't that I was a rookie at this game. After all, I had traveled through a fair share of wilderness areas since entering college nine or ten years before. I'd taken lengthy canoe trips in the Okefenokee Swamp and the

Everglades, several week-long backpacking trips in the mountains of Wyoming and Arizona, whitewater boating excursions to Wisconsin and North Carolina, and even spent six weeks studying wildlife in Africa, but compared to where we were now, those areas were tame.

Or *seemed* tame: memories under stress can play strange tricks. I slowed my breathing and began to concentrate on the country at hand. I laughed at how I was blowing Katmai's dangers, real and otherwise, out of proportion. A few bears? I'd seen grizzlies before. Windy as hell? Couldn't be any windier than that Oregon coast storm I was in. Rough water? I couldn't remember how many times I had been trashed on the Chattooga River of *Deliverance* fame. When I noticed that the sky was indeed growing more ominous, I remembered something a Vietnam vet friend of mine used to say when things got heavy: "Don't mean nothing."

"What was that?" Judy asked, turning around.

"Oh, nothing. Just thinking out loud is all."

Judy's presence acted as an anchor. I felt a tremendous warmth for my partner, paddling steadily up in the bow. She helped set the tone of our journey through her eagerness and quiet, steadfast strength. I sometimes had difficulty expressing my feelings, but there were many things I loved about her that I rarely put into words. Her honesty, integrity and intelligence were always unwavering, but equally as endearing were her spirit and willingness to march off into the backcountry, provided she could get the time off from work. I'm sure there are many outdoorsy women who would enjoy spending a couple of weeks kayaking in bear country. Until meeting Judy, however, I never was involved with one. The same age as I, she hadn't made any wilderness trips until we met, though she always thought she would enjoy them. Judy had learned quickly how to handle herself in the outdoors. So far we had made a good team on all our trips together, whether canoeing or backpacking. As we traveled deeper into Katmai, I knew that this, our first kayak trip, would follow that trend.

Only four miles away, beyond a narrow, two-pronged glacial moraine that divides Naknek Lake from the Iliuk Arm, was our first day's objective. While we were still in the lee of several low mountains, the lake was calm, and paddling was deceptively easy. Tomato-red sockeye salmon, the two-foot-long males resplendent in breeding colors, jumped out of the water ahead. Bald eagles, their white heads turning from side to side, watched the proceedings cautiously from nearby birch trees and stunted white spruce. We were interrupting their dinner, and we were hungry for our own, so we hurried by.

Nearing the moraine, we began to lose the protection afforded by the mountains. The wind swirled over the water and waves curled under the boat. I tightened the cinch strap on my sou'wester rain hat and made sure that my life jacket was fully zipped. From calm to chaos in minutes—Katmai is a land of extremes, even by Alaskan standards.

Katmai can be a violent place, shaped and molded as it was by volcanoes and ice. The Aleutian Range—the backbone of the peninsula and part of the "Ring of Fire" along the Pacific Rim— bisects the park. Within Katmai are a half-dozen volcanic peaks higher than 7,000 feet. Some of these emit smoke and steam; all are adorned with multilobed, snowy glaciers. South of the range is a narrow coastal strip along Shelikof Strait. This 100-mile-long zone contains wave-battered headlands, offshore islands and deep fjords. It is unspoiled and rarely visited. On the north side of the rugged mountains is the vast watery system toward which we were headed. Naknek Lake, the largest of Katmai's lakes, drains through the Naknek River into salmon-rich Bristol Bay, an arm of the Bering Sea.

Katmai's weather is as unstable as are the volcanoes in the Aleutian chain. The lowlands are often covered with rain-laden clouds and low, blinding fog, especially in August, the wettest month. According to park records, the sky over Katmai in summer is clear only about 20 percent of the time. "Perfect" weather—no wind, no rain—can be expected only irregularly. Battering winds and gusty rainstorms, we were told, can appear suddenly, and presented the greatest danger to us as lake boaters.

When we reached the half-mile-wide gap separating Naknek Lake from the Iliuk Arm, we tried to find shelter, but were met by a strong southwesterly wind that drove us on. Unaccustomed to using our boat in inclement conditions, we wished we hadn't been so eager to leave the headquarters campground. The Klepper was being hit squarely by a cross-chop. Swells hammered our chests and foamed over the covered deck. Our only option was to continue paddling and look for a protected cove.

A wave hit me broadside in the face; ice-cold water trickled down my neck. I windmilled methodically with my double-bladed paddle, a repetitive movement that left me free to reminisce.

After Judy and I had made a successful two-week backpack trip to Denali National Park, I had imagined myself an Alaskan veteran. During that trip we hiked among the spectacular mountains and observed many species of wildlife—including grizzlies, Dall sheep, moose and caribou, several of which I'd never seen before. However, as wild as Denali was, as heavy as our packs felt on some steep mountain climbs, we were never more than a day or two's march from the gravel road where bright yellow shuttle buses ran every hour back to the park headquarters. That proximity to motorized locomotion was the escape hatch our journey to Katmai didn't have. An impulsive thought came to me as I gazed over the wind-tossed lake whose forty-five-degree temperature could immobilize even the strongest swimmer in minutes: As far as traveling through the Alaskan wilderness was concerned, I had a lot to learn, and this trip was bound to teach me.

A shout from Judy snapped me out of my reverie. She was pointing to a spot of land off the bow. It wasn't much, but the tiny hook-shaped inlet could provide the shelter we needed. Stiff, creaky and wet, we were grateful to step onto firm land—until we noticed a twin set of long-clawed prints in the sand. "Griz tracks," I said in a hushed voice, afraid the animal might hear. Judging from their crisp edges, the tracks had been made not long before our arrival. They merged into a deeply rutted path that ran in and out of the woods. We had been so preoccupied with paddling that we had given little thought to wildlife, but now a slight chill ran down my back and my eyes darted nervously from beach to forest. The unseen presence of the Alaska brown bear had a powerful effect on us.

"Well, we might as well get used to them," I said as we examined the grizzly spoor. My size-twelve rubber boot fit inside the largest of the paw impressions with inches to spare. "We're probably going to see tracks wherever we land."

"I guess," Judy replied. "But it's still scary."

We pitched the tent atop a spongy layer of green moss and grass within a thicket of drunkenly leaning spruce. Although the woods were quiet and we were tired, we didn't sleep easily that night.

Judy's Journal
9 p.m.

Lying in the tent listening to the rain and for bears. Lar's wet sleeping bag (one of the "waterproof" storage bags leaked) is against my back. Everything is damp. I feel a little hyper. We've had a draining day with travel and all. Paddling was not too bad, but the wind seemed to keep changing directions and strength. The waves were pretty high . . . still, we should expect much rougher. It's light outside, making it hard to sleep. Anyway, I would like to stay up a while longer. As I said, listening for bears. . . .

I too was listening for bears. I recalled another restless night in another national park. On the first day of my first backpacking trip in Yellowstone National Park, I crested a knoll and spotted a herd of elk grazing peacefully in a small meadow. Some of the calves dozed in the warm late afternoon sun; others were tugging at their mothers' teats. I dropped my pack and watched unnoticed from behind the fringe of lodgepole pines. Suddenly the adult elk stiffened, heads turned toward the meadow's far end. Following their stares, I saw a golden grizzly weaving through the dry grass. The bear saw the elk and quickened its shuffling pace. The cows dashed off as the bear broke into their midst. Calves old enough to run on tottering legs kept at their mothers' sides. Others remained hidden in the grass, relying on their immobility to escape discovery. The grizzly's acute nose wasn't fooled. Zigzagging across the meadow, it flushed a panicked calf from its hiding place. I watched as the bear gave chase. In a series of lightning-quick bounds, the grizzly caught the young elk and killed it instantly with a blow to the head. A few of the cows drifted back and stood to the side of the bear. One of them in particular, probably the calf's mother, refused to leave but was powerless to intervene.

It was the witching hour. I was too scared to move ahead and unwilling to turn back. I spent the night in a state of nervousness, excitement and fear. Maybe Walt Whitman never saw a grizzly bear, but something he wrote more than a century ago expressed exactly how I felt as I lay there in my sleeping bag under the stars: "Seems as if something unknown were possibly lurking in those bushes, or solitary places. Nay, it is quite certain there is—some vital unseen presence."[1] For the first time I was in grizzly country, and that "unseen presence" was a flesh-and-blood *griz* straddling a dead elk calf a few hundred yards from my camp. That night the bear instilled in me an animal alertness I didn't know I had.

There were other grizzly sightings that Yellowstone trip, six in all. Gradually, with each encounter, my dry-mouthed fear subsided. I became a confirmed bear watcher, relishing the opportunity to draw upon my savage ancestry, to refine the simple but lost instinct of looking around. Wild places without grizzlies offer their own rewards, but my love for the bear, for the essence of wilderness it represents, was something that excited me in much the same way that others are excited by lofty mountains or raging rivers.

The night eventually turned dark and gray. Sunrise, if one could call it that, was even more bleak. A low ceiling had settled over the lake country in the early hours, bringing with it a monotonous drizzle and gusty winds. We were shielded for the moment, but if we left the cove we wouldn't be for long. Sweeping across Naknek Lake were the same rollers we had dueled with yesterday. It was a day to sit tight—read books, talk, go for short walks—but we didn't know that then. We thought strong winds and storms were to be expected almost continuously on the Alaska Peninsula. To complete this trip, we figured we'd have to paddle with or without the weather's cooperation.

Seaworthy though it was, the Klepper took a beating on the open water. The rising waves hit us abeam, ahead and astern, sending our seventeen-foot boat on a wild roller-coaster ride with no end in sight. Doused by spray, water trickled down our necks and into our laps. The sprayskirt helped, but only so much; three-foot breakers always managed to leave some water behind. The sloshing under the deck, plus the fact that my seat was immersed in numbing water, made it clear that several gallons of unwanted ballast had joined our already considerable load.

For five nonstop hours we paddled hard, unable to appreciate the lake's attractions as we inched toward a distant headland. Only by watching the slowly passing shoreline could we see that we were making any progress at all. We finally called it quits only five miles from our previous camp. Spotting a slight shelter, we raced toward land before the next wave came tumbling down. Wet, stiff and bedraggled, neither of us wanted to admit that if this was typical Katmai weather we might not accomplish our trip's goal.

While unloading the boat, we took stock of the situation. The wool and synthetic clothing we were wearing was soaked through; our high-tech rainsuits had failed to do their job. Our own body heat would dry our clothes, but a few bags of gorp (nuts, sunflower seeds, raisins and M&Ms) were beyond reclamation; inside the plastic bags was an inedible pulp. Worse, Judy's binoculars had been dunked and were fogged inside and out.

"Don't mean nothing," I said, squeezing the water out of my shirt.

"Could be worse," Judy agreed, draining out her rubber boots.

We set up our tent and started the gas stove. With spare dry clothes on and hot drinks in our bellies, even the wind-whipped rain couldn't dampen our spirits. We had shelter and plenty to eat, and were dry and warm. Only a gnawing question remained about what tomorrow's weather would bring.

Judy's Journal
9 p.m.

Again, we took in quite a bit of water today—the lake was rough. Things got wetter than we anticipated. I was scared at first, but after a while got used to the big swells and finally enjoyed them. We're camped in a grassy area above the beach. Signs of bear and moose abound. Lots of birds. Wish I could see them better, but my binocs (which were around my neck) got wet when some waves hit me in the face. I feel edgy tonight and would love to talk, but I think Lar is already asleep. He's been really quiet on this trip so far, which is not like him; maybe he feels some pressure. I don't think we said over twenty words today. . . .

I was dreaming of being tossed around like a bottle in the ocean when a nudge and Judy's voice broke the spell. "Larry, wake up! Look outside." Clearing my head of cobwebs took a second, but when I rolled over and peered outside the tent, I instantly sobered up. In the twilight I could discern some hulking brown shapes moving in and out of the mist about a hundred yards away.

"Bears?" I asked.

"Yeah. I spotted them a moment ago. They seem to be coming closer."

"How many?"

"Three, I think—a mother grizzly and two small cubs."

Sure enough, the animals were getting larger. If they continued on their present course down the narrow gravel beach, in a few minutes they would be directly in front of our camp. They didn't seem to be aware of us yet, but we didn't want to be trapped inside the tent when they realized we were there. We slipped out of our sleeping bags, threw on our clothes and quietly crawled outside. The spruce and poplar were too small and spindly to climb, so we got the boat ready in case we had to escape to the lake.

We need not have hurried. The bears were having too much fun where they were to notice us. The pint-sized cubs seemed to relish rough-housing in the shallow water, splashing and dunking each other like unsupervised children at the neighborhood pool. One of the honey-colored twins climbed onto his sibling's head and dunked him. He, in turn, yelped when his other half bit him on the ear. Not content to sit on the sidelines and referee, their ever-watchful, quarter-ton mother entered the foray. Towering over her offspring, she gently rapped them with her flapjack paws—the same paws that can bend a bar of steel.

Mesmerized by the performance, I held my breath as the big sow plodded dripping out of the lake. With a mighty shake of shaggy fur, she sent spray flying, then, looking back at her cubs, belched a low growl indicating playtime was over. Obediently, they scampered after her on wobbly, unsure legs. We were relieved when they started off in the other direction. I was finally able to put down the paddle in my hand and loosen my grip on the boat.

During breakfast we discussed the bear episode. Although we had several close contacts with grizzlies in Denali's backcountry, and I had seen ten or more grizzlies on backpacking trips in Yellowstone National Park, every new bear observation was unique and thrilling. With no weapons at our disposal—firearms are not allowed in Katmai National Park—we were virtually defenseless against a bear attack. In some strange way our impotence only added to the mystique of traveling through grizzly country. Having a kayak at our disposal was handy and somewhat reassuring, but the bears' speed—they have been clocked at forty miles per hour—would not always leave time to get the boat into the water.

Before we finished breakfast, the weather changed abruptly. The sky was still overcast, but the wind and rain ceased. We packed the boat without delay, concerned that this lull might not last. Our destination was the Bay of Islands, about twelve miles away. We wanted to spend a few days exploring this archipelago of forested outcroppings, considered by some to be the most enchanting area in the Katmai lake system.

By mid-morning the dreary clouds had lifted, giving us our first glimpse of the Aleutian Range. The brilliant sun and clarity of the sky made everything intense. Distant, snow-capped peaks seemed to float before our eyes. The lake became glass-calm, the mountains mirrored on its surface. Leaning overboard, I stared into the clear turquoise waters. Without the glare I was able to peer into another world. Smooth rocks, big and small, littered the bottom. Passing salmon darted like quicksilver thirty feet down. I raised my head and felt dizzy. These lakes were as clear as gin and equally intoxicating.

Above and on the water was an assortment of birds delighting in the resurgence of sun as much as we were. Three bald eagles soared overhead, their white heads indicating they were all mature birds. A pair of loons uttered their haunting cry in between dives for fish. Flocks of ducks—scaups, goldeneyes and mergansers—bobbed like black and white corks a few hundred yards offshore. In a few months these waterfowl would be gone: Katmai's lakes start to freeze in November and don't begin to thaw until late April.

Paddling at a steady two-to-three-knot clip, we soon glided past an unnamed point of land that jabs into the main body of Naknek Lake. From here to the Bay of Islands we would be paddling east along the slopes of Mount La Gorce, a 3,183-foot summit named in 1919 for a member of a National Geographic Society expedition to Katmai. Even if a south wind did develop now, we would be protected by this tundra-covered ridge.

We approached the first group of islands about noon. Stopping for lunch on a tiny islet, we were surprised to find others had been here before. The big cloven tracks of a moose and the much smaller, dog-like prints of wolves were clearly etched in the wet sand. It was possible the wolves were stalking the moose, but since the trail led into a jumble of rocks the outcome remained a mystery.

The further we penetrated into the Bay of Islands, the more we liked it. The peaceful, enclosed waters were a welcome respite from the wide-bodied Naknek Lake. Furthermore, good campsites were common on many of the islands that dot the bay. Although bears as a rule are less likely to be encountered offshore, we did discover recent sign almost everywhere we stopped. There was hardly a moment while on land when we could really let down our guard.

For three days we paddled into the bay's labyrinth of inlets and lagoons, exploring hidden passages in our search for wildlife. Bald eagles, gulls, grebes, ducks and swans took off each time we rounded a new bend, and always serenading us was the maniacal laughter of common loons. Most memorable, though, was a pair of curious river otters who repeatedly dove and resurfaced around our boat one afternoon. When satisfied that we were too big to eat and too clumsy to play with, they departed with their peculiar sea-snake swimming motion, chirping excitedly to each other as they continued their rounds.

The abundance of waterbirds was evidence that Katmai's waters are rich in fish. Rainbow trout, lake trout, Dolly Varden, grayling, arctic char, whitefish, northern pike, and several species of salmon inhabit Katmai's lakes and streams. The sockeye salmon form an especially important link in the food chain. The salmon die en masse after spawning in August through October, providing a readily accessible food source for bears, eagles, otters, gulls and other fish-eaters. During this period the grizzlies concentrate in abnormally high numbers around a few select spawning streams, putting on jelly rolls of fat to fuel their bodies during their long winter sleep.

Because we already had adequate staples—about two pounds of food per person per day—and because bears are attracted to anything with a fishy smell, we had decided beforehand not to fish except in an emergency. Besides, I seriously doubted that I could catch anything with the spool of line—no rod or reel—and two general purpose lures that I had brought along.

The only thing that marred the otherwise halcyon days in the Bay of Islands was the arrival of bugs. Whenever the wind died down to less than a slight breeze, swarms of humming mosquitoes and flies converged over our heads. Mosquitoes I could handle— they were big, slow and easy to kill. However, the whitesox—a white-legged blackfly whose bite I consider far more unpleasant than the mosquito's sting—nearly drove me crazy. Persistent pests, their sole mission in life is to crawl over warmblooded beings. Their bite is quite painless, as it injects both an anesthetic and an anticoagulant. However, an hour or so later the affected area starts itching and oozing blood. The repellent that we smothered ourselves with didn't deter them in the least. Even a complete covering of clothes (and headnets when things really got bad) didn't thwart their probing attacks. For some reason, the whitesox preferred tall swarthy men to short fair women. Judy was annoyed by the flies, but rarely bitten. I was both annoyed and bitten. Despite my best defenses, a few always managed to sneak behind my ears and under my collars and cuffs. The welts they left behind festered for days.

We would have liked to stay in the Bay of Islands longer, despite the bugs, but our schedule dictated that we leave for our next destination to the north.

"We'll be across with all our stuff in two hours," I promised Judy, as we beached the kayak. It was early morning and we were at a neck of land that separates the Bay of Islands from Lake Grosvenor. "According to the map, the portage is only a mile long." She merely nodded her head as if she'd heard that line before.

Like most trails in Katmai, this one was originally made by generations of lumbering bears. The most recent tracks in the muck belonged to a moose and a grizzly with cubs. Carrying grossly overloaded backpacks on the first leg, we slowly picked our way through the poorly drained muskeg and thickets of alder and willow. Only then did we return for the kayak—we were saving the worst for last. The brochure lists the Klepper Aerius II at eighty pounds, but with rudder, sprayskirt, paddles and tie-downs, it probably weighs closer to 110. Our Klepper was not equipped with a carrying yoke, and was far more at home on the water than on our shoulders or cradled under our arms. Sharing the awkward load, we reached the other side in time for a late lunch.

As I lay in the grass, sweat-soaked, catching my breath, I wondered why Judy wasn't also wincing with pain. After all, I was the former all-around athlete, the one who worked out daily, with a job that kept me physically active. By contrast, Judy was a health care administrator, and like most bureaucrats, a physically demanding workday for her was taking the stairs from the third to the fourth floor. Yet something she never brags about is that she can do seventy-five push-ups at a crack. "It must be genetic," she said, when I tried to pin her down for a biological explanation. "My whole family is squat and low to the ground, built on the order of Eskimos or French voyageurs." She wasn't kidding—her older brother's nickname was Eskimo, and it wasn't because he liked the cold.

We repacked the boat and squirmed inside, glad to be paddling again. Immediately upon leaving shore it was evident that Lake Grosvenor was a wilderness gem. Stretching for eighteen miles between low, rounded mountains, the lake is like a wide, watery canyon, intimate yet spacious. According to that government tome, *Dictionary of Alaska Place Names,* the lake was named in honor of Gilbert H. Grosvenor (1875-1966), editor of *National Geographic* during the Society's early exploration of Katmai. The lake is infrequently visited; we shared it with no one, which only enhanced its appeal.

Judy's Journal
> After the portage, we paddled about eight or nine miles until 6:30. Camped on a rocky outcropping of a large island. Had a late supper—instant tomato soup, pilot biscuits, freeze-dried lasagna and peas, and for dessert, a chocolate bar. Pretty good. Breezy tonight, no bugs! When we finished eating, Lar wondered if we'd see the full moon, as it was due tonight and the sky was clear. Amazingly, as he stood up and looked across Lake Grosvenor, a huge creamy-white ball crested the mountain on the other side. It was beautiful! It's moments like this that make me feel overwhelmed to be where we are. . . .

We embarked early the following morning with the intention of taking the entire day to reach the Grosvenor River, at the east end of the basin. The mile-wide lake was unruffled, its waters the bluest of blues. By staying in the middle we could study both shores simultaneously as we watched for wildlife. Our vigilance was rewarded by the sight of a lone moose wading the shallows and a small grizzly walking the bank.

We put down our paddles and absorbed the view. Judy stretched her arms wide as if to capture the scene forever. A quote I had seen under a sea kayaking photograph ran through my mind: "When you find a place in which you are comfortable, it becomes your own." I was comfortable. With the anxiety of the first few days now past, I was confident of our ability to handle almost anything.

In the late afternoon, as we neared the far end of the lake, we began looking for suitable campsites. The sloping shoreline was heavily forested all the way to the water, leaving no room to set up a tent.

"Let's take the next spot that looks okay," Judy suggested, turning around to face the stern. "I'm sure we'll . . ." Her face suddenly stiffened. She gazed over my shoulder. "Hold on, take a look behind you."

I swiveled quickly in my seat. "You mean that cloud?"

"Yeah, isn't it weird? I've never seen one like that."

A few miles away, in the direction from which we had come, was what appeared to be a small fog bank sitting on the lake. Despite the absence of any noticeable wind, the grayish-white rampart seemed to be rolling toward us at a fast clip, but it was hard to say for certain.

"Just a cloud," I said casually. "No big deal. The weather's perfect."

We were a half-mile from shore, aiming toward the Grosvenor River, when it hit. Without warning we were engulfed by a gust of icy air, followed by blasts of stinging rain that roared between the mountains. Only then did we realize we were in the grips of a *williwaw*, and how quickly it could turn clear cruising into a desperate struggle.

Caused by up- and down-drafts near glaciers, river valleys, large bodies of water and open tundra, a williwaw is a violent windstorm that arises suddenly, with wind velocities often reaching 100 miles per hour. The winds weren't quite that strong—yet—but they were definitely becoming more violent. I wasn't afraid of the kayak capsizing; familiar with its reputation, I knew the Klepper could ride out far worse than this. But I was afraid of the jagged shoreline at the end of the lake. The wind was pushing us closer to it quickly.

"Just a cloud, eh?" I heard Judy shout above the howl. "This is more like a hurricane!"

"Okay, so I was wrong. I'll apologize later. Let's make the river inlet or else we'll get pounded against the rocks."

The wind lashed at us, nearly strong enough to wrench the paddles from our hands. We tapped all the energy we had. Blinded by my water-smeared eyeglasses, and unable to see much beyond the bow, I was having difficulty keeping the boat on course with the rudder.

"We're going the wrong way!" Judy cried. "The river is over there!" When I told her I couldn't see, she began shouting directions—"right! . . . left! . . . straight ahead!"—until somehow we drove the Klepper into the sheltered mouth of the Grosvenor.

The forty-five-minute struggle left us completely exhausted and numb. We sat limply in the boat, shielded by a small promontory overlooking the gentle stream. The cove was totally calm, blissful. A water bug skimmed over the glassy surface; pondweed bent gently in the current. By contrast, just a few feet away the williwaw still raged, tossing white-plumed waves high over the lake. We weren't sure how long the gale would persist, and now that we were in a safe harbor we really didn't care.

In a few hours the storm ran its course, letting us enjoy the Grosvenor River even more. During the next couple of days we relaxed in our new camp near the spot where we had entered the river. When the mood struck us we went for short kayak trips on the sluggish stream; other times we just loafed by the tent with a good book. With moose, beaver, whistling swans and hundreds of bright-red salmon swimming in the area, we never lacked company. No bears stopped in to visit, but plenty of telltale sign let us know they were close by.

We broke camp early when it was time to move on. A light rain and temperatures in the low forties sent a shiver through my body. I put my rain outfit on over wool pants, a pile sweater and polypropylene long johns. Over that went calf-high rubber boots and a blaze-orange life jacket. The dark, moody weather seemed likely to stick with us the rest of the day. I tucked a high-energy pemmican bar in my pocket to snack on later.

The serenity of the Grosvenor River was soon a memory as we followed its current three miles to the Savonoski River. Compared to the narrow, tree-lined, slow-moving Grosvenor, the swift, wide and deeply braided Savonoski appeared more like the Yukon. Clouded dishwater-gray by glacial silt and volcanic ash carried down from the mountains, it was a startling contrast to the other clearwater streams and lakes we'd seen thus far. Spinning whirlpools, huge mud flats, expansive sandbars, uprooted trees and ice-cold glacial water made us sit up straight and concentrate on reading the river. There were many channels to choose from, but only one that would take us down safely.

River running wasn't the only thing on our minds as we careened from bank to bank. The twelve-mile-section of the Savonoski that we were paddling—between its confluence with the Grosvenor River and where it empties into the Iliuk Arm—was reportedly prime grizzly habitat, among Katmai's best. We had been cautioned to run this stretch in a single day to avoid spending the night in the bear-infested area. I expected to see a big griz on every gravel bar, and scanned the banks and gravel bars repeatedly. When the boat nearly collided with a large rootwad, Judy opined that it might be better to forget about bears for awhile and watch the river instead.

Although we didn't see any of the giant bruins during the five-hour ride, we felt their eerie presence at each stop. Long-clawed tracks led in all directions, and fish-filled dung, still steaming, suggested they had been there not long before. The feeling that these ghost-bears could materialize at any instant made us dread the thought of getting stuck in some dead-end backwater channel and being forced to get out and walk the boat.

We were still wondering where all the bears were when we pitched camp that evening near the mouth of the Savonoski, not far from the Iliuk Arm. No trees impeded the view. After spending so much time among forests the past week, the surrounding low-bush country was a welcome change.

A short walk away was the Ukak River, a tumbling, ash-choked torrent that has its origin in the Valley of Ten Thousand Smokes. Innumerable rocks appeared to be floating on its waters, an odd sight since I had always been led to believe that rocks don't float. Closer examination, however, revealed that the "rocks" were actually chunks of pumice—light, porous cobblestones varying in size from that of peanuts to tennis balls. Bobbing in the swirling eddies as buoyantly as plastic foam, the grayish-brown pumice served as a reminder that Katmai's principal volcanic area was only a few miles away.

It was an ethereal night: the lake waters and rivers sparkled under a rising moon; a wispy breeze massaged my face and kept the mosquitoes and whitesox subdued. Sitting around the tiny gas stove, Judy wrote in her journal while I prepared dinner. Waiting for the water to boil, I pondered how past experiences had led me to a place as remote as Katmai.

With visions of becoming a big game hunter in Africa or an explorer like Peary or Scott, I had wanted to escape the city since I was a small boy, but I never knew how. Reared in a typical north Chicago suburb, "wilderness" for me meant north-central Wisconsin, where my uncle owned a modest fishing resort. During our annual family pilgrimage there, lasting four to five days at the most, I would sneak off by myself, wandering, fantasizing, prowling through the posted six acres of pines, hoping to see a whitetail deer, or, dream of dreams, hit the jackpot with a glimpse of a rare and elusive black bear. I saw neither during my treks.

After two years at the University of Missouri, where I studied to be a journalist, I made a fateful, week-long trip to northern Arizona's White Mountains to visit my cousin Bud, a game warden for the Arizona Department of Fish and Game. If ever there were a radical, mind-altering trip to affect me, this was it. Bud was doing exactly what I wanted to do with my life. I was impressed with his closeness to the land and the responsibilities of his job. Upon my return to Missouri I changed majors and schools. I transferred to the University of Arizona in Tucson, graduating with a degree in wildlife biology.

While studying wildlife among the lonely splendor of Arizona's Sonoran Desert, and the canyons and mountains of Texas, Utah and California, which I visited during school breaks, I acquired a passion for wild things and wild country that grew stronger with time. Still, even after dozens of backpacking and paddling trips through some of the finest wild lands remaining in the continental United States, I wanted desperately to go to Alaska and see real wilderness, wolves and grizzly bears. A few years after college I finally found my conservation job. Not long after that I made it to the "Last Frontier." Judy, whom I had met on a Sierra Club outing, joined me on that inaugural trip.

I was still adrift in the past when Judy suddenly grabbed my arm. "Did you hear that?" she whispered.

I shook my head. "Hear what?"

"Over there . . . in the bushes." She pointed to a clump of low-growing willows and alders on the perimeter of our camp.

My chest muscles tensed. "What'd it sound like? Could it have been a bear?"

She was about to answer when the words froze in her mouth.

A blood-curdling scream in the brush caused us to jump. It sounded exactly like a maniacal woman. The thought of encountering a crazy person in this lonely expanse was somehow more horrifying than the possibility of running into a grizzly. As we stumbled toward the river, leaving our dinners in the dirt, a series of growls and moans sliced the air. Nearby shrubs rattled.

We were about to make a headlong dash down the steep cut-bank when I glanced upon a pair of liquid amber eyes staring back at me through the foliage. Seconds later, out stepped a big tawny cat larger than a bobcat: a Canada lynx! The lynx looked placidly at us as it padded noiselessly over the pumice and gravel. It stopped a mere twenty yards away, licked its paw, sat down on its haunches, and studied us some more. Not feeling threatened, and certainly not threatening us, the cat got to its feet, yawned, and melted into the alders.

I waited, hoping to glimpse it again. Determining its location was simple: we got goosebumps listening to vocalizations we thought no cat could make. Some resembled a woman crying in pain; others were like an old man in a spasm of hacking coughs. Finally, after five minutes, all was still except for the gushing of the river. The lynx never reappeared.

Soft light filtered through the tent the following morning. The day promised to be clear and warm, a welcome change from the previous day's weather. After a breakfast of instant oatmeal and steaming hot cups of tea, we packed the kayak in record time; with more than half our food gone, the chore was becoming easier. Ten miles away lay Mount Katolinat, the mountain we had chosen to climb. We were eager to study it and plot our route up its prominent sides.

Helped by a brisk tailwind, we cruised along the south shore of Iliuk Arm, reaching Katolinat's base by mid-afternoon. The mountain's lower elevations definitely seemed formidable. Since the mountain is densely forested with a patchwork of spruce, alder, willow and poplar from the shoreline to about 2,000 feet, it appeared that we would have some serious bushwhacking to do before breaking out into the clear. Once out of the alder jungle, however, the openness of the alpine tundra and bare rock led all the way to the 4,730-foot summit.

Scouting for a campsite near the mountain's base, we glimpsed a thin strip of beach ahead. We curtailed the search upon discovering the area was crawling with bears. Five grizzlies ambled down the shoreline in our direction. Another half-dozen were milling around the mouth of Margot Creek, three-quarters of a mile away. All this ursine activity meant the creek was a hotbed of spawning salmon; it also meant that camping in the vicinity was clearly not in our best interests.

We watched the bears while drifting in the kayak, wondering about our next move. There was an acre-sized island a half-mile from shore that we had noticed before. We figured this would be a safe place to camp in an emergency since it was covered by nothing more than boulders and grass.

"What do you think, Jude?" I asked. It was getting late. I needed to get out of the kayak. "The mainland or the island?"

"Let's go for the island—definitely."

Hundreds of herring gulls clamored and squawked as we approached. They had been using the surrounding rocks for a roost and didn't like being disturbed. After we landed, they soon settled back down to squabble among themselves.

"Looks okay," I said, glancing around. "Doesn't seem to be anything here that would attract bears—especially since they'd have to swim pretty far to get here."

"Oh, yeah?" came Judy's annoyed reply a moment later. She had been coursing the island like a bird dog and was pointing to the ground. "What's this?" Several unmistakable soft, squishy mounds lay at her feet.

I kneeled down to inspect the brown mass. "Looks like the remains of a humongous dinner of sushi."

Her shove nearly pushed me in it. "Come on, get serious," she implored. "There's bear sign all over this place!"

It was true. To my amazement, it appeared that grizzlies swam over here regularly. Furrows through the knee-high grass and scattered fish remains were ample evidence of their more recent visits. Our new campsite, the only one around, was not the safe refuge we had envisioned. To ease our jumpy nerves, we kept the kayak near the water, with life jackets and paddles close by.

All that evening, before darkness forced us inside the tent, we could make out a dozen or so hulking forms moving in and out of the brush along the shore. A few of the bears waded chest-deep into the stream. They stared intently at the shallow water, then, with an explosive eruption, dunked their shaggy heads beneath the surface, and if lucky, surfaced with a thrashing sockeye salmon gripped in their jaws. Other grizzlies paced the beach, stopping to sniff the air with quivering noses, then "bear-paddled" out to deeper water where there was a string of belly-up salmon. Mouthing half-rotten carcasses, the animals would swim back to shore and carry their prizes into the brush.

Nothing happened to alarm us that night. Even the gulls behaved more passively than usual. When I poked my head outside the tent at daybreak I saw why. An opaque white fog cloaked the lake basin, cutting visibility to zero. All the gulls were temporarily grounded. And until the fog lifted, so were we.

We had a leisurely breakfast, then broke camp and sorted through our gear. Today was the start of our Katolinat climb, and we had a lot to do. By the time we were ready, the mist was beginning to dissolve in patches. As each gauze-like layer burned away, a little more of the familiar world appeared. Nearby islets, Margot Creek, tundra lowlands and, finally, pinnacled mountaintops emerged.

When we could see well enough to navigate, we loaded the kayak and paddled to Katolinat's base. We stopped often to scan the creek and shoreline for bears, but saw none. Upon landing we spread out all our belongings to finalize our packing. The stove, pot, tent, sleeping bags, some spare clothes and food would go into our backpacks; the leftovers and the kayak we would hide in the forest, next to the lake.

We were busily fumbling with our backpacks when an uneasy sensation crept over me. I slowly raised my eyes and looked down the beach. Only twenty-five yards away a chocolate-brown grizzly was blankly, innocently staring at me. "Judy, don't move," I said as calmly and softly as I could. "There's a bear right behind you." She stiffened, kneeling beside her pack. Her eyes flashed the message, "Okay, now what do we do?"

Instinct told me to run, but common sense prevailed. If we didn't flee, chances are we wouldn't excite the bear's predatory instincts. I froze. A quick glance indicated that the tree branches in the nearby forest were not beyond an adult grizzly's reach. "Get your paddle," I said quietly. "Walk very slowly to the boat."

We gingerly picked up the kayak and eased it into the lake. The bear didn't move, but its darting, coal-black eyes followed us every inch of the way. We made scarcely a sound as we stepped inside the Klepper and sat down. A few quick backstrokes and we were bobbing safely in deep water. The griz was still watching us from shore. "Whew! That was close," Judy said, breathing hard from the excitement. "But what about our gear?"

Still neatly laid out on shore was a large investment of camping equipment and plastic-bagged food, not to mention the fate of our trip. We were armed with only our voices and tinny police whistles. If the grizzly wanted to rummage through the supplies, we were in no position to stop him. The bear blinked, swung his head and turned as if totally uninterested. With the characteristic, flat-footed gait, he shuffled into the forest, only to walk past our clearing a minute later on his way to Margot Creek.

A few minutes later we were back on the beach. We glanced repeatedly toward the forest and down the beach as we continued our packing. Finally, the backpacks were loaded and ready. We carried the kayak a short distance into the woods and propped it upside-down against some trees. The food and remaining supplies we suspended head-high up a nearby spruce, obviously too low off the ground to do any good, but we felt better all the same. We knew it was a gamble to leave everything here while we were gone, particularly since well-worn bear trails criss-crossed through the forest, but if we wished to climb the mountain there was no other way.

Our climb of Mount Katolinat wouldn't even make a footnote in the annals of mountaineering history, but it was a significant accomplishment for us. Halfway up the mountain, I was already formulating the story I would tell my friends: "First there was the struggle to scramble through the thick belt of lowland forest and boot-sucking muskeg; then there was a steep uphill slog with hordes of mosquitoes, not to mention brown bears, lying in ambush in the tall grass. . . ." I tried to tone it down, but it was all true.

It took hours of pushing through deep grass, bogs and shoulder-high brush before we were allowed to enter the dry alpine tundra of the high ridges. Carpeted with matted plants and mosses and bare rock, the ridges had the charm and ease underfoot of the Scottish Highlands.

Once in the high country the trek became easier; route-finding was simplified and there were no bugs. On the green tundra hillsides we saw ptarmigan, hoary marmots, ground squirrels and their nemesis, the golden eagle. A few more grizzlies also showed up. They had abandoned fishing for the time being and were busy digging for rodents and roots.

A blanket of dense fog covered our camp at 2,400 feet the following morning, but we climbed on anyway, thinking that we'd get above the clouds. It was an uncertain victory. Unable to see farther than fifty yards, we finally turned back when all the routes led down.

On the thirteenth day of our trip, a Friday, bright sunlight streamed through the tent's golden walls, waking me up. I nudged Judy. "Time to climb, dear." She groaned and rolled over, doing her best to play dead. "C'mon now," I shook her harder. "We've got a long day ahead."

By mid-morning Judy was functioning almost normally, which was gratifying because our route back up the mountain was steeper and rockier than we first thought. Three hours beyond camp we jubilantly reached the summit. We realized then that what we thought was the summit yesterday was actually a thousand feet below. This wasn't the first time I had been totally fooled by fog. But even if we had made it yesterday, we would have been cheated of the view that now filled our eyes.

Hundreds of miles of untracked wilderness surrounded our aerie. Low mountains, rolling tundra and a myriad of lakes were visible to the west and north. Looking east through binoculars we identified the Savonoski's mouth, the Bay of Islands, and the very portage we had taken to Lake Grosvenor. To the south was volcano country, most notably the Valley of Ten Thousand Smokes and its three rivers, Lethe, Windy and Knife, and Mount Griggs, at 7,600 feet one of the highest peaks in Katmai. Beyond the Aleutian Range, across Shelikof Strait, was what we thought might be Kodiak Island.

Even with this grand vista before us, our enjoyment was tempered by a growing concern about the safety of our boat and gear below. I tried to put it out of my mind. If necessary, the walk back to Brooks Camp wouldn't be too bad now, provided we could get past Margot Creek and its small army of bears.

Judy's Journal
> We decided to stay up in the tundra one more night rather than rush back to the boat. I'm glad we did because my feet were killing me. We moved camp a little lower on the mountainside, to a spot closer to running water. Today was so warm that I actually had an opportunity to wash up, which feels wonderful physically and mentally. Larry said I was smelling like a wolverine, and I must admit I did smell worse than he. As I write, the sky is turning all pink and purple, and it's starting to get chilly. Lar's taking sunset pictures of the lake. Across the ravine, on the other side of the ridge we're on, is a big silver-tipped grizzly. Guess I'll have to sleep with my fingers in my ears again. . . .

The trip down took half as much time as the ascent. When we finally converged on the cache my heart sank. The suspended food

Judy Bradford on the slopes of Mount Katolinat, looking back at Naknek Lake.

bags were untouched, but the kayak had been moved a few feet and looked slightly crumpled.

While Judy began hauling gear to the lake, I surveyed the damage. The normally sleek, heavy-duty rubber hull was now loose and wrinkled. Rolling the boat over, I discovered four parallel five-inch tears at the center-line. A hasty examination revealed that one of the twin flotation air chambers running the length of the craft had been punctured. My guess was that a curious bear had taken a swipe at the kayak with its razor-sharp claws. A rush of leaking air had startled the animal and scared it away. Considering that the grizzly just as easily could have turned our boat into a pile of tire patches and ready-split kindling, I counted us lucky. That is, until I heard Judy's frantic call from the beach.

"Larry, let's go! Some bears are headed our way from the creek."

"Come on back, help me get the boat to the water!" I yelled. I didn't want to be on land when the bears arrived.

We each grabbed an end of the kayak and sped through the forest, banging into trees, stumbling over fallen logs, trying to go in different directions. Despite our haste, the grizzlies were almost upon us when we reached the beach. While I dragged the kayak into the shallows, half expecting water to gush in at the seams, Judy sprinted back into the forest to retrieve our paddles and life jackets.

I was already pushing off as she threw me a paddle and fell into the boat.

A half-minute later, three grizzlies converged at the site where Judy had just been standing. The leader, a big boar with massive shoulders and head and long, ivory-colored claws, was dancing with aggressiveness. Gnashing his teeth and "woofing" in short hoarse blasts, the bruin charged to the shore. Fortunately, we were already a few boat-lengths away in deep water. With a final husky growl, the upset animal backed away, glaring at us over his humped shoulder. We weren't sorry to see him and his two friends continue on their way. They had proved their undeniable sovereignty.

The deflated air chamber made the kayak list, but as long as the lake remained calm we would be all right. All the tears in the hull were just above the waterline. When the bears rounded a bend and there were no others in sight, we returned to the beach to pick up our supplies. Tossing everything inside, we shoved off and paddled tipsily toward our tiny island camp of four days ago.

On the way, though, we made a slight detour to watch the bears at Margot Creek. It was such a fine afternoon for the Alaska Peninsula—no wind, clear skies and temperatures pushing the seventies—that we couldn't resist spending a few hours observing the action. Seven grizzlies were scrounging the beach for spawned-out salmon, and three or four more could be seen inland along the stream. We cruised to within a few hundred feet of the animals and idly drifted. A couple of the brownies paused to look us over, but after a brief, bored glimpse, continued their activities unperturbed, as if we were part of the scenery or perhaps some odd-shaped log.

Bears are solitary creatures, possessing a fierce sense of hierarchy. When two bears meet, the less dominant one will run off. Grizzlies do kill one another on occasion, but for the most part they existed amicably in this area of unusually heavy concentration. Only a few times did we see a cranky individual growl and feint a charge toward a neighbor who had strayed too close.

The majority of bears walked the shoreline around the creek's mouth, sniffing the air for the pungent odor of decaying fish. With a glut of dead sockeye—over a million salmon a year spawn in the waters of Katmai—only twice did we see bears actually chase down a live fish, pouncing on the thrashing salmon with lightning speed and frightening claws. Grizzlies savor the delicacy of the fat-rich brains, skin and roe of salmon, as these parts are much more important than protein to tide them over the winter. These bears often took only one or two bites before leaving in search of a tastier morsel. This apparent wastefulness created a windfall for the hundreds of gulls and a few bald eagles who flocked nearby. The birds swept in as soon as a bear abandoned his meal, pecking, screaming and flapping around the tattered carcass. In less than a minute, a five-pound, pink-fleshed salmon was reduced to bones.

The swimming bears of Katmai gave us the greatest thrill. During the warmth of the day the grizzlies took to the water, cooling off their heavily furred bodies by wallowing in the lake. When hungry all they had to do was follow their noses to a dying or dead fish floating offshore. With their dish-shaped heads poking above the water and their heavy breathing reverberating over the lake, the grizzlies dazzled us with their swimming speed and acute sense of smell.

We took a last, lingering look at the grizzlies through the fading light. Darkness was closing in fast. A freshening breeze ruffled the water. We headed toward the island; a crippled boat was no place to be in tossing waves.

I paddled sluggishly. Emotionally, I was torn between two polarities. I was relieved that the trip was almost over, not having truly relaxed since our arrival, but I hated to have it end: the classic "approach-approach" conflict, I recalled from a psychology class, which inevitably leads to frustration.

Whenever I unfolded a map of Alaska, I found myself frustrated. Among the vast emptiness, I saw bears, moose, caribou, wolves and a lifetime's worth of fascinating journeys. I saw a wealth of wilderness areas—parks, refuges, monuments, preserves—of which Katmai was only one. I was already planning which places I wanted to visit in the upcoming years. The list was long. By the time I was drawing Social Security, I reckoned, I should be wrapping up my Alaska odyssey.

The next day we would be returning to Brooks Camp, ten miles away. Then a series of plane hops would take us back to Illinois, a place where bears and wilderness survive only as faded memories. As we approached the island, I made up my mind to return to Alaska soon, next summer for sure. I felt more at peace now. So many dreams, so much to do. Seeing even a small part of wilderness Alaska was going to be a life-time occupation. Taking it one step at a time was the only way I'd get it done.

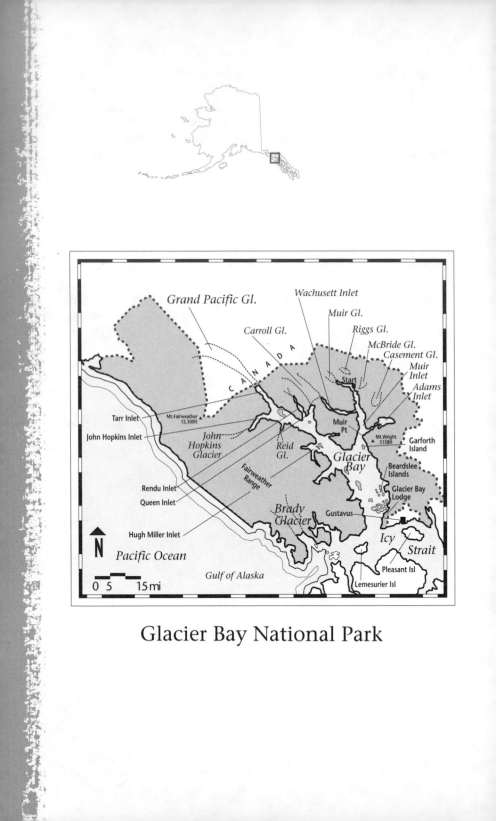

Glacier Bay National Park

Of
Rocks,
Ice and
Glacier
Bay

CHUNKS OF ICE CLOSED around us as Judy and I delicately nosed our kayak through the ice-choked sea. The face of Riggs Glacier loomed ponderously overhead, its intense aquamarine hue softened by the heavy gray mist. Double-bladed paddles braced against the frigid water. The boat stopped.

With the tidewater glacier a quarter-mile away, we dared go no closer. Pinnacles and spires on the ice front seemed to be at the point of toppling any moment. House-sized icebergs, most of their bulk concealed from sight, floated ominously off our bow. A small boat too close to the glacier could be capsized by waves from a falling pillar or a rolling berg. I stuck my thermometer into the water; my hand recoiled from the cold. The temperature was 36 degrees Fahrenheit; the sea water wouldn't get much warmer though it was already early August.

As we sat contemplating the frozen, 150-foot high palisade, the kayak was being tugged away from the glacier by the ebb tide. The eons-old ice also moved with the flow. The clatter of the bergs' hard, abrasive surfaces sounded like wind chimes tinkling in a breeze. We prodded the smaller pieces away from our boat when they drifted near. Their sharp edges could abrade our Klepper's thin rubber skin.

Following an open lead back to camp, we were delighted to see numerous black-eyed harbor seals poking their small, pointed faces up between the floes. Suddenly the seals disappeared. A second later we were startled by a loud rumble that sounded exactly like thunder. The glacier was calving! We looked behind us and saw a geyser of water shoot skyward as a huge rectangular slab weighing hundreds of tons tumbled from the ice wall. The slab plunged deep into the sea and then slowly emerged. Waves roared out from the glacier's snout. Hundreds of screaming kittiwakes and arctic terns hovered, twisted and dived into the turbulence, snapping up fish and invertebrates brought to the surface by the upwelling. The blanket of ice covering the surface flattened the long, low swells, and by the time the waves reached us they were minor ripples. Our kayak rocked gently as we poked through the shifting bergy-bits on the way back to camp.

I peered through the fog toward shore, searching for our tent, which was anchored atop one of the few flat rocky shelves above high tide. Nestled between the glacier's lateral moraine (an accumulation of rock and rubble at the side margins of a mountain glacier) and a mound of dirty black ice and smooth polished cliffsides that rose straight into the clouds, the tiny two-person shelter seemed to emit a golden glow. How different from the luxuriant forest we had left at Bartlett Cove, near park headquarters, the morning before. How different it was here compared to what we had found in Denali and Katmai parks, many hundreds of miles to the north.

Just a year before, while waiting for a Grumman Goose to airlift us out of Katmai National Park on the Alaska Peninsula, Judy and I had talked to a pair of veteran park rangers at Brooks Camp. Both were hard-core wilderness travelers. The man had made ascents up several Alaska peaks and had been to wild areas of the state that as yet I only dreamed about; the woman had kayaked and climbed from the high arctic to Patagonia in southern Chile. They had taken an interest in our lake-circuit kayak trip and advised us of some other places to consider for another trip up north.

After hearing of our interest in wildlife and noting that we owned a Klepper kayak that had never been in saltwater, they recommended Glacier Bay National Park and Preserve in the upper Panhandle section of southeastern Alaska. They delighted in describing the abundant wildlife-watching opportunities and superb sea kayaking found there. By the time they finished, I was convinced Glacier Bay was where we would go next. Judy and I were excited about adding an ocean trip to our experiences, and Glacier Bay, with its tidewater glaciers and Ice Age landscapes, sounded like a perfect first saltwater trip. My only disappointment was that there wouldn't be as many bears in Glacier Bay as there were in Katmai. Not as keen on bears as I am, Judy found the news a relief.

By the time we were ready to take our Glacier Bay trip, we were both looking forward to another sojourn in the Alaska wilderness together. After Katmai, I had made week-long backpacking trips to Utah's Capital Reef National Park and the Badlands in South Dakota, as well as a ten-day canoe trip through the remote lower canyons of the Rio Grande between Texas and Mexico. Judy hadn't been able to accompany me on any of these journeys, or several others since we had first met. Consequently, she needed to be renourished by the wilderness more than I. And what better place to have worries fall away like autumn's leaves, to paraphrase John Muir, than in the ice kingdom of Glacier Bay?

At the end of July we arrived at Bartlett Cove, the headquarters/ visitor complex in Glacier Bay National Park and Preserve. A day later we were still eagerly awaiting our first glimpse of the sun. A nonstop drizzle had made us and everything else sopping wet. Streamers of fog in every shade of gray shrouded the forest. We could hear the seabirds screeching out on the water, but couldn't see them.

"You should have been here last week," the ranger said as I registered for our backcountry permit, "four days without a cloud in the sky." He explained that such an occurrence was exceptional in an area averaging seventy-five inches of precipitation annually. When I asked for a weather forecast, he grimaced. Looking out the window, he said, "What you see is what you get."

That evening Judy and I loaded our kayak and some gear onto the motor launch that was to take us up-bay to Muir Inlet and the Riggs Glacier the next morning. After the boat was stored, we headed back to the walk-in campground to spend the night. The campground was buzzing with activity. While we were away, a marauding black bear had shredded a tent near ours and had seriously damaged an unattended folding kayak. We weren't even in the backcountry yet and were already on full bear alert.

At 7 a.m. the *Thunder Bay*'s horn blew, signalling that it was about to depart. We had been up since five o'clock and were still groggy from lack of sleep. Taking refuge from the cold drizzle in the heated cabin, we joined about forty other passengers, mostly West German, Swiss and Japanese tourists, huddled inside. A couple of backpackers and Judy and I were the only ones planning to leave the ship. Everyone else would be returning to Bartlett Cove that evening. The lodge there, I was told, had a big roaring fireplace, comfortable beds and superb food. Upon hearing that we were going to spend the next eighteen days in the wilderness, a small group of passengers treated us to cups of steaming hot chocolate and plied us with questions. I wasn't sure if they admired what we were doing or merely felt sorry for us.

Through the rain-streaked windows, I watched the jungle-green forest as we passed. I regretted not having more time to spend around Bartlett Cove and the nearby Beardslee Islands. Clustered near the mouth of Glacier Bay, with the Gulf of Alaska's Icy Strait and its riptides not far away, this area of protected islands and mainland coves would have furnished a week or more of excellent kayak touring. A guided nature walk the day we arrived at the park had only teased us into wanting to know more about this complex ecosystem. It was difficult to imagine that this mature, 200-year-old virgin forest, thick with stately spruce and hemlock covered with mosses and lichens, was not too long ago buried under a river of ice.

The boat chugged on. The moody weather, affected by the moisture-producing Gulf of Alaska and the warm Japan Current, took a turn for the worse. Rain pelted the roof and fog spun a silky web around the vessel. The monotonous hum of the engines lulled some of the passengers to sleep. Through sporadic breaks in the mist, the rest of us watched an ever-changing landscape. The rain forest had disappeared within an hour of our leaving Bartlett Cove, replaced first by mountain slopes laced with wispy cottonwoods, then by bushy alders and willows. Everyone scrambled on deck as we passed our first big iceberg. Nearly as large as the boat, it was a frosty bluish-white and glowed with a clear inner light. A throng of gulls and a solitary bald eagle perched on the berg's peaked high side.

Finally, around mid-afternoon, the land turned barren—no greenery, merely rock and rubble. The engines slowed as we approached the protruding snout of Riggs Glacier. We were forty-five miles from Bartlett Cove, as far up Muir Inlet as the tour boat could go.

The tourists watched as the crew helped us lift our kayak and gear over the side of the high rail and onto a slippery ledge near the edge of the glacier. I then jumped ashore, but Judy hesitated. She had visions of being totally humiliated, not to mention gravely wounded, by slipping on the rocks as she leaped out of the boat. With the crowd urging her on, she drew in a deep breath and took the plunge, landing solidly, if not gracefully, on high ground. The *Thunder Bay* pulled away. Within minutes it melted into the fog and rain. We were glad to be free of the noisy craft but were also a little forlorn. The tour boat's cabin was warm and secure, the people friendly. Standing in the rain, alone, staring out across an inlet full of ice floes, we were chilled and slightly disoriented. I knew from past experience that the feeling would soon pass, but right then I couldn't imagine a gloomier place to be.

Located about sixty air miles northwest of the state capital of Juneau, Glacier Bay National Park and Preserve is one of Alaska's most visited national parks and one of the few that includes a deep arm of the sea. Declared a national monument in 1925, and redesignated a national park and preserve in 1980, Glacier Bay has astounded visitors for a century. Approximately 3.2 million acres in size, with many narrow inlets snaking their way among spectacularly glaciated mountains and gray-blue ice fields, its boundaries enclose an area larger than Yellowstone, Great Smoky Mountains and Acadia National parks combined.

Consisting of a sixty-five-mile-long main trunk with two arms and a dozen or more crinkled fingers, or fjords, Glacier Bay lies within a large horseshoe rim of snow-and-ice-covered mountains that includes the Fairweather Range to the west and the Saint Elias Mountains to the north. Both ranges are the birthplaces of a large number of tidewater glaciers and glacial systems found in the upper reaches of the park. Mount Fairweather, its gleaming white summit 15,320 feet above sea level, watches over all.

No one can make a visit to Glacier Bay without learning something about glaciers. Their effects, both subtle and dramatic, are in evidence everywhere. The process by which a glacier is born is a curious thing. Much of the snow that falls each year in Glacier Bay's high country does not melt and is slowly transformed into ice. When the ice mass reaches sufficient thickness, volume and weight, gravity pulls it slowly down the path of least resistance. When a glacier finally reaches the warmer lower elevations, where the melting rate equals the rate of accumulation, a terminus, or snout, is formed. When this snout abuts the sea, as do thirteen of the park's glaciers, a tidewater glacier results. The surging tides, which can fluctuate as much as twenty-five feet daily, gnaw constantly at the ice walls, undermining and weakening their seaward extension. The innumerable icebergs in Glacier Bay's upper inlets exemplify the dynamic nature of this confrontation.

Because much of southeast Alaska is either water or steep mountains, highways connected to the outside have never been built in Glacier Bay. Visitors must arrive either by sea or by air. We flew in by jet aircraft to the outlying village of Gustavus, and from there were bused twelve miles on a dusty, little-traveled gravel road to the visitor center at Bartlett Cove. With our Klepper kayak, we planned to paddle the park's main sea lanes and several of its smaller, seldom seen inlets. The nearest tidewater glaciers to Bartlett Cove are in the Muir Arm, about fifty miles away, and in the West Arm, about sixty-five miles away.

Fifteen years ago, sea kayaking was virtually unheard of. A few odd, eccentric folks paddled their Kleppers and Folbots in coastal waters around the world, but by and large sea kayaks were phantoms from Eskimo and Aleut history. Now, by some estimates, sea kayaking is the fastest-growing segment of paddlesport, which is only fitting because ocean coastlines provide some of the most scenic environments a paddler can find.

Sea kayaking as a means to see the backcountry has become increasingly popular in Glacier Bay, but the number of kayakers in the park at any one time is never large. The great majority of Glacier Bay visitors see the park from aboard a cruise vessel. Each summer scores of these large oceangoing ships ply the park's sheltered waters as part of a much longer tour through the west coast's Inside Passage. Their presence in what would otherwise be a pristine wilderness has long irked self-propelled travelers seeking solitude. More controversial is the contention that motorboat traffic may be responsible for the departure of most of Glacier Bay's humpback whales, one of three species of whales found in the park and the most endangered. Restrictions on the number of motor-powered boats in the bay have been implemented within the past few years to protect the park's wilderness and sea life. These changes were accomplished by the park staff working with the cruise ship industry (which has enormous political leverage in Alaska) to develop a suitable compromise plan.

Our camp near the Riggs Glacier moraine was ours alone. With rain puddles everywhere, no protection from the wind and hard rocks for beds, this wasn't surprising. Only a decade before the site had been under more than 300 feet of glacial ice, and though the glacier's recent withdrawal had left its leading edge more than a mile away, this was still a rough area. The backpackers who had been dropped off with us were not tethered to the sea and had headed out in the fog to places unknown. They planned to rendezvous with the *Thunder Bay* at a later date, because it would be virtually impossible to hike back to Bartlett Cove. Around us for miles on end were ice-topped mountains creased by gullies and ravines and piles of dirt and stone.

From the door of our tent we could see where Riggs Glacier meets the ocean. Even at this distance it was immense, forming a vertical apron of ice nearly a mile wide. Still, it is a relatively minute fragment of the overwhelming ice sheet found here two centuries earlier.

At the end of Muir Inlet, about four miles away, Muir Glacier poured out of a mountain amphitheater. Named after the great naturalist, explorer and geologist, John Muir, who had made his first visit to Glacier Bay in 1879, Muir Glacier is a veritable ice cube machine. The majority of the inlet's countless bergs are shed from its serrated face. We tried to paddle nearer to its snout but were stopped a considerable distance away by tightly packed brash, or pan ice: small pieces of ice rubble often found around the faces of tidewater glaciers.

The sight of glaciers and icebergs has long brought people to Glacier Bay. Lured by John Muir's popular essays and lectures, and a story appearing in an early *National Geographic* that described the bay as "grand and impressive beyond description," since 1890 tourists have boarded steamers to see the place for themselves. Many people were so impressed that they made the long journey, often at considerable expense and discomfort, more than once. Glacier Bay was hailed as one of the wonders of the world.

The region's history was the topic of conversation during our dinner of macaroni and freeze-dried vegetables, served up under a makeshift tarp. Afterwards we walked along the beach in the vicinity of the camp. So strange and captivating were the sights and sounds that I could understand what had drawn people to this area a century earlier. Gargantuan mounds of rubble and beached icebergs stranded at high tide created a harsh and unforgiving, yet hauntingly beautiful landscape. In the morainal debris was the constant clatter of rocks; landslides were common. By contrast, the stranded icebergs, from brick-sized bits to truck-sized chunks, were more sedate; the only sounds they emitted were made by beads of liquid sapphire and indigo sweating off their crystalline faces. On

Judy Bradford dwarfed by a stranded iceberg in Muir Inlet.

the face of the glacier was the main show. Sheaves the size of rail-road cars tumbled down into the sea, creating grand splashes, waves and roars. I imagined I could hear the groaning, grinding and popping of the glacier as it inched over the bedrock.

We had trouble sleeping—not because we were worried about bears, as we had been in Katmai, for this far up bay the chances of encountering a grizzly or black bear were slim—but because the rumble of rending ice and the reports of falling fragments sounded as if we were in a war zone.

At daybreak, lead-colored light filled the tent. Rain pattered on the nylon walls, and the air felt cool and damp, typical for a north-ern climate influenced by warm ocean currents. We left Riggs Glacier at ten o'clock, paddling south down Muir Inlet through the mist and rain. To starboard was a cliff-like wall known as White Thunder Ridge, which runs steep and sheer for five miles. On our port side was a far friendlier shore, where we could pull out if neces-sary. Icebergs still dotted the water and in places prevented access to land, but their number decreased as we worked past the snout of McBride Glacier, the last tidewater glacier we would encounter in Muir Inlet.

We had lunch at Nunatak Cove. Above the shrubby haul-out was a 1,205-foot high rounded knob, or *nunatak*, which had been above the ice line when glaciers covered the entire inlet. I studied the map and peered up-bay to where we had last camped. It had taken us four hours to cover eight miles. We had our first channel crossing coming up. Facing more than a mile of open water, I was concerned about running into tour ships or sudden winds. The less time we spent in the middle, the better.

The west shore of Muir Inlet seemed distant as we eased away from Nunatak Cove. Our destination was Wachusetts Inlet, a fifteen-mile-long, nearly ice-free fjord that had been completely smothered by Plateau Glacier as recently as 1929. The heavily loaded Klepper sliced sluggishly through the water. Without any definite points of reference, I had difficulty estimating our speed.

About a half-hour from shore, just when we were getting into a cruising mode, we stopped to watch wildlife at a stony isle named Sealers Island, so called because a seal hunting blind built by Tlingit Indians was found here in 1926. There were no seals on the island when we approached, but it was hectic with oceanic birds not often seen outside their breeding grounds. Drifting offshore in the gentle swells, we identified an assortment of species perched on crags, ledges and shelves: glaucous-winged and mew gulls, black-legged kittiwakes, pelagic cormorants, common murres, arctic terns, pigeon guillemots, tufted puffins and marbled murrelets. Also on the glassy waters around the island were thousands of waterfowl and seabirds: red-throated loons, northern phalaropes, common mergansers, white-winged and surf scoters, oldsquaws and several other types of ducks. Their exotic names matched their strange shapes, colors and behavior. Over 200 species of birds have been recorded within Glacier Bay's boundaries, and we anticipated seeing many more birds in the days ahead.

I fixed my binoculars on a bald eagle sitting statuesquely by a sea stack. Three harbor porpoises surfaced and blew a few feet from our boat. Their sleek gray bodies twisted sidelong in the water. We knew that Glacier Bay's fertile waters also held orcas, a much larger species of porpoise often erroneously called "killer whales," but no large black dorsal fins typical of these animals were seen.

Finally tearing ourselves away from Sealers Island, we paddled steadily until we reached Wachusett Inlet, named in honor of the U.S.S. *Wachusett*, a survey ship that entered Glacier Bay in 1881. Too tired to be picky, we settled on a camp a few miles inside the fjord's mouth on a sloping beach of shingled rock. Closer to the inlet's head, some ten miles to the west, the landscape was more austere—thousands of acres of gravel, with no plants of any kind. The country was sullen, raw, lifeless. We set up the tent a short walk from shore. If all went according to Glacier Bay's grand successional plan, in another century or two a spruce-hemlock forest would cover the ground where we now camped.

When the British explorer George Vancouver sailed through Icy Strait in 1794, Glacier Bay was little more than a dent in a shoreline of ice. Captain Vancouver confronted the seaward terminus of a huge sheet of ice more than 4,000 feet thick, twenty miles wide, and extending more than 100 miles to the Saint Elias Range of mountains.

When John Muir arrived almost a century later, the formidable wall of ice that had repelled Vancouver had retreated forty-eight miles up the bay. Water filled the channel the ice had clogged. A ten-mile-wide basin and adjoining narrow fjords were waiting to be explored. Muir was startled to find a developing forest in the vicinity of what was soon to be named Bartlett Cove, land that had been ice covered just ninety years earlier. The region was undergoing phenomenal changes never before witnessed by scientific observers. Muir and others realized that Glacier Bay offered a golden opportunity to learn more about the forces that shaped our earth.

Scientific evidence indicates that much of southeastern Alaska was once under ice. But about 10,000 years ago, relatively recently by geological standards, the deep freeze began to thaw. A general global warming trend had begun to melt North America's extensive continental glaciers. The bulk of Glacier Bay's glaciers began to fade. Ice-drowned inlets, valleys and major rivers slowly began to emerge.

The newly exposed land remained idle and barren until enough nutrients were laid down to support the simplest of plants. First were the pioneer plants, a black crust made of lichens, algae and fungi, followed by buttons of green moss, dwarf fireweed, strands of dark brown horsetail and low dense mats of mountain avens brought in by windcast spores and seeds or contained in bird droppings. Next came the prostrate willows, soon to be overshadowed by willow and alder thickets. Then the cottonwoods moved in to replace the alders. Centuries passed, until much of the once-bare rock was covered by a coniferous forest typical of that found today along the northern Pacific Ocean coast.

For several millennia this complex forest community, inhabited by voles, shrews, martens, foxes, bears, moose, mountain goats and wolves, continued to thrive. About 4,000 years ago a cooling period known as the "Little Ice Age" began. This new Ice Age, while not approaching the "Great Ice Age" or the "glacial epoch" of Pleistocene times that began more than two million years ago and ended about 10,000 to 15,000 years ago, was nonetheless impressive. Glacier Bay was again smothered with ice nearly a mile thick.

Vancouver's eighteenth-century visit coincided with the beginning of another warming trend. The latter half of the eighteenth century marked the onset of one of the most rapid glacial retreats in this planet's history. Currently, most of the glaciers on the bay's east side are continuing to shrink. Muir Glacier, made famous by its easy access, has receded five miles in seven years; if this trend continues, it will soon beach itself above high tide. As the glaciers melt, ground that has been covered for thousands of years is exposed. In fact, Glacier Bay's topographical maps are constantly being revised because of the sudden changes caused by the withdrawing ice. Within ten years of re-emerging, shoreline that hasn't seen sunlight in forty centuries supports thick beach grass and small shrubs. Wachusett Inlet is in this phase.

Judy's Journal
10 p.m. and still light out.

> Arrived in Wachusett Inlet about four o'clock. Amazingly, it didn't rain from then until now. We even managed to dry out our stuff a bit. The ground under my sleeping bag and foam pad is rock-hard because rocks is what it is. I'm still extremely comfortable, though. Could it be because I have too much 'built-in' padding? We both seem much more relaxed on this trip than we did at Katmai. I think it's because the paddling has been pretty easy so far—no strong winds or dangerous waves; *plus*, except for the black bear at Bartlett Cove, we haven't seen any bears in the backcountry and almost no sign. However, Lar just reminded me of the story a ranger had told him at Bartlett Cove. A few years ago a hiker was killed by a grizzly on White Thunder Ridge. Beside the partly eaten body was a camera. When the rangers developed the undamaged film, the last pictures on the roll were of a grizzly walking toward the guy. . . .

"I don't believe it," I gleefully remarked, unzipping the tent door after a restful sleep. "We've got bright sun and blue skies!" This announcement even got Judy out of her sleeping bag at 5:30 a.m. The inlet's waters were a sheet of blue-green glass. Last night's high tide had scattered ice on shore that glittered like diamonds. Fifty yards away, in a little tidal pool, a pair of red-throated loons gave us an ear-piercing vocal performance.

We took the tent down and packed up our gear. We munched a couple of cardboard-tasting granola wafers for breakfast, then carted the boat and gear to the water's edge. An eight-hour paddle lay ahead, well within our ability provided we got an early start. Our plans were to recross Muir Inlet and enter Adams Inlet, another glacially eroded fjord. I folded up my rain jacket and hat, but packed them close to my seat in case of sudden squalls.

During the long trip from Wachusett Inlet south to Adams Inlet the great feeling of being outside in such a magnificent place more than made up for any trifling discomfort (such as numbness from sitting). The weather pitched in to make the day complete. We encountered no rain and little wind. Blue patches of sky showed through thin cirrus clouds, and we basked in summery temperatures.

At the mouth of Adams Inlet, we waited for an hour so that we could paddle in on slack tide. We had been cautioned that tidal currents in the narrow entrance could reach speeds of up to ten miles per hour. I used the break to study the topographic map attached to the spraydeck. Ringed by the 4,500-foot-high Chilkat Mountains, Adams Inlet is a ten-mile-long shallow saltwater basin formerly occupied by the Adams and Casement glaciers. Geese and other waterbirds are common along its estuaries and tidal flats, where they molt during midsummer. We were glad that the park service had declared the inlet off-limits to tour boats and most motorcraft.

It was mystifying to me how anyone could accurately predict the high and low tides for any given day and location and put that information in a simplified table, but precisely when it was supposed to, the ebb tide turned to flood. We jumped in the kayak and pushed off from shore.

The current picked up momentum and I began to feel as if I were on a wide, slow moving river. For several miles the inlet is less than a mile across, backed by low brushy bluffs on the north and steep rock-faced escarpments to the south. We scanned the craggy cliffs for mountain goats. Members of the same family as antelope and sheep, these dingy-white creatures—the most sure-footed of all North American mammals—flourish in Glacier Bay's inaccessible retreats. Or so we were told. All we saw in the highlands were soaring black ravens.

We passed several potential campsites with sloping beaches and access to drinking water. Eventually we chose one that looked particularly inviting, at the outwash of a hanging valley. This tributary glacial valley, laced with waterfalls, was perched hundreds of feet above the floor of the main Adams Inlet. I climbed a nearby esker, a meandering, steep-sided, sand-and-gravel ridge that was formed beneath a glacier by the depositional action of meltwater streams. I could see most of the inlet from my 100-foot-high perch, and looked for boats, tents and people. After a few minutes I slid back down the esker to meet Judy. As in Wachusett Inlet, we had the entire basin to ourselves.

An hour of intense work always follows the decision to make camp. First, Judy and I dragged the kayak a few feet up on the rounded rock-and-pebble shore. Next, we unloaded a small mountain of gear that had taken an hour to load that morning and lugged it fifty yards to our tent site. Only then did we return for the empty boat. With each of us cradling an end, we carried the ungainly beast to a secure spot above high tide. We decided that maybe it wouldn't be a bad idea if we made Adams Inlet a two-night camp.

Once we had put everything in order, we scrutinized our surroundings. The torrent that had created the outwash near camp roared down from a slot-like chasm between smooth granite ridges. Over the years the glacier above had worn loose a good chunk of the mountainside. Meltwater had channeled boulders, gravel and fine sediment down the slopes to the sea. Near the stream's banks, the sound of rolling rocks was so loud that we practically had to shout to be heard. On higher ground ringing the inlet dense thickets of struggling alder and willow gave the land a greenish tint that belied its harsh nature. Closer to sea level, hugging the ground to escape the wind, mats of yellow dryas and creeping willows survived among a mosaic of other hardy pioneer species.

Given a choice between camping in a lush rain forest or country scraped bare by ice, I invariably prefer the latter. I have always been drawn to the openness of deserts, prairies, marshes, savannas and tundra. Without tall vegetation, wildlife watching is much easier: the eye can roam unobstructed. With our backs pressed against a boulder, we gazed across the inlet. Terns, gulls, Canada geese and ducks were everywhere we looked. Their chatter was mixed with the sweet trill of song sparrows, the sharp cry of parasitic jaegers, the cackle of willow ptarmigan. Across the inlet, a mile away, a big bull moose looked conspicuous standing in a tangle of knee-high brush.

Scoping out the terrain through binoculars, I searched for an animal that I wanted to see in the wild but never had. The closest we had gotten to a wolf thus far on both our Alaska trips was finding fresh tracks. "I'd trade five grizzly and ten moose sightings for one wolf," I half-joked. It would be another year, another Alaska journey, before I realized this dream.

At 10:30 p.m., while it was still light, I sat outside scribbling in my journal while Judy read a book in the tent. After a few minutes, I put my pen down. There was too much happening on the inlet to concentrate on written words. A half-dozen porpoises shot fine mists of spray above the calm water as their hot breaths met the cool downdrafts from Casement and Adams glaciers, and fifteen or twenty harbor seals cavorted near the creek's mouth trying to corral a school of fish. I was musing on how grand nature is when a swarm of whitesox, those tiny biting blackflies, chose this moment to make their first appearance on this trip. Hearing me curse, Judy asked how I was doing. "Great, except for the bugs," I said, trying to sound cheery. "I think I'll stay out a little longer." A minute passed. I squished a mass of the flies under the heel of my hand. They retaliated with several more bites on my neck. "Okay, I had enough nature for this evening. Make room, Jude, I'm coming in."

Rest days are often anything but restful. Instead of breaking camp the next morning, we stuffed our daypacks with a few necessities, launched the kayak on a flood tide, and went for a morning paddle further inside Adams Inlet. According to the map, there were places called Howling Valley, Girdled Glacier, Berg Creek and Tree Mountain to explore.

Not even a trace of clouds shielded us from the sun as we glided easily to the east. "Seems odd without the threat of rain," Judy commented, staring up at the satin-blue sky. I didn't notice. I was too busy trying to take a picture of a porpoise circling our boat. Every time I got my camera ready and focused, the porpoise would surface somewhere else.

We had lunch at the edge of a two-mile-wide gravel delta devoid of any vegetation. We climbed a small hill overlooking the braided stream. The scene reminded me of an abandoned quarry. Silt, sand, mud and rock covered what was once a mature forest. Only scattered low-growing plants softened the ground, species that have somehow managed to grab a toehold in these inhospitable conditions. My curiosity was piqued, and I suggested that we exchange our rubber boots for hiking boots and climb higher for an overview of the entire inlet.

"The alders don't seem too bad," I noted, studying the belt of shrubs on the mountainside. "Neither does that avalanche chute we'll have to follow."

Judy gave me a doubtful sidelong glance, meaning: Not too bad? Where have I heard that before? "Okay, lead on," she acquiesced.

We stayed to one side of the braided stream as we climbed. Draining out of Adams Glacier, a shrinking ice field that now lay several miles inland, the water was icy and fast moving. Rock flour—finely ground, silty rock produced by abrasion at the glacier's base—colored the stream a milky white. There was no way to tell how deep the channel was, especially since we didn't have hiking staffs or ice axes. We decided not to cross.

On our side of the river bar were more than enough items of interest. Groups of tree stumps, half-buried in the gravel, told the story of an ancient forest which once covered much of Glacier Bay. The relics of Sitka spruce and cedar had been overrun by an advancing glacier, then exhumed by its last retreat. We touched the millennia-old skeletons, called *interstaidal* trees by geologists, rubbing our fingers over the gnarled, petrified wood. By studying their age and distribution, scientists can determine past climates and the extent of previous glaciations.

The first part of our climb was harder than I had imagined, and that should have told me something was wrong. Dislodged rocks and loose gravel slid down the jagged slope, but that was nothing compared to what we next faced. Few things are as irritating as trying to get through a thick band of head-high alders, especially while going uphill. At the 1,200-foot contour, we were stopped in our tracks by the impenetrable, interlocking trees.

"This stinks," I groused, trying to limbo my way under the downsloping branches. "Maybe we should forget the ridge. What do you think?"

No reply. I turned around to find Judy trapped in an impossible position, with one leg wrapped around an alder prong, the other dangling two feet off the ground. By mutual consent, we retraced our steps down to shore.

We timed our departure from Adams Inlet early the following morning to coincide with the ebb. It was another clear, crisp morning. I stripped down to an undershirt and shorts while packing the boat. Judy bemoaned her failure to bring sunscreen. "Never mind," I counseled. "This can't last."

In two hours we were safely through Adams Inlet. Muir Point, at the mouth, provided a convenient place to stretch our legs. In 1890, John Muir built a simple cabin at this very location, which he occupied for the summer season. It was strange to think that Muir Glacier, presently twenty miles to the north, was then only one mile away. All that remains of the cabin today is a pile of chimney stones overgrown with moss, and even these are nearly impossible to find because dense alders surround the site. Just being near the spot where Muir once resided was enough for me. His wonderful essays on Alaska and the wilderness have inspired my own travels many times. I stared up the long watery channel where a glacier used to be and wondered if Muir would recognize this place today.

Ahead was a six-mile, open-water crossing. In a fully loaded kayak in a calm sea, our paddling speed was usually two to three miles per hour. True to form, it took us exactly two-and-a-half hours to reach Sebree Island at the mouth of Muir Inlet. Two miles long and shaped like a tear drop, the island was named in 1890 for Uriel Sebree, a U.S. Navy commander who had participated in relief expeditions to Alaska. There was no one on the island when we landed, but we did find a botanical oasis. Intermixed with the alders, willows, cottonwoods and young spruce were delicate wildflowers, wild strawberries and blueberries. While on our hands and knees plucking the fruit, we were joined by a variety of songbirds who flitted around the bushes. Within minutes, I added juncos, yellow-rumped warblers, Swainson's thrush, fox sparrows and hummingbirds to our Glacier Bay checklist.

I was on my belly taking flower pictures, and Judy was searching for wild strawberries, when we were startled by a loud whooshing sound. We got up and stood frozen, staring out into the bay. In a few moments, along the near horizon, a jet of spray gleamed skyward, followed a second later by the forceful whistling sound of an exhalation. I could barely contain my enthusiasm—a whale!

This was the first cetacean I had ever seen. Even a half-mile away, it looked gargantuan. When it kicked for the bottom, I could tell it was a humpback, the most common large whale in Glacier Bay; its thickset body, distinct hump in front of the dorsal fin, and large flukes with white underneath helped identify it. I could only guess the size of this individual, but I knew that most humpbacks grow to about fifty feet.

Tracking with my binoculars, I followed the whale as it cruised steadily up-bay. With only its smooth back arching above the waterline, the whale surfaced with a loud sigh, filled its blowhole with air, then vanished for several minutes before reappearing a quarter-mile from its last position to repeat the breathing cycle.

Up until the late 1970s, twenty to forty of these giants routinely returned to Glacier Bay each June after spending the winter in the Hawaiian Islands or off the Pacific coast of Mexico. In the cold, sheltered waters of Glacier Bay, the whales found abundant quantities of herring, capelin, shrimp and small crustaceans known as krill. During the summer of our trip, researchers estimated that only five humpbacks were using the bay, which matched exactly the whale sightings we had. The year before, nineteen humpbacks showed up, but halfway through the season, all except three suddenly left. There is much speculation about this alarming and abrupt decline in numbers. Some researchers theorize that increased tour boat traffic in the late 1970s caused the whales to abandon Glacier Bay; humpbacks, they contend, are bothered by noisy boats. Others, including the tour ship industry, argue that the whales may have left because of a cyclical food shortage. Whatever the reason, the elimination of the humpback from Glacier Bay's ecosystem would be everyone's loss.

For two days after we left Sebree Island we paddled up the west arm of Glacier Bay. The widest point from shore to shore in this broad inlet was approximately six miles, which made us wary of the strong downdrafts that occasionally sweep down the bay from the ice fields to the north.

Three weeks for most people is more than adequate for a vacation, but in Glacier Bay, it isn't nearly enough time. We cruised past places such as Tidal Inlet, Vivid Lake, Composite Island, Queen Inlet and Rendu Inlet, that we would have liked to explore, but couldn't. It is difficult to comprehend the size of Glacier Bay National Park until traveling slowly through it by one's own power; it would take several kayak tours to explore just one of Glacier Bay's arms. Beyond the tidal zones are what John Muir called "the chaste and spiritual heights"—mountains and hidden valleys that have rarely if ever seen the footprints of a human being.

Eventually we reached Gloomy Mountain, a good point from which to make the three-mile passage to the Gilbert Peninsula on the other side of the arm. The bay was calm and there was no wind as we crossed, but a blanket of silent, cold fog hung above the water. Fortunately, we encountered no big ships; even with radar their captains wouldn't have been able to tell our Klepper from a floating piece of ice.

From the peninsula, it was an uneventful twelve-mile paddle to Reid Inlet, where we arrived around dinner time to the accompaniment of "white thunder." At the head of the inlet was the squat

The camp near the terminus of Reid Glacier.

Reid Glacier, nearly beached at low tide. Although the weather was overcast and drizzly, the inlet was nonetheless a welcome place to be. We had traveled far, and all we wanted to do was eat a hot meal, relax and look around.

In the morning, before exiting Reid Inlet for the next fjord up-bay, we made a pilgrimage to what is known as the Ibach cabin. It was low tide when we reached the entrance to the inlet. We beached the kayak at the edge of a sandspit a hundred yards from the boxy one-room house. The wooden-planked cabin looked nearly as weathertight as it was when Joe Ibach built it in 1940 as a home away from home.

A prospector by trade, Ibach arrived at Glacier Bay early in the summer of 1924, the year a fight was being waged in Washington, D.C., for the establishment of Glacier Bay National Monument. Ibach was not a "conservationist" and was on record as being opposed to the creation of a park, but he was as much a part of Glacier Bay's fabric as the brown bears and wolves. In his thirty-two-year association with the Reid Inlet area, Ibach and his wife, Muz, achieved almost legendary status as part of Glacier Bay's history.

I felt strange approaching the structure. Except for the barn swallow nests plastered to the eaves and the peeling red paint, the place looked as if it were still occupied. I half-expected Joe himself to come shuffling out the front door. Around the cabin, on what had once been a terraced vegetable garden, were three spruce trees about twenty-five feet high, which seemed odd since the nearest conifers of this size were many miles to the south. The spruce had been planted as seedlings by Muz. She and Joe had filled in the terraces, bag by bag, with dirt boated in from their homestead on an island in Icy Strait.

The door to the cabin was ajar, the rectangular frame slightly twisted. I peeked in: bed, table, chairs, stove, wallpaper from torn-out pages of cataloges. No one was home. The last year at Reid Inlet for Joe and Muz was 1956. In 1959 Muz died in a Juneau hospital. She was buried on Lemesurier Island, at the mouth of Glacier Bay, near their big house. In the spring of 1960, despondent and drinking heavily after Muz's death, Joe made a last visit to the old Reid Inlet cabin. The next day he shot himself. At the bottom of his hand-scrawled will was the note, "There's a time to live and a time to die. This is the time." He was laid to rest alongside Muz.

Since leaving the East Arm we had not seen more than a handful of icebergs; apparently the ebb and flow of the tides kept them recirculating in the bay's upper reaches. We reentered the ice world, though, when we rounded the dogleg entrance into Johns Hopkins Inlet. First Lamplough Glacier dazzled us with its half-mile-wide, 200-foot-high wall of solid ice, then the entire chasm appeared as if the mountain had suddenly fissured.

Icebergs and floes were everywhere. The landscape was in turmoil. Ten miles away, at the head of the inlet, the massive Johns Hopkins Glacier, impossibly crevassed as it curves out of the high Fairweather Range, is bucking the trend within the park by growing instead of shrinking. During the last half-century, the glacier, which retreated more than eleven miles between 1892 and 1929, has been slowly advancing and thickening. It has advanced more than two miles since 1935. We were hard pressed to say whether Johns Hopkins Inlet or Muir Inlet was the most spectacular in Glacier Bay. Glacially speaking, Johns Hopkins was the more impressive. Within the narrow, brooding fjord nine separate ice masses descend the walls.

The rumble of ice and rock falls, primeval sounds from the bowels of the earth, echoed off the skyscraper cliffs as we paddled inside. How could any warm-blooded creature live in here, I wondered. But they do, in great numbers. As many as 2,500 harbor seals call the inlet their home during the summer months. The adults gather on the densely packed icebergs to mate and raise their pups.

These platforms are relatively secure from attacks by orcas, or killer whales, their chief enemy.

A score of the inquisitive seals circled our boat, studying us with bright, glistening eyes set in small, oblong heads. They were only the advance guard, however—the seal's population center was closer to the glacier's face. Sprinkled over the pancake floes were hundreds of the sausage-shaped bodies, drifting on frozen water-beds of the sea.

We had been cautioned that tent sites were rare within the inlet. The walls were sheer, smooth and scoured, hardly good places to haul out with loads of heavy gear and a burdensome kayak. Since we planned to spend three nights at camp, our intention was to get as close as possible to the snout of Johns Hopkins Glacier. This would be our best and last opportunity during the trip to observe a highly active tidewater glacier.

By proceeding slowly and scouting out promising gaps in the west wall, we managed to locate a suitable camp a couple of miles from the glacier's front. The little bench was not the easiest place to reach by kayak—we had to do a balancing act with one foot in the boat and the other on slippery rocks to unload—but the site was relatively flat and secure, gave us access to high-country hiking and best of all, had a sublime view. Directly across the narrow fjord the heavily crevassed Kashoto and Hoonah glaciers, branches of the much larger Brady ice field hidden in the 6,000-foot mountains, spilled into the sea. Behind our camp, rising into the scattered clouds, were equally impressive granite ridges which the topo map indicated had glaciers of their own.

"I think we're stranded," Judy announced. While I was preparing dinner, she had walked to the water's edge. "Our take-out is turning into a cliff face. The only way up—or down—is with ropes." I consulted the tide tables, checking the date, the hour, the fluctuation of the tide. In six hours our launch spot would be twenty-five feet above the waterline. We would only be able to get out at high tide.

No matter. We were in no hurry to leave. At dusk, alpenglow transformed the surrounding peaks into hot shades of reddish-yellow and pink. Icebergs funneled toward the inlet's mouth as the ebb tide kicked in. Seals were bellowing. And every so often we'd hear white thunder, followed by an enormous splash, as a section of the glacier's face toppled into the water. At one point I noticed a cup of finely woven grass supported in the crotch of some willow branches. When I parted the leaves, a pair of yellow warblers scolded me for coming too close to their nest. I leaned over for a quick peek. Inside the well-secured little receptacle were four pin-feathered, big-mouthed nestlings, so delicate, so vulnerable, yet equal to the magnificence of the glacier that overshadowed us all.

I am not a religious person, but standing there that night, watching the power of ice over rock, moon over tides, I mused over the religious beliefs of the Tlingits, Haidas and Tsimshians, the people of the tides, forest and sea, who had been on Alaska's southeast coast for countless generations before the arrival of the white man. Their totem was the Great Raven that guarded the great lights—the sun, the moon and the stars. To them, a belief in the spirit of nature made one truly alive.

In *Glacier Bay*, William D. Boehm described the Tlingits' fascination with storytelling, passing their legends from generation to generation. I remembered the legend of the icebergs:

> One legend of the Hoonah Kwan people, the group that once inhabited Glacier Bay, concerns the tremendous ice fields that covered their hunting and fishing grounds. In former times, the legend says, the Hoonah Kwan people fished and hunted with great success around the Beardslee Islands. Then a young girl, Kahsteen, who was being kept in seclusion at the onset of puberty, called the glacier down from the north out of spite for being kept alone. The glacier responded, forcing the people to retreat from their homes and move southward toward the mouth of the bay.
>
> When they found out that Kahsteen had called it, the tribe wanted to leave her behind so the glacier would no longer chase them. But Kahsteen was young and might bear many children, so a barren old woman, Shaw-whad-seet, took her place and the people moved to a protected place called Hoonah. Tlingits say that, although Shaw-whad-seet could not have human children, after the glacier covered her she could have ice children; these are the calved icebergs in the waters of Glacier Bay.[1]

A new generation of "ice children" was being born as I watched. The noises made by the glaciers became louder the quieter the inlet became. Cold, blistering noises, grinding, churning, sliding, splashing. We had heard Johns Hopkins Inlet referred to as the wildest fjord in the park. As far as we were concerned, things couldn't get much wilder.

Of course, everything is not perfect in paradise. While I was watching the light and ice show, the whitesox became increasingly annoying. Rather than put up with their assaults, I retreated into the tent. Actually, I was looking forward to crawling into my sleeping bag. I was engrossed in an extraordinary book. *Mawson's Will*, by Sir Douglas Mawson, is an incredible, true story of Antarctic exploration in the early 1900s. The book describes Mawson's 1912 expedition, in which one of his companions fell into a crevasse and was lost; the other died of food poisoning. Mawson, an Australian geologist who had been one of the Shackleton party that found the South Magnetic Pole in 1909, staggered on alone 165 miles to his ship. As I lay in the tent warm and dry, I nevertheless shivered while reading Mawson's account of his epic sledging trek. Our journeys seemed like a Sunday picnic by comparison. But a wilderness trip's success or failure is not measured by the quantity of hardships. For now, a peaceful Glacier Bay was exactly where I wanted to be.

After breakfast the next morning we undertook a combination paddle/climb. Dropping the kayak to the water at high tide, we paddled to within two miles of the face of Johns Hopkins Glacier. The pan ice was far too congested to go any further. We spent several hours sitting in the boat, mesmerized by the dynamics of moving ice. Occasionally a sound like high-explosive artillery rang out as a huge, rectangular block broke off its unstable front. After the splash, the floating ice pans in the fjord rearranged themselves as if they were part of a cosmic geometric puzzle.

The word *awesome* is overused today, but awesome best described what was before us. We became part of an inexorable life force as the ice began to flush out the inlet on the ebb flow. Observing the harbor seals from camp had been wonderful, but being among the bergs provided us with an even more intimate glimpse. Thousands of liquid black eyes stared at us as we jostled among the floes. It was likely that the pups had never seen kayakers before. Born between late May and mid-July, they were half the size of their mothers and had short, coarse, yellowish-gray coats resembling the adults'. A sudden roar at the ice wall didn't affect the young seals at all, because they were accustomed to the glacial cacophony.

The latter half of the day we devoted to the climb. A mile from camp was a fairly steep but possible avenue of ascent to the mountain heights. We both considered ourselves in pretty good physical shape, yet while kayaking is a wonderful conditioner of the upper body, it makes for atrophied legs. We were soon breathing hard. Judy was afraid that by the time the trip was over, her legs would be even shorter and her arms would be so beefy she'd never be able to wear a sleeveless dress to work again. "Maybe for our next trip we should try backpacking," she said. "That way I could spend the next few months balancing out my body." As a matter of fact, I had been thinking about a trip to the Arctic National Wildlife Refuge for the summer of the following year and was glad to know that she was up for a long trek.

The vegetation decreased as we went higher. Prostrate arctic willows and dryas merged into bits of moss and minute perennial herbs. These in turn tapered off until there were only loose, unstable boulders made slick by runoff from above. As we sat down to contemplate our hard-won view 3,500 feet above the sea, a flock of gray-crowned rosy finches fluttered in from nowhere to a pool of water near my feet. The size of pet canaries and almost as tame, the birds dipped their yellow beaks into the water, then tilted back their heads to swallow. From the pool they hopped to a snowbank, where they gleaned iceworms, segmented black earthworms about an inch long and the diameter of a darning needle. Found only on glacial ice and perennial snow, iceworms feed off algae growing on the snow. After preying on a few of the wiggling creatures, the finches lifted off with a whir of wings.

I refocused my vision and studied the terrain below. We were above Johns Hopkins Glacier, in a position that allowed us to see the route of the glacier as it flowed into the sea. The pale blue ice, sharp-cut and deeply fractured, poured like a river between the lofty mountains. Toward the inlet's mouth were enough wild lands and waters for months, if not years, of wilderness journeys. Muir, upon his first general view of Glacier Bay, called it "a solitude of ice and snow and newborn rocks, dim, dreary, mysterious." To me, this was country to come back to for certain.

One of the paradoxes in Glacier Bay is that with so many tidewater glaciers, there are only a few locations where kayakers can actually touch the pillars of ice. On our way out of Johns Hopkins Inlet, we arrived at the face of Lamplough Glacier at low tide. The glacier's terminus was surrounded by relatively dry, glacial till of different-sized rocks and boulders that were bulldozed forward. If our calculations were correct, we'd have about two hours before the glacier's snout would again be flooded. Judy volunteered to watch the boat—on the thin strip of gravel there was nowhere to tie it off—while I roamed among the towering seracs to take photographs. A dozen steps from the water I found a crack between the glacier's walls. The crack opened into a shallow cave. Shut off from direct sunlight, the glacier turned from pale white to shades of luminous blue as the pressure became greater, squeezing the air out of the ice. I touched the rough surface. It was hard as a diamond, and equally clear. The curved walls were scalloped as if they had been artistically chiseled. Softball-sized rocks and specks of gravel floated strangely within in suspended animation.

I continued, stepping cautiously. I was only a hundred feet from Judy and blazing sunlight, but for all practical purposes, I was lost in another world. Quiet, sensual, protective, the ice cave was like a womb. A low rumble followed by a tremor reminded me that an ice cave could also be a tomb. Keeping my head low, I scurried for safety.

We decided to return leisurely to Muir Inlet during our final week. A slightly different route would allow us to visit new country. At Blue Mouse Cove in Hugh Miller Inlet, we made camp at the tip of a small rocky island facing out onto Glacier Bay. Granite boulders, round and smooth, sat poised on the glacial, polished ledge where we pitched the tent. Everything would have been perfect except for the reappearance of the whitesox. I gamely tried to stay outside and enjoy the spectacular view as long as I could, but the bugs were winning both the battle and the war. Judy had more sense and was already inside starting a new book. I was brushing the bugs off my head and shoulders before diving into the tent when I noticed a strange, multiheaded creature crawling on the mussel-covered intertidal rocks. After a startled double take, I realized the mythological sea creature was actually four baby river otters. Popping in and out of the wave-washed rocks, they resembled toy jack-in-the-boxes as they tried to get a better look at me. I was about to call Judy, but a sharp "peep-peep-peep" stopped me. The mother otter had returned from hunting and didn't appreciate the predicament her babies were in. Arching out of the water, she bared her pointed teeth at me and growled and hissed. Taking the cue, the youngsters crawled over her and hung on as she swam away.

The following day we recrossed the West Arm, aiming for a spit of land called Caroline Point on Muir Inlet's west side. At the spit was a huge iceberg, the largest we had seen thus far, floating slowly out to sea. The berg served as a platform for scores of gulls and a few bald eagles cashing in on the free ride. Passing counter-current to the iceberg was another humpback whale. We followed the geyser-like spouts as the whale surfaced and dived.

Normal Glacier Bay weather finally returned. The dry, warm

days of the last week were no more. When we started on the long, open-water crossing to Garforth Island, our rendezvous point with the *Thunder Bay*, rain was coming down lightly, the temperature was in the low fifties and a dismal fog hovered above the water. The other shore was visible, but only barely. Halfway through the passage, the fog lowered and we were blinded. I pulled out the compass—the first time I had needed it on the entire trip—and placed it on the topo map, adjusting the bezel. I was even more impressed than Judy when Garforth Island appeared out of the mist.

Judy's Journal
August 17, Garforth Island.
    Everything is damp, but we're altogether happy. Right now we're under a small orange "space blanket," whose overflow of rain water is slowly filling our dwindling water supply. Our island camp is reminiscent of the forest near Bartlett Cove, only the spruce and hemlock here are not nearly as large; it's been awhile since we camped under real trees. We assumed the island was bearless, until Lar stumbled upon a large mound of berry-filled droppings— *fresh* berry-filled droppings. Our day waiting for the boat has been spent reading, napping, eating, singing old seventies' tunes, and, for me, thinking of dry clothes, cherry pies, vanilla ice cream, pepperoni pizzas and crackling fireplaces.

We would have been content to continue exploring Glacier Bay's wilderness, but the trip we had planned for so long was nearly over. The *Thunder Bay* would pick us up at any moment.

We were almost finished packing the boat—we would have to paddle out to meet the *Thunder Bay* because of the rocky shoreline around Garforth Island—when a large, flapping bird landed on top of a nearby spruce. A mature bald eagle perched motionless, surveying his watery domain. I made a move to get my binoculars, which attracted the attention of the regal bird. When I looked up, the eagle was staring straight at me with piercing yellow eyes. Our gazes locked for only an instant before the eagle lifted his white-feathered head and let loose a wild cry. With powerful leg thrusts and a few pumps of his mighty wings, the huge fish-eater sailed off the tree and disappeared into the low-hanging fog.

Judy and I looked at each other and grinned. We would also be gone soon, but Glacier Bay, like the eagle we had just seen, would remain a part of us for a long, long time.

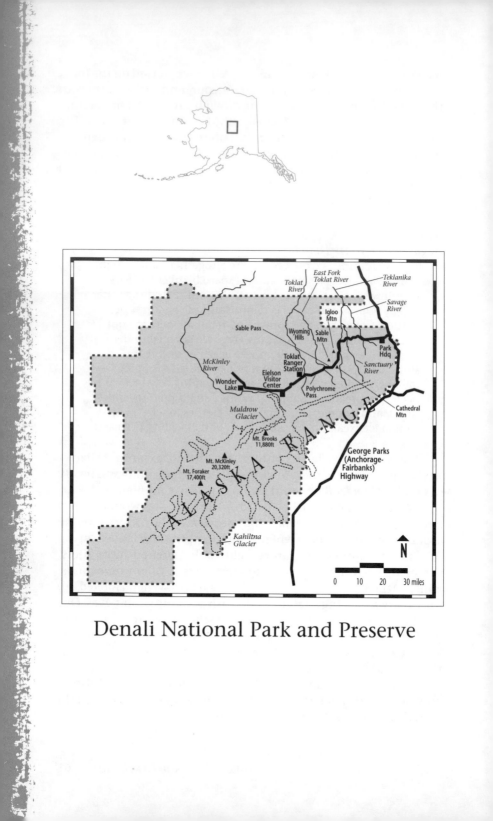

Denali National Park and Preserve

In
the
Shadow
of
Denali

CHOOSING A COMPANION for a strenuous backcountry trip is possibly the single most important decision in determining the success or failure of that trip. When I initially decided to visit Denali in winter, Charlie was the first person I thought of asking; happily for me, he said yes. Quiet and even-tempered, he is one of the most stable, dependable friends I have, always eager to travel to new places. I could count on him to be in top shape.

I first met Charlie when I walked into the only wilderness supply store in Peoria, Illinois. He sold me my first pair of cross-country skis and introduced me to winter camping. We were soon spending many of our long weekends and vacations together back-packing, skiing and canoeing in wilderness areas across the United States. During the years leading up to our Denali trip, we competed to see who spent more nights in the backcountry. We each averaged fifty per year, with Charlie always slightly ahead.

I was glad that Charlie would finally make it to Alaska, al-though the cost of this trip had put a severe dent in his savings. Lately he had been hinting that if he enjoyed this first journey to Alaska, he might want to accompany Judy and me to the Brooks

Range that summer. "The best investment I can make with my money right now," he said, when we talked economics, "is to spend it on experiences like this."

That night brought an April Fool's Day surprise like no other for Charlie and me. The weather in Denali National Park took a drastic turn for the worse. The temperature plummeted as wind-driven sleet splattered off the walls of the dome tent. We emerged from our sleeping bags. Still dressed in our ski suits, we fumbled for parkas and gloves before unzipping the door.

Charlie crawled out. I followed. The cold air stung my face, snatched my breath away. Through tearing eyes, I could faintly discern the bulk of Mount McKinley, at 20,320 feet the highest mountain in North America, across the Thorofare River. I briefly wondered if anyone was up there now, holed up in a snow cave among its glaciers and ice-rimmed ridges. If so, they were probably more secure than we were at the moment. Completely exposed on the barren tundra, with the snow less than a foot deep, we had nowhere to dig, nowhere to hide. The closest trees were along the Toklat River, a long day's ski away. While Charlie jammed our skis and poles into the thin layer of snow to help secure the tent, I attached extra pegs to every available anchor point.

At midnight we were rudely awakened from our uneasy slumber. The tent was shaking violently. We pressed our hands against the walls to keep them from caving in. Fearing some of the pegs had torn loose, Charlie went outside for another look. When he dove back inside, his face was a mixture of amazement and terror. "Only a few pegs are holding! Half the grommets have ripped out. It's a wonder the tent has stayed upright as long as it has."

Before we could contemplate our next course of action it happened: an ear-shattering roar was followed instantly by the sickening pop of tearing seams. A heartbeat later I was underneath all my gear, the victim of an unintentional, lightning-quick somersault. I was stunned and disoriented, but otherwise okay.

"Charlie, you all right?" I shouted. The wind nearly drowned out my words.

"Yeah. What happened?"

I groped in the darkness for my headlamp. Along with my stocking wool cap, it had been knocked off my head. The flashlight beam illuminated the disarray. The tent was upside down. Books, cameras, stuff sacks, jackets, boots, water bottles were scattered across what had been the ceiling. The tent began to vibrate and move. I braced for the next blast to send us careening over the rolling tundra.

Charlie reacted instantly. "Find the door. Let's get out of here and collapse this thing!"

We rolled the tent to clear the door and emerged into the biting gale. Spindrift flooded inside. We bent low to keep our balance as a wall of wind tried to lift us off our feet. While Charlie unhooked the fluttering rain fly, I clutched the tent to keep it from sailing away. Then we wrestled the bent aluminum poles out of their sleeves and flattened the dome, much as a sky diver would gather a flapping parachute upon reaching the ground.

We dove back into the dark, shapeless nylon sack. Our only option was to lie fully dressed in mashed sleeping bags with the flailing tent fabric grasped tightly to our chests. The wind was still doing its best to send us on an airborne trip.

Cold and uncomfortable, I was unable to sleep. My mind raced back to the day when our Denali ski journey began. Was it really just ten days ago that the train pulled up to the railroad station?

"McKinley! McKinley Station!" the conductor announced. Charlie and I awoke from a bored slumber. After a year of planning, capped off by an overnight flight from Chicago and an eight-hour rail ride from Anchorage, it was a relief to be finally at Denali National Park. Accompanying our excitement was an undercurrent of nervousness as we prepared for the cold and snow outside. We had three weeks of ski-packing ahead before we were due back at the train station.

The yellow-and-blue cars ground to a halt. I am not fond of train travel, but the journey on the Alaska Railroad had been an opportunity to experience a side of Alaska that few tourists see. I had been on the train before during summer; the cars then were packed with camera-toting vacationers, who, like I, had boarded in Anchorage for the 130-mile run up to the park. Now my only fellow passengers were a couple of grizzled sourdoughs who had jumped aboard with snowshoes under their arms when the train made an unscheduled stop in a trackless, forested wilderness, and a plump, long-haired woman dressed in a heavy plaid wool jacket and denim dress who was leaning against the window snoring.

I asked the conductor, a veteran of twenty-five years on the Alaska Railroad, how the train could make any money during the winter. "It doesn't," he replied matter of factly. "Doesn't need to. We're owned by the federal government." I learned that negotiations were underway that would allow the U.S. government to sell the railroad to the state of Alaska. It now has been sold to the state government, which is trying to turn the losing venture around.

Charlie and I were the only ones to get off at McKinley Station. The sourdoughs were continuing to Fairbanks, and I supposed the plump woman was too, since she was still asleep. The train station, the scene of so much activity during the summer, was now deserted. I glanced around, trying to remember details of this place from my past visit. Everything looked so different.

While we were unloading our cross-country skis and backpacks from the baggage car, a stocky, middle-aged man strode up to us. His tattered down parka, patched blue jeans and tape-wrapped insulated pac boots were a far cry from our high-tech stretch ski suits, pile jackets and bright Gore-Tex outerwear.

He introduced himself as Dennis, the man we had been expecting to meet. He ran Denali Dog Tours and Wilderness Freighters, a commercial dog-team service licensed to operate within the park. During the past few months we had corresponded with him about caching food and fuel for us at two locations along our route. This way we would have to ski with only a week's worth of supplies at a time. Dennis told us he was leaving early the following morning on a ninety-mile journey to Kantishna, an abandoned mining town near Wonder Lake just outside the park. On the way, he would drop off our food bags at prearranged caches, the furthest fifty-five miles away. At a cost of less than a dollar a pound for cartage, we thought we were coming out ahead on the deal.

When the transfer was completed, we hoisted our double-decker packs. After Dennis left, I was free to let out a groan. Even with the bulk of my food removed, my internal frame sack still weighed over sixty pounds. A bit of adjustment was necessary before the load felt right, then we skied west on the main park road toward the headquarters to obtain our backcountry permit.

It became apparent as we glided past the shuttered buildings, closed hotel and deserted information station that except for a few dog mushers and park patrols, we would have virtually the entire six-million-acre park to ourselves. By contrast, backpackers who visit Denali in summer often have to wait several days before they are allowed to enter the backcountry. It was this solitude, as well as the anticipation of observing Denali's abundant wildlife, that appealed to us most about this off-season trip.

We rustled up an off-duty ranger at the headquarters office. She was surprised to have visitors drop in at this late hour. While filling out our permit, she explained that only a skeleton crew worked in the park in the off-season. "After the first snowfall, the only visitors we generally get are a few mushers, snowshoers and skiers. Winter is my favorite season here. Right now Denali is wilderness at its best."

The sun set as we made camp in a grove of black spruce and quaking aspen a half-mile past the headquarters. Stepping out of our skis, we sank to our knees in the fluffy snow. I stomped out a flat spot while Charlie unpacked the tent. The experience acquired during a number of ski and snowshoe trips together allowed us to work efficiently and with few words.

The deep bass hoots of a great-horned owl acted as an alarm clock. Seven o'clock, time to get moving. I glanced at the thermometer hanging outside the door. Ugh! Fifteen below. I moved sluggishly as if my heart were pumping thick, summer-weight oil. Ordinarily simple chores such as getting dressed and stuffing sleeping bags become increasingly complicated when the temperature falls much below zero Fahrenheit. I pulled on my black nylon ski suit over the polypropylene long johns I had worn to bed, then I put on two pairs of dry wool socks and slipped my feet into down booties and mukluks. Only when I had my down jacket and pile pants on was I ready to crawl out of the tent.

When I emerged I noticed a half-dozen brown shapes moving silently through the dark spruce. When the animals stepped into a sun-dappled clearing, I recognized them as Alaska moose. Over seven feet tall at the shoulder and weighing close to 1,200 pounds, these ungainly looking Denali residents are unmistakable. Able to traverse deep snow where caribou and Dall sheep flounder, the long, spindly legged moose plodded down a steep ravine that led to a frozen creek, then vanished into a thick streamside tangle. The clouds of steam emanating from the moose's bulbous noses reminded me just how cold it was.

Only after the sun had warmed the air a bit did we break camp. We didn't have to consult the map, since initially we planned to follow the snow-packed park road through the wooded terrain.

Built in 1927 as a result of pressure to open up the new Alaskan park, the sinuous, ninety-mile road, mostly gravel, cuts through the heart of Denali, one of the greatest spectacles in North America. It rolls across lowland spruce forests and high tundra, passes over wide, braided rivers, meanders up mountain passes and skirts lofty ridges. Visitors in summer are allowed access to Wonder Lake, near the base of Mount McKinley, through a combination of shuttle buses and regulated private vehicles. When the first major snowfall blankets the ground, however, usually in mid-September, the road is closed to motor vehicles, including snow machines. For nearly eight months of the year, the lane becomes a part of the wilderness. Snowdrifts make the road blend in with the surrounding landscape. Wildlife moves back into areas that were abandoned during the summer.

Two long days' travel over a distance of thirty miles took us past the Savage River, Mount Margaret, the prominent 4,275-foot Mount Wright, and the Sanctuary River. We had gained almost 1,500 feet in elevation since leaving the headquarters, but now we were greeted by a fairly level route surrounded by pleasantly undulating hills. From the top of an open tundra pass, which marked the highest point between the Savage and Sanctuary rivers, we paused to gaze upon Mount McKinley. This was Charlie's first view of the legendary peak. He was impressed when I told him that the *lowest* point on the mountain visible from here was 12,000 feet high! Towering above the distant horizon, the snow-capped waves of rock urged us on.

As we skied up and down the sloping hills, we found ourselves in a perpetually changing corridor, with the unbroken icy peaks and domes of the Alaska Range to the south, and a smaller series of mountains—the Outside Range, or "outer hills," as Alaskans call them—to the north. Occupying the wide valley between the mountains and the rounded humps of the outer hills was a mosaic of open, unprotected tundra—windswept, treeless meadows and slopes where small shrubs, sedges, herbs, mosses and lichens lay under a thin blanket of snow—and thin, wavering taiga forests adjacent to the river valleys. Only the *taiga*—a Russian term meaning "the land of little sticks," which describes the stunted, wind-sheared trees—offered a respite from the incessantly blowing breezes that swept across the countryside.

We weren't the only ones attracted to these windbreaks of spruce, interspersed with deciduous trees of modest size. Searching for a campsite along the glacier-fed Teklanika River, we were scolded by energetic red squirrels as we skied under their globular nests of twigs and moss. They were temporarily quieted when a pair of raven-sized goshawks whizzed through the tree canopy, surprising us as much as they did the squirrels. A moment later a flock of a hundred or more willow ptarmigan, the pure white grouse of

Charlie Roger looking back at the Alaska Range; Mount McKinley is the highest peak.

the winter north, scattered when the accipiters glided into their midst. Skiing further, we crossed the tracks of moose, wolf, lynx, ermine and snowshoe hare. As harsh as Denali is in winter, it appeared that we would have plenty of warm-blooded company.

Charlie and I shared the trait of being early risers, which was one of the reasons I was out of the tent at 6:30. The other reason was that it was my turn to fire up the camp stove to melt snow for water. I had finally started the temperamental thing when I saw something out of the corner of my eye. A dog-sized animal—a red fox? a wolf?—had burst out of a clump of willows a hundred yards off and was loping across the tundra. I reached for my binoculars.

"Charlie! Hey, man, get out here!" I gasped.

A black-and-tan wolverine, rarely seen even by longtime residents of the bush, had its nose to the ground sniffing the snow. Its low-slung body, buffy chevron stripe across the chest, and short bushy tail made identification easy. Suddenly, the big weasel stiffened and looked up. Something, not us, must have frightened it. With a surprisingly fast gait for such a squat animal, the wolverine lurched across the clearing and disappeared into the spruce forest.

We waited and watched for awhile, hoping the wolverine would reappear. When it was clear it wouldn't, we broke camp and began our own slow-motion advance through the forest. The moment to detour from the road had arrived. Rather than skirt the high slopes of Igloo Mountain, where the road went, we decided that the easiest route was to follow the Teklanika River to the south side of Cathedral Mountain, then veer west to Sable Pass.

Leaving the trees behind, we gingerly skied atop the frozen river, unsure whether it would support our weight. We need not have worried. The river's cover of snow had almost completely blown off, leaving bare and bubbly ice four feet thick. The only real dangers were open holes and fissures, which we encountered periodically. We kept searching the ice ahead to avoid falling into the cold, clear water that lay underneath.

We had applied layer upon layer of wax to the bottoms of our fiberglass skis, but it was stripped away almost instantly by the abrasive ice. With no grip, I felt as if I were riding a motorcycle with bald tires on an oily road. Sometimes I spun out wildly with total loss of control; at other times my legs wanted to do a split. Skiing with a diagonal stride was out of the question. I soon learned that the proper technique was to keep the skis parallel and push forward by constant double-poling. When conditions were right, I could maintain a blistering pace. It was only a matter of time, though, before an accident would happen. I was double-poling, moving at a fast sprint with the wind at my back, when an ice bubble forced my skis to cross. *Whump!* I pitched forward and sprawled flat on my face, pinned to the ice by my gargantuan pack. Charlie rushed over to see if I was all right. "No bones broken," I muttered as he helped me to my feet.

We made camp at the base of Cathedral Mountain, back within the strip of taiga bordering the Teklanika. At first glance the adjacent countryside appeared barren and lifeless, but each time I looked through my binoculars something different appeared: a cow moose and calf at the edge of a distant stand of willows; a golden eagle skimming over the tundra headed for its evening roost; a small band of Dall sheep, easy to spot as tiny white dots against a brown, snow-free hillside. I was at peace with my surroundings and myself.

After dinner an icy wind flowed down from the glaciers. Grand vistas and wildlife observations notwithstanding, our sole desire was to get inside the tent, curl up in our sleeping bags and read. Charlie had recently become addicted to bird-watching, and studied his field guide for species we might encounter here and in the Brooks Range. I preferred to leaf through the sheaves of park information I had brought. This wasn't the first time I had read the brochures and pamphlets, but now that I was here, the facts, interpretations and natural and human history were more meaningful. Warm and cozy in my heavy down bag, my head propped on a pillow of spare clothes, the wind bouncing harmlessly off the side of the tent, I stuffed a chocolate bar in my mouth and opened a brochure that lay on my chest. If this wasn't utter contentment, nothing was.

Geology is a good place to begin describing the park. Denali National Park and Preserve lies within the great bow-shaped arc of the Alaska Range, a 600-mile-long mountain chain stretching across Alaska's lower third. The park is located at the northern limit of the last great continental ice sheet that covered the northern hemisphere 10,000 to 14,000 years ago. Although most of Denali's glaciers are mere remnants of what they were in the past, numerous ice fields still cascade down from many of the higher mountains. The glacial influence on the area is evident everywhere. Broad U-shaped valleys, wide gravel bars, and low hills dotted with glacial melt ponds show where the moving ice shaped the land.

"The park," stated the brochure, "exemplifies interior Alaska's character as one of the world's last great frontiers offering an opportunity for wilderness. It remains largely wild and unspoiled, as the early explorers and pioneers found it." All I had to do was look out the tent door to see that this was true. The wide, low plains of taiga and tundra seemed to stretch forever, as did the surrounding hills and low mountains that merged with the Alaska Range. Some national parks I've visited in the lower forty-eight—Big Bend in Texas, Capital Reef and Canyonlands in Utah, Yellowstone, the Everglades, South Dakota's Badlands—approach Denali in providing me with what I feel is quintessential wilderness. However, whether it is a state of mind, my personal bias, or a reality, I believe the only true wilderness left in the United States is found in Alaska. In *A Sand County Almanac*, which became the bible of the environmental movement of the 1960s and early 1970s, Aldo Leopold wrote that wilderness encompasses many things, but more than anything else it is a place "big enough to absorb a two weeks' pack trip, and kept devoid of roads, artificial trails, cottages, or other works of man." In Alaska there are still many places large enough to absorb backcountry trips of a month or more without encountering the works of man. Denali is one. Despite many regrettable man-made intrusions, Denali National Park and Preserve still remains an area that, in Leopold's words, qualifies as "a sanctuary for the primitive art of wilderness travel."[1]

The park is many things to many people, but for me it is first and foremost a world of animals. I was interested to learn that park researchers have deduced that some 2,700 caribou, 2,500 sheep, 2,700 moose, 111 wolves, 200 black bear, and 200 grizzly bear inhabit Denali's open, rolling tundra, spruce forests and river valleys. This is in addition to a variety of smaller creatures, including wolverine, lynx, marten, hoary marmot, beaver, red fox and 157 recorded species of birds. Because of its amazing concentration of wildlife, one researcher has compared Denali's lowlands to the Serengeti Plain of Africa. A United Nations agency designated Denali as an International Biosphere Reserve, an honor given to only a handful of parks worldwide. There are few places on this planet where it's possible to view moose, caribou, Dall sheep and grizzly bears in the wild; in Denali, as Judy and I had done during our summer visit, it is relatively simple to see and photograph them all in a single day.

It comes as a surprise to many that protection of Denali's wildlife, not the majestic Mount McKinley, was the impetus behind the park's establishment. Charles Sheldon, a prominent hunter/naturalist and president of the Boone and Crockett Club, spearheaded founding of the park in 1908. His interests focused on the area's large mammal population, particularly the heavily hunted Dall sheep, one of only two species of wild white sheep in the world. His goal was to have the area set aside as a "game preserve," a model for national parks to come.

However, while the handsome and articulate Sheldon lobbied in the nation's capital for wildlife protection, the summit of Mount McKinley was attracting the real attention. A race was on to see who would be first to reach the top. From 1903 to 1913, there were no fewer than eight earnest attempts to scale the mountain. In 1910 four Alaskans, calling themselves "The Sourdough Expedition," pioneered the long and arduous Muldrow Glacier route and succeeded in climbing the slightly lower north peak, a phenomenal feat considering they had only crude homemade equipment and bulky supplies of food. Three years later, Sheldon's friend, Harry Karstens (who later was appointed the first superintendent of the park), and Archdeacon Hudson Stuck, Walter Harper and Robert G. Tatum won the race when they became the first human beings to stand on McKinley's South Peak, the true summit of this lofty massif.

When the national park was established in 1917 it was given the same name as the mountain: McKinley. The designation was hotly disputed, just as it had been in 1899 when the mountain itself had been named for the former senator—and later president—William McKinley. The majority of Alaskans thought both labels were ludicrous. McKinley never laid eyes on Mount McKinley or the park and had exhibited no particular interest in either. It wasn't until 1980, with passage of the Alaska National Interest Conservation Act, that half the wrong was righted: the park was renamed *Denali* ("the High One" or "the Great One"), the Athabaskan Indian name for the mountain. However, to the disappointment of many Alaskans and mountaineers, fierce politicking by legislators from President McKinley's home state of Ohio persuaded the U.S. Geological Survey to leave the mountain's moniker unchanged.

Although name changes proved to be an emotional issue, they were only a minor concern of this landmark conservation act, signed by President Carter. Of far greater importance was the fact that the parkland tripled in size. Currently Denali National Park and Preserve embraces more than six million acres, an area larger than the state of Massachusetts.

I folded the pamphlets and returned them to their plastic bag. It was dark outside; Charlie was fast asleep. Tired as I was, I had been so engrossed I didn't know where the last two hours had gone. My head was swimming with new-found information. I had no intention of climbing Mount McKinley. I'd leave that to the thousands of people who attempt that challenge each year. My interests lay in the shadow of the "High One," an attitude shared by Alfred Hulse Brooks, the famous pioneer of the U.S. Geological Survey in Alaska for whom the Brooks Range was named. Exploring the area around McKinley at the turn of the century, Brooks applauded those who had designs on the summit. "But as for me," he wrote, "I am satisfied to have been able to traverse the great lowland to the base and to climb the foothills."

It had been five hours since we left our camp at the Teklanika River. Our leaden packs were feeling heavy and our legs tired from the steady uphill grind. To continue west into the park we had to cross Sable Pass. At 3,895 feet above sea level, the pass wasn't particularly high, but the views were sublime. Although Mount McKinley was still many miles to the southwest, the sight of this ice-covered massif, considered by many to be Alaska's most impressive feature, was still overwhelming. With a vertical relief of some 18,000 feet above the wide tundra plain before it, a greater rise than that of Mount Everest from base to summit, McKinley could accurately be called the tallest mountain on earth. Most of the other snow-capped peaks that surround the High One are dwarfed by its sheer size.

I put the big mountain out of my mind and concentrated on traversing the pass. This was not where I wanted to spend the night. Treeline in the park is about 2,000 feet, except in some protected river valleys, where it may extend to 2,800 feet. Sable Pass was therefore treeless and covered with a heavy mantle of snow. No birds ventured here—there was nothing to eat. The only mammals there were hibernating. I tried to convey to Charlie how different this place was in the summer. In just a few months, the barren landscape would be ablaze with colorful arctic wildflowers. Marmots, ground squirrels, voles and lemmings would grow fat on the tundra plants. They in turn would fall prey to weasels, foxes, hawks and eagles. Grizzly bears, too, find the highland meadows to their liking, so much so that Sable Pass is closed to hikers during the summer season.

Whenever I mentioned "grizzly," Charlie perked up. He had

never seen a grizzly bear and didn't really want to except from a safe distance. "There's nothing to worry about," I pointed out. "On this trip we have as much chance of seeing a grizzly as we do of seeing a giraffe."

I was stretching the truth. Depending on location, physical condition and the sex and age of the bear, Alaskan grizzlies usually retire to their winter dens in late October and emerge in April or early May. I had read of instances of grizzlies awakening even earlier from their long sleep, but their excursions usually last from only a few hours to a few days.

Four miles of easy downhill skiing brought us to the East Fork River. This wide and braided stream is a major tributary of the Toklat River, which in turn drains a large part of the park. We pitched the tent among some scanty willows at the edge of a snow- and ice-covered gravel bar around which the braided river intertwined. There was so much overflow ice at this point, created when running water underneath the ice breaks through and freezes on top, that the river resembled a large skating rink. The overflow had made odd-looking islands out of a few solitary spruce trees. I snapped a series of pictures of this unusual sight when the ice glowed a crimson pink with the setting sun. There were times during the journey when I cursed the photography gear—my pack was heavy enough without an additional ten pounds of glass and metal, but moments like these made me glad to have a quality 35mm SLR camera and an assortment of lenses. It was one thing to have the image etched into my mind, and quite another to be able to view it years later with my eyes.

I focused my wide-angle lens on Charlie melting snow over the stove. We had pushed deeper into the belly of the park and were now midway between the Alaska Range and the Wyoming Hills. As far as I knew, we were the only human beings for a hundred square miles around. Dennis and his dog team were probably far ahead. I took one last picture, then put away the camera. At 7 p.m. there was still enough light to read, but not enough for Kodachrome film. I listened to the rifle-crack sound of the ice expanding with the cold. Charlie motioned me over—the water was boiling. At that moment nothing was more appealing than a steaming mug of tomato soup.

That evening, as I lay in my sleeping bag, writing in my journal, I jotted down some notes about the day. We had picked up three days' worth of food at our Igloo Creek cache, which, when added to our next depot, left us twelve days' worth of food before returning to Igloo for the last of our supplies. The temperature had been in the teens this afternoon, and now stood at ten degrees. After more comments on weather, animal sightings and the quality of skiing, I focused on something that was beginning to bother me. I couldn't discuss it with Charlie, because his uncommunicativeness was part of the problem.

I always knew Charlie to be rather quiet even among his closest friends, but since starting on this journey his taciturn demeanor had become more pronounced. We had just gone through an entire day without more than a few minutes of dialogue, even though I wanted to talk. Emotionally, I was beginning to feel as if I were doing the trip solo. Charlie and I were still on very friendly terms, but something seemed to be lacking in our friendship—a bonding, a confidence, a comfortable conviviality that good buddies are supposed to have. I didn't want to make too much of it, yet I had to try and analyze the situation. If his solemn mood was in fact just his nature, there was nothing I could do. But if his solemnity was due to the newness of the region, the cold, the prospect of a grizzly encounter, the goal we had before us, perhaps I could help. I remembered that Judy had noted that I, too, was uncharacteristically quiet my first few days in Alaska, but once I began to relax I was able to open up. Ready to nod off, I decided to not let Charlie's quietness bother me. Just act like it's normal and let Charlie work it out for himself.

Our campsite must have been a courtship arena for all the local ptarmigan. With a winter diet of dry berries, leaves and the buds of birches and willows, the gregarious birds were attracted to the knee-high brush that lined the watercourse. The amorous grouse chattered throughout the night and into the early morning. Their repetitive "tobacco . . . tobacco . . . tobacco" call, plus an assortment of cackles and chicken-like clucks, made me wish I had brought earplugs. Neither of us got much rest, which may have contributed to our decision to stay another night at the East Fork.

We loaded up our daypacks after breakfast for an exploration upriver. Nine miles from camp, tucked away into the folds of the Alaska Range, was a long tapering glacier at the head of the East Fork. It was tough slogging, hardly what we had in mind when the notion of a "rest" day was originally conceived. A strong wind blowing north out of the mountains, coupled with a river bed of uneven ice, slowed our pace to a crawl. Every hour or so we'd paste on a triple coat of new wax. A hundred yards later we'd be skiing on waxless slats.

Five hours after leaving camp we reached the source of the East Fork in a high rocky basin of the Alaska Range. Fantastic pyramid-shaped peaks, some two miles high, towered over us. The sight of the glacier, a pearly-blue tongue of frosted ice hanging from a somber peak, lured us onward. At the edge of the glacier was a chute that led into its inner chambers. We took off our skis and cautiously entered the ice cavern, walking, sliding, slipping, ascending, until we could proceed no further. A vertical wall of ice blocked our path. I peered into the frozen mass. Suspended within like stars in a galaxy were small boulders, rocks and grit plucked from high up the mountain, locked in suspension for hundreds, perhaps thousands, of years. I began to shiver. It was time to head back down.

Our return trip was exhilarating, the longest uninterrupted ski run I had ever been on. A steady, hard wind propelled us down the crusty snowpack. The slope of the river bed was only a few degrees, but the sensation of speed was fantastic. Sometimes the wind pushed too hard; frequently we had to snowplow or turn back into the breeze to slow ourselves. It took us only an hour-and-a-half to get out.

After the satisfying day, that night the darkness of the tent made it easy to talk. I broached the subject that I felt awkward bringing up earlier. "Charlie, I've been trying to read your mind, but you haven't given me any clues. Are you having a good time out here?"

He put his hands behind his head and sighed. In the dim light, with his pointed beard and hooked vulterine nose, he reminded me of Gandolf, the wizard, from Tolkien's *Hobbit*. "Yeah, I'm having a good time. Now quit playing Dr. Freud and get some sleep." He rolled over and cinched up his hood.

The next day we followed one of the braids of the East Fork past the base of the steep, rugged cliffs and turrets of Polychrome Pass. The 1,500-foot-high wall, volcanic in origin, was a kaleidoscope of color. Bands of red, purple, yellow, brown and green merged together, interrupted only by rock slides and ravines. On the other side of this rocky rainbow was the Toklat River ranger cabin, where Dennis had agreed to deposit our most distant cache.

Polychrome is Dall sheep country, some of their best winter range in Denali. Through binoculars we counted about thirty of the dingy-white animals clinging to the mountain. The sheep choose the inaccessible, windswept ridges for the lichens, grasses and forbs that are exposed, plus the available escape routes from predators. The largest band consisted of ewes and yearlings, while a hundred yards away were a half-dozen mature rams identifiable by their massive curled horns. All the animals appeared healthy and fit, which may have been a direct result of the mild winter.

The snow veneer on Polychrome Flats was hard packed and fast, allowing us to make good time. In five hours we covered the twelve miles from our East Fork camp to the Toklat ranger cabin. When we got there, I groaned as I dropped my pack. I waited for Charlie to reveal some pain, but he remained characteristically stoic. "You think your shoulders are sore now," he jabbed, showing no sympathy, "wait until you add another sack of food to your load."

Dennis had placed our big orange bag, containing a week's worth of food for each of us, plus spare fuel, flashlight batteries and paperbacks, in a ramshackle shed behind the deserted, locked cabin. We had been concerned about wolverines bothering the supplies. But when we opened the loose-fitting door, a little red squirrel greeted us. The feisty animal, perched atop the chewed-open orange bag, was busily stuffing its face with my trail mix of nuts, raisins and M&Ms. "Get out of here!" I yelled, throwing my gloves at the rodent. The squirrel had nowhere to go but out the door. A blurry red streak blasted past me and scurried up the nearest tree.

The damage to our supplies was minimal. We sealed the tear with duct tape; only about four ounces of my precious food had been consumed. In what I thought was a touching, magnanimous gesture, Charlie offered to give me a couple ounces of his gorp when I began to starve. He knew how prodigious my appetite was, having more than once accompanied me to an all-you-can-eat buffet.

After quickly packing our food and supplies, we skied the frozen, rocky Toklat to a small grove of spruce trees downstream of the cabin. Low, hump-backed mountains rose on either side of the river. The largest of these was Mount Sheldon, a 5,570-footer named for Charles Sheldon, who had spent the winter of 1907–1908 in the nearby Wyoming Hills. Sheldon's sojourn of hunting and exploration convinced him that the Denali wilderness should be set aside as a national preserve. His experiences also provided background for *The Wilderness World of Denali*, published in 1939. I found Sheldon's tales of excitement in Alaska's subarctic absorbing.

I had other reasons to be fond of the Wyoming Hills. This was where Judy and I had camped and hiked during our first sojourn to Alaska. We were seduced by the area's superb mountain scenery and wildlife, as Sheldon had been three-quarters of a century before. The wide, braided river acts as a natural pathway connecting the rugged Alaska Range with the lakes and spruce forests of the northern lowlands. During our late summer visit we had seen caribou, bear, sheep, fox and other animals on a regular basis. Charlie, growing tired of my persistent raving about the area, suggested we spend the next three nights along the Toklat.

We searched the vicinity for a campsite that would offer us a view of the valley as well as protection from the wind. Finally, we pitched the tent near a thin line of spruce trees. Here there were only a few inches of snow, and in spots none at all, as opposed to a more secure spot deeper in the woods with two or three feet of fine, dry snow and no view.

"Funny, isn't it?" Charlie remarked as we unbagged the tent. "Folks at home probably think we're hip-deep in snow with thirty-below temperatures, but there was more snow in Peoria when we left than we've got right here!"

I checked the thermometer to see if my body parts would be safe for the night. No problem, eighteen degrees, a veritable heat wave. With the longer days, the worst of winter was over. Although temperatures near park headquarters may fall below minus fifty degrees Fahrenheit in January and February, during March and April the average daytime temperature is between twenty and thirty-eight degrees *above*. By the middle of May, rivers would be breaking up and only patches of snow would remain at lower elevations. The period between late winter and early spring generally offers the best cross-country skiing in Denali.

The next couple of days we spent rambling among the snow-spotted slopes of the Wyoming Hills, which separate the two main forks of the Toklat. I knew from reading Adolph Murie's landmark wildlife study, *The Wolves of Mount McKinley*, that a large number of Dall sheep spend the winter here, migrating over from the main Alaska Range where they live during the summer.[2] Related to the bighorn sheep of the Rocky Mountains, Alaska's Dall sheep are completely at home on or near steep, rocky areas, where they use their incredible climbing skills when threatened by wolves and grizzlies. The sheep are attracted to the windblown plateaus and ridges of the Outer Range for the grasses, creeping willows and sedges they contain. A telephoto shot of an adult, full-curled ram with the Alaska Range as a backdrop would be the justification I needed for carrying the heavy 200mm lens.

Hiking the Wyoming Hills was a welcome change from ski-packing the lowlands. Without heavy packs, and not having to concern ourselves with deep or slippery snow, we practically floated up the frozen, rock-hard tundra slopes. One route took us toward a precipitous ridge that was half-concealed in the clouds. Only when we neared the apex did we become aware that a large band of white sheep had us under observation. The animals acted leery at first—perhaps because they hadn't seen a human being since the previous summer, but even when they resumed grazing, we gave them a wide berth. Winter offered the sheep enough challenges from wolves, starvation and accidents; we didn't want them to expend valuable energy avoiding us.

There was more to view in the high country than Dall sheep. Beneath our perch the mile-wide Toklat River drainage and adjacent hills were full of potential ski touring options. The Alaska Range unfolded to the south as far as we could see.

We huddled against an embankment and watched for wildlife. It was a quiet, reflective time, until a freshening breeze swirled over the hillside. The sky turned gray and dreary. We stiffly got to our feet and headed back down the mountain. I thought of the sheep as we glided into camp at dusk. I last saw them bedded down in the open, their rumps to the wind.

Dark, ominous clouds rolled past as we sat around the blazing stove. We had to melt about five pots of snow to get one pot of water. On a calm night this process might take a half-hour. Tonight, though, with the wind penetrating the stove's wrap-around screen, it was over an hour before our freeze-dried dinners were ready. We dug ravenously into the plastic-bound concoctions wrapped in air-tight aluminum foil. Shrimp Creole. Chili mac. Beef stroganoff. A side order of peas. All doused with fat dabs of high-calorie margarine and home-bagged spices. Taste really didn't matter. I gulped it all down without chewing in an effort to get to the last chunks before they turned ice cold.

Soon after eating we retired to the tent. I snuggled into my sleeping bag, cringing at the first touch of the icy nylon. In a few minutes the down cocoon warmed to the temperature of my body. With a Farley Mowat paperback about the Far North propped up on my chest, I was as comfortable as I would have been in my own bedroom.

The wind continued unabated the next day, but that didn't keep us from prowling the hills. Protected by several layers of clothing, we herringboned and sidestepped as far as possible up the slopes until the crusty snow merged into bare tundra. Then, leaving our skis upright so they would be clearly visible on the return trip, we ascended a long, narrow ridge to the 5,000-foot contour. We

Larry Rice at the campsite in the shadow of Denali.

hoped that near the summit of the Wyoming Hills we would have unhindered views in every direction.

We were about a minute from reaching our destination when I noticed a trio of dark objects below, moving purposefully in a tree-less gully a quarter-mile away. "Are they what I think they are?" I whispered. I was shaking, more from excitement than the cold.

At my side, Charlie already had his binoculars glued to his eyes. "I think so. . . . I'm sure so. I'll be damned. Wolves!"

Hiding behind tufts of short grass, we watched with fascination as the tundra wolves loped across the narrow valley in single-file procession. Wolves come in several shades from black to white, but these animals all exhibited the more common gray coats. Even at this distance, there was no mistaking them for their smaller cousin, the coyote, an uncommon resident of the forested eastern sections of the park.

Moving effortlessly at a pace that could cover fifty miles in a single night, the animals left the valley for the high country, climbing the crest of a knife-edged mountain across from us. I focused on the leader. Every so often he would stop and stare off into space, probably scanning for weak or careless sheep. I doubted the wolves would find any; in the last few minutes the sheep had calmly drifted away. The wolves continued their upward journey, their canine outlines silhouetted perfectly against the jagged skyline. The pack followed the scree to the peak. I blinked and they were gone.

The morning's temperature was a balmy thirty-two degrees. A warm front had moved into the park while we slept, ushering in moist air and a low, dull sky. Hills we had climbed earlier were lost in the clouds. The Alaska Range had disappeared.

We broke camp without conversation, interested in getting an early start on the trail. I studied the map a final time, trying to calculate exactly how far we had to go. Fifteen miles of open tundra separated us from Thorofare Pass, at 3,900 feet one of the highest points on the Denali road, and from there it was another five miles to a remnant glacial terrace above the Thorofare River, our furthest destination on the trip. We had a lot of skiing to do, but were anxious to go. The last two days without packing had given our shoulders a welcome rest.

When we neared Thorofare Pass in mid-afternoon, the gloomy overcast was gone. The warm front had punched through, leaving a cirrus-tattered sky in its wake.

"Well, I'll be . . . look at that!" Charlie called. He was already at the top, hunched over onto his poles, gazing toward the southwest. I put on my dark sunglasses and hurried to his side. All of Mount McKinley burst into view from top to bottom for the first time. The mountain's mass was overwhelming: it dominated the horizon although still more than thirty miles away. Other snowy summits—Mount Brooks, Mount Mather, Mount Silverthrone, Mount Carpé, with elevations of 11,000 feet and above—were dwarfed by McKinley's bulk.

The magnetism of the mountain pulled us on. We raced down the pass, glided past the shuttered Eielson Visitor Center and made camp a couple of hours later in a wide-open trough with the Alaska Range to the south and bumpy foothills to the north. From the tent door I watched the sinking sun slowly illuminate the massif in shades of orange, red, pink and purple—hot, fiery colors that belied the icy barrenness found all along its sculpted slopes.

Many other big mountains are technically more difficult to climb, but positioned as it is less than 250 miles from the Arctic Circle and perpetually gripped by winter conditions, McKinley has the reputation of being one of the most severe climber's destinations in the world. According to one well-known mountaineer, a McKinley summit bid "is about 90 percent trying to stay warm and alive, and only about 10 percent climbing."

In the three-quarters of a century since Denali was first climbed, 10,000 people have struggled up its slopes. Nearly half of them made it to the top, another fifty-three died trying, along with hundreds of cases of illness and injury, mostly frostbitten fingers and toes. Climbed in all seasons and in all manners, by the very young and the very old, the downside of the mountain's majesty is that it has become a very busy place. A record 916 climbers attempted to scale McKinley in 1988, prompting the National Park Service to consider installing an *outhouse* at the 17,000-foot level for sanitation purposes.

As I sat there eating my dinner, ruminating over how human beings can love even the likes of Mount McKinley to death, the full moon we had been anticipating all week broke over the Alaska Range. A pale milky light bathed the snow-covered lowlands in muted brightness. The air was calm, peaceful. Sitting outside by myself, I was adrift in a sea of tranquility. It was a long time before I slipped into the tent.

In the morning the mountain was gone, three-and-a-half vertical miles of rock and ice swallowed by fog. Everything felt damp and beads of moisture collected on the inside walls of the tent. Worse, the rising temperature turned the snow into a sloppy mess. It was a good day *not* to move camp.

Although the air was warmer, it felt much colder with the higher relative humidity. We got dressed in our usual multilayer outfits and sat outside on foam pads. There wasn't much to see with the mountain vistas blotted out, but after a hot breakfast chased away the chill, we decided that we might as well ski. I only had one more paperback left, and I wanted to save it for the luxury of reading at the end of a hard day.

Rather than drop down to the Thorofare River gravel bar far below, we did a zigzag climb back to the park road, which was about a half-mile from our camp. Immediately upon reaching it, we crossed a string of fresh wolf tracks in the snow. The animals were going east, the same direction from which we had come. We stopped often to listen and look. A large flock of tiny snow buntings whirred by us, and every so often a rock ptarmigan would appear, but we saw no mammals.

Charlie expressed his surprise that we hadn't seen any caribou on this trip. I doubted we would. The caribou's winter range is in the lowland country north and west of the park, many miles from where we planned to go, where they subsist on vegetation—mostly lichens, dug from beneath the snow with their broad front hooves.

In late April and May the caribou begin drifting toward the eastern section of the park, staying primarily on the south side of the Alaska Range. In late June or early July they recross the mountains and complete the circle back toward the western end of Denali. It's during this period that hundreds of caribou are seen along the park road, delighting bus riders and backpackers alike.

Having never seen a caribou, Charlie was understandably disappointed. "I guess that's just one more reason I'll have to go to the Arctic Refuge with you and Judy this summer."

A maxim of winter camping is: Stay warm by staying dry. We were better off when the temperature remained below freezing, as ice is easier to cope with than water. After only a few miles our boots and socks became soaked. My fancy insulated ski overboots had worked splendidly at home during trial tours, but Denali's marble-hard snow had shredded them to ribbons. Charlie's simple stretch-rubber oversocks hadn't fared much better, but at least they didn't fall off his feet. We had spare, dry wool socks, both heavyweight and liners, but without some sun our boots would probably remain wet for the rest of the trip.

The warm front covering Denali had other effects besides turning snow into slush. It generated a restlessness in certain animals generally dormant at this time of year. Retracing our route back to camp, we received a jolt. In front of our ski tips were the unmistakable tracks of griz: a five-toed footprint, as long as my boot, but almost twice as wide, with claws extending well beyond the toes. Not only were the depressions obviously of recent origin, they angled precisely toward our camp. We skied cautiously behind the bear trail, knowing that a bear just out of its winter den might be more cantankerous than usual. To our relief, a few hundred yards from the tent, the grizzly tracks veered up a ravine and were lost among a pile of boulders. Later I learned that this observation on the final day of March was the earliest grizzly bear sign recorded in the park in several years.

We had an early dinner, then made a quick retreat into the tent. The wind had picked up, and with it came a sticky sleet that lashed the taut rainfly of our dome tent. There was still plenty of light, but visibility was limited. I burrowed into my sleeping bag, trying to convince myself that this was just another average, low-level gale that would burn itself out in a couple of hours.

At 7 p.m. the wind began to get worse, although the tent continued to hold up well. I started reading *Brendan's Voyage*, by Tim Severin, to take my mind off the storm. In 1976, the author and a small crew sailed from Ireland to Newfoundland in an open leather boat to show that a sixth-century Irish monk, Saint Brendan, could have crossed the Atlantic in an identical vessel made of oxhides, thus proving that Irish monks may have been the first Europeans to set foot in America. The terrible weather they encountered made me shudder, and the story increased my feelings of gloom and apprehension. Our tent was as exposed as a raft in a stormy sea.

A few hours later the wind grew much stronger. The tent rocked back and forth from powerful gusts, which caved in the side panels. Just after midnight on April 1 our dome tent broke loose from its anchors and turned turtle.

The night spent clutching the collapsed tent to our sides was long. Neither of us said much. Finally a ray of sun stirred me from a restless slumber. I checked my watch through puffy eyes: eight o'clock. Morning always brings a new outlook on life, a fresh start. Almost always. This morning the staccato rattling of the wind-whipped nylon gave me a headache. I nudged Charlie. He snarled. Eight hours huddled cheek-to-cheek had made him as grouchy as I was.

I squirmed to the door and peered out. Visibility had improved dramatically. Mount McKinley and the rest of the Alaska Range poked through the stringy clouds, trailing streamers of snow off their wind-blasted peaks. Down at ground level, a skim of spindrift swept across the tundra. The skiing would be brutal on our return to the Toklat River, the nearest place with trees for shelter, but anything was better than remaining in this hurricane tunnel. Cold and stiff, we decided to move on.

We emerged from our bags, only to discover that we each had on some of the other's clothes, a real trick since I'm a head taller. "Here, take your pile jacket," Charlie groused. "And here's your hat and vest."

"Thanks," I replied. "You mind checking to see if you have my underwear on?"

Once we were properly attired we went to work on the rest of our equipment, which was scattered in the creases and folds. While one of us packed, the other held off the flapping tent and pinned items down to keep them from blowing away. A half-hour later we were ready to face the wintry world of Denali.

We skied through the wind for the next seven hours, taking only brief breaks to rest. Sunshine or not, this was still a whopper of a storm. Several times I was nearly knocked flat. I used my poles like outriggers on a canoe as we lurched toward the safety of the trees.

We were both slightly beat up when we arrived at the Toklat River. The wind was still blowing, but not nearly as hard as before. Not taking any chances, we set up the battered tent on a slab of deep snow in the thickest stand of spruces we could find. The evergreens' conical spires bent to the breeze, but inside the security of the forest there was scarcely a ripple of air.

After doing my chores I suddenly felt drained. Immediately after dinner I crawled into the tent and drifted off to sleep. All night I tossed and turned, my mind unable to turn off the sound of the morning's ghoulish winds. (My nightmares would have been worse had I known just how widespread and severe the storm had been. The high winds spewing out of the Gulf of Alaska served up the worst disaster to hit Alaska since the 1964 earthquake struck Anchorage. The night our tent blew over, winds clocked at over 130 miles per hour tore through Anchorage. Damage was reported to exceed $25 million. An Anchorage meteorologist said the windstorm was the strongest the city had ever experienced. Miraculously, no deaths were reported.)

We had a late start the next morning. There was no reason to ski hard. Our plan was to travel slowly on the return journey, taking the opportunity to study the park's wildlife at greater length and take several side trips into the foothills and river valleys we had skirted on the way in.

The seasons were unfolding at a rapid pace. The days had become as long, then longer than, the nights; temperatures were more moderate. Bare patches of earth, moist with melting snow, were expanding so quickly we began to wonder if we might soon have to carry our skis.

Charlie and I began to talk a little more, any tenseness between us left behind with the storm. I don't know what precipitated the change. But my guess was that the pressures and anxiety felt earlier had been dwarfed by our faith in our own abilities.

When we paused to take a rest, I noticed Charlie staring in amazement at my shoulder. "What?" I asked. He gently scooped up something with his hand and opened his closed fist in front of my face. A delicate, pale blue butterfly fluttered into the air and sailed off with the breeze. First grizzly bears, now butterflies. Winter was on its way out in Denali, and before long, so were we.

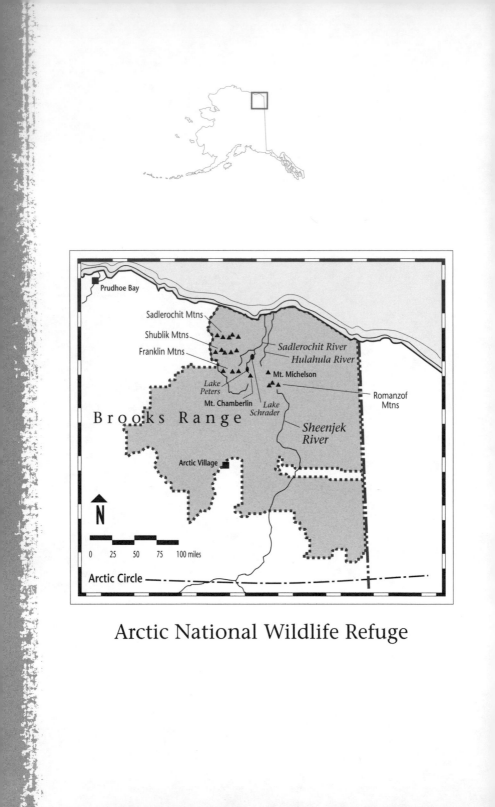

Arctic National Wildlife Refuge

Arctic Refuge: Beyond the Brooks Range

THE CLOUD COVER HAD become progressively thicker the farther north we flew from Fairbanks. When we approached the Brooks Range, even the highest peaks were blurred by the gray blanket. The sky above was blue, but visibility below was zero. Tom, our bush pilot, had warned us that there were only a few places on the northeast side of the Arctic Divide where a floatplane could touch down. We had only a short time to search for Lake Peters and Lake Schrader before fuel constraints would force us to return to Fairbanks, 300 miles away, to await better flying weather.

We were nearing the point where we'd have to turn around when Tom suddenly bent his head down. "There they are!" he shouted over the steady drone of the Cessna 185 Skywagon. I leaned over his shoulder and looked down. More than a mile below us, barely visible through a small hole in the bulging clouds, two long and narrow lakes nestled against steep somber mountains. "Better hold on," he cautioned us while fiddling with the controls. "We're going to drop quick before that hole closes shut."

I felt my stomach lurch as the plane nosed toward the ground. I hoped Judy and Charlie remembered where the air-sickness bags were. They had been crammed into the rear cargo compartment along with extra aviation fuel containers and our backpacks for the past two-and-a-half hours.

The altimeter plunged from the 9,500-foot cruising mark. Gripping the map on my lap, I stared intently out the window. Somewhere in the clouds at our altitude was Mount Chamberlin, the second highest peak in the Brooks Range. I wondered if Tom knew where it was. I had met our pilot only yesterday, but from our brief encounter, I was completely confident of his abilities and knowledge of matters related to flying. Tall and lean, with closely cropped hair, Tom was a retired Air Force colonel who ran a one-man air charter service. During the flight north, I learned that he had flown many combat missions in the Pacific during World War II. He had once been shot down and spent many days in a life raft in the ocean before being rescued. A knack for survival serves an Alaskan bush pilot well. Nevertheless, part of my self-appointed role as unofficial co-pilot was finding the 9,000-footer before it found us in the fog.

When the needle hit 5,000 feet, the low-hanging cloud bank dropped away abruptly. I had only a moment to relax. Coming up quickly below us was one of the finest wilderness areas in North America—the North Slope of the Arctic National Wildlife Refuge.

Sitting on the edge of my seat, my face pressed to the plexiglass, I was spellbound. I had long dreamed of traveling far above the Arctic Circle to the northeastern corner of the state. It had taken me twenty-nine years to get here, and from what I could see, it was worth the wait.

As the plane descended, I hungrily absorbed the scene. Stretching east to west, splitting the refuge in half, were the stark, fluted mountains of the Brooks Range. The upper slopes were still cloaked in by the clouds, but the foothills and smaller outer ranges—areas in which we would be hiking—were clearly visible under the cirrostratus. Contrasting with the high country was the verdant arctic coastal plain. From the air, the treeless tundra resembled a rumpled green carpet that eventually smoothed out until barely a wrinkle remained. Numerous winding rivers and streams sliced through this great open expanse, their waters rushing swiftly to the ice-covered Beaufort Sea, buried under a blanket of fog only forty miles away.

Tom circled the plane low over Lake Schrader, searching for the best approach to a pair of deserted, ramshackle cabins that stood near the east shore. After noticing a channel through a submerged gravel bar, Tom set the plane down gently on the clear blue water and skimmed to a stop. I unsnapped my seatbelt and swung open the door. Only the sound of water splashing against the aluminum floats broke the intense silence. The air was cold and sharp. The tundra smelled rich and earthy. Tom instructed us to off-load the Cessna before the fickle arctic weather changed for the worse.

After reconfirming our pick-up date, Tom eased into the cockpit and waved good-bye as we nudged the plane away from shore. Soon the Cessna was just a speck in the overcast sky, buzzing toward a notch in the mountains. The three of us stood on the deserted beach, watching our link with the outside world disappear. Except for Kaktovik, a small native Alaskan community on Barter Island at the edge of the refuge in the Beaufort Sea, the closest village was 100 trackless miles to the south.

Judy sucked in her breath, trying to take in the vista before us. I could tell she was both nervous and excited about this trip. Charlie was even quieter than usual, but I attributed his reticence to the fact that this was his first fly-in trip to Alaska. The remoteness was overwhelming. There were no park rangers to greet us; no backcountry permits to fill out; no suggestions on what routes to choose; no warnings about river crossings, hypothermia or grizzly bears; no one to aid us in the event of accident or injury. We would be totally self-reliant for the next three weeks.

Another difference between this and past trips was that I was now part of a trio instead of a duo. There would be some adjustments for us to make in the following days. Judy didn't know Charlie as well as I did, but when I had suggested we ask him to join us in the Arctic Refuge, she immediately agreed. Charlie's outdoor skills would be of benefit to us, and having three in our group instead of two had several advantages: assistance in case of an emergency, splitting the cost of the chartered airplane, sharing the weight of communal gear. Most significantly, though, we enjoyed Charlie's company and friendship. Because we were friends with similar outdoor experience we had no "leader"; our choice of routes, campsites and other decisions affecting the group would be subject to democratic approval. I had every reason to believe we would make a close-knit team.

Leaving our packs at the cabins, we climbed a small knoll for a better view of the surrounding countryside. I could see for miles across the rolling tundra. The hillocks to the north were smooth and Irish green, wavelike undulations swelling to the horizon. To the south reared sharp and angular mountains, their snow-capped peaks and hanging glaciers hidden in the clouds. But the most arresting sight was the turquoise-blue waters of Lake Schrader and Lake Peters. The largest lakes in the refuge (each is five miles long, separated by a mile-long channel) were named after two geologists, but their Inupiat Eskimo name, Neruokpuk, meaning "big lakes," is far more descriptive.

As usual before heading into the Alaska backcountry, Judy and I sat down, propped our elbows on our knees, and methodically surveyed the surroundings with binoculars. Charlie did the same with his more powerful spotting scope mounted on a lightweight tripod. Ostensibly we were looking for some of the more than 160 animal species that inhabit the North Slope, but in reality we searched for two top-of-the-food-chain creatures: *Ursus arctos*, the grizzly, and *Homo sapiens*, our fellow human beings.

Although I was sure we would see grizzlies in the next few weeks, I didn't expect to see any of our own species, except perhaps sheep hunters at a distance. In the arctic there are only three seasons: June, July and winter (snow usually covers the ground at least nine months a year). Mid-August and later, the only period we could break away for our visit, is generally considered a marginal time for extended hiking trips in the North Slope because of the unpredictable weather.

"There's some caribou," Charlie announced shortly from our lookout. "Far away, but I think you can see them with binocs." It took me only a few seconds to locate the group of brown-and-white animals grazing peacefully on a distant ridge. Even from a mile away, I could discern the multitined antlers of the males, and the less showy, simple, short spikes of the females. They were undoubtedly stragglers, since most of the North Slope herd had already migrated south. Further study of the landscape revealed some waterbirds on the lake, a red fox darting along a sandbar and a few fat ground squirrels near the cabin. No bears.

Judy was the first to notice the ground squirrels edging toward our stuff sacks of food. We hurried back down before any damage was done. The rodents—called sik-siks by the natives because of the their two-note call—were reluctant to leave. If they were this careless around us, a bear would someday have an easy meal. I ran after them, trying to teach them a lesson. They scurried to safety beneath the wooden buildings.

We rummaged through our packs, making last minute decisions about what to take and what to leave behind. In the planning stages of our trip, we had determined that two hikes of about equal duration into different areas of the refuge would be better than one long trek. A ten-day load across tundra is acceptable; a two-week load is pushing it; anything more verges on torture. The first trip would take us north through the Sadlerochit and Shublik Mountains, isolated outer ranges of the Brooks Range; on the second hike we would follow the Sadlerochit River to its headwaters in the Franklin Mountains, stopping often to explore hidden valleys and canyons in the heart of the Brooks Range.

While out on the first trip we would store spare food and supplies in five-gallon plastic buckets and cache them inside one of the cabins. The tightly sealed containers were definitely water- and rodent-proof, but only possibly bear-proof. I had asked Tom, who had flown over into the area on several occasions, whether he thought we would have any trouble with grizzlies invading our cache. "I don't think bears will bother it," he answered. "To tell you the truth, I'd be more concerned about humans."

With his wry sense of humor we thought he was joking. Nevertheless we stacked the buckets in the rafters of the larger cabin and left notes attached to each explaining our situation. This was done as a courtesy in case the cabins' "owners" came by.

Built before the establishment of the refuge and currently owned by the Arctic Research Lab, the windowless shacks were boxlike and dark. We were tempted to pitch our tent at their front door—the day and a half of nonstop traveling with little sleep the previous night had left us exhausted—but the area around the twin cabins was heavily littered with fuel drums, plywood, rusted cans and the usual junk. The buildings were eyesores in an otherwise pristine land. We decided to hike out for a mile or two to country where it was possible no one had camped before.

"Everybody ready?" I asked, bent over from my pack. I leaned against the cabin's walls to keep from toppling over.

I heard Judy groan, then Charlie added to the ruckus. "Did anybody weigh these things at the airport?" Judy asked, cinching up her waist belt.

"I hope not," Charlie answered. "If I knew what this sucker weighed, I wouldn't carry it!"

We fastened the cabin door with a loop of wire over a nail, took a last glance around, and headed toward the rolling hills behind the lake. The caribou across the lake had already begun their long journey across the Arctic Refuge. We were about to begin ours.

Established in 1960 by executive order of the Secretary of the

Interior, the Arctic National Wildlife Refuge is the second largest and most northerly of the 420 units in the National Wildlife Refuge System. Because of its animal life, size and remoteness, it has long been of interest to conservationists and those seeking land completely unsullied by man. It is the last place in North America, and perhaps the world, where a complete range of arctic and subarctic ecosystems survives intact. The refuge originally consisted of 8.9 million acres, but the passage of the Alaska Lands Bill in 1980 added 10 million more acres to the refuge's southern and western boundaries in an effort to preserve important migratory areas for the Porcupine caribou herd (one of the largest herds in Alaska), as well as valuable habitat for wolves, wolverines, bears and moose. Now encompassing nearly 30,000 square miles, or approximately one-twentieth of Alaska, the refuge protects a vast, undisturbed (but not unthreatened) arctic environment large enough to be biologically self-sufficient.

After walking only a few hundred yards, I knew why so few backpackers came here—it wasn't entirely because of the remoteness and expense. At first glance, tundra appears to be the perfect hiking surface. Seen from the air, the valleys beckon with the appearance of smooth, emerald meadows. But in truth the tundra may be one of the worst hiking surfaces on the face of the earth, the ultimate conditioner for flabby legs.

We faced wet, spongy moss at the outset. The North Slope is covered with an abundance of marshy areas because of a permanently frozen layer a few inches below the surface. Only about six inches of precipitation fall on the North Slope each year, far less than in most North American deserts, but because of the underlying permafrost shield, very little moisture is absorbed into the soil. Most of the water that falls as rain or snow stays on the surface, forming the thaw lakes, meltwater ponds and shallow streams and puddles that create considerable obstacles to two-legged travelers.

The soft, pillowy surface was preferable, though, to the unavoidable sedge tussocks we soon encountered. Visitors to the arctic inevitably have to deal with these tussocks. The mushroom-shaped mounds of grass, each matted cylinder about a foot wide and a foot high, grow close together, separated by small moats of stagnant water that can't seep through the permafrost. Staggering across them, we were forced either on top of the wobbly humps or into the ankle deep pools at their base. If we stepped wrong, a face-flattening tumble could result. No matter how we proceeded, it was a slow and laborious business. We tried to keep our leather hiking boots dry for the first few miles by following ridge tops and detouring around wet areas, but eventually we abandoned this tiring technique and resigned ourselves to soaked feet. We had brought lightweight running shoes to wear around camp.

During the next few days, as we slogged toward the Sadlerochit Mountains, we usually managed to find campsites on dry heather overlooking a meandering river valley or a cottongrass meadow. After ditching our packs and setting up the tent, we collapsed on the ground, tired, hot and thirsty. In these moments of repose, without the weight of packs dulling our brains, we discussed what little we knew about this arctic preserve.

The refuge is a complex area, not the frozen, trackless wasteland the uninformed think it is. The Brooks Range, actually the most northerly extension of the Rocky Mountains, curves through the refuge and divides it into almost equal-sized north- and south-draining slopes. Deep valleys reach far within the mountains to the base of glaciated peaks.

South of the Arctic Divide, the valleys are strikingly warmer and more fertile than those found on the opposite side of the mountain barrier. Moderating winds from the Yukon River basin flow up the river drainages, bringing temperatures that may reach the mid-seventies, while beneath a fog layer along the coast temperatures may be below freezing. Stands of spruce and clumps of aspen grow in the south-sloping valleys, although above the 4,000-foot level only the hardiest of plants survive.

North of the Brooks Range a handful of lesser mountains (foothills, really) contain valleys and ridges that conceivably have never seen a human footprint. Beyond these outer ranges is the coastal plain, covered by a thin, frayed carpet of grasses, sedges, lichens and other low plants, and intricately patterned with hundreds of freshwater ponds. Here, each spring, one of the great migrations of the animal kingdom occurs. Escaping the tormenting flies and heat of areas to the south, some 180,000 barren-ground caribou cross over the harsh mountain passes and head for their ancestral breeding grounds on the North Slope. The cows drop their precocial calves, then disperse eastward in July to the neighboring Yukon Territory in Canada. Their seasonal migration may cover over a thousand miles per year.

Caribou were a source of inspiration and frustration to us. These ungainly beasts are profoundly beautiful in their own way. After a summer of feasting on lichens and forbs, the animals were fat and vigorous, their pelage in its prime. I envied the broad cloven hoofs and powerful legs that carried them easily over the tussocks, soft tundra and rocky ridges. Unlike the caribou, we found that even our best efforts resulted in only a tortoise-like crawl.

Charlie and I had been busy staying in shape since our return from Denali the previous spring. We thought that our daily work-out routine of jogging, pull-ups and push-ups would be adequate for this trek, but it really wasn't. The five miles per day we jogged at home on flat roads could only serve as a warm-up for what we were doing now. What we should have done is enroll in an Outward Bound course for three weeks before heading north for Alaska.

Judy had proved that she could handle heavy loads during our past trips, but so far our hike in the Arctic Refuge had been more difficult. Her bulging orange pack weighed nearly half as much as she and was almost as tall. For several months prior to the trip, she had worked hard to be ready for it. She worried about being left behind as Charlie and I plodded ahead. She had never been on a trip with Charlie, but he had legendary status among our friends for his ability to haul heavy loads. I have a reputation, too, I have been told, of being competitive, so Judy had the added worry of being caught in a marathon death march across the tundra. During the final weeks before departure, as she trained by packing a cement sack up the bluff behind our house in hot, sultry weather, she repeatedly reminded me that the focus of our trip would be wildlife study, not a grueling "survival of the fittest" challenge.

Another reason for our weariness was the weather and the bugs. Without any wind, the fifty-five-degree temperature under sunny, unpolluted arctic skies seemed uncomfortably warm. The mosquitoes were abundant and hungry. The pestilential insects swarmed around our heads whenever we stopped to rest. I counted twenty-three mashed corpses on my shirt-sleeve after a single swat. Contrary to Alaskan lore, they weren't the size of small birds or any meaner than the southern mosquitoes I was accustomed to, but they were formidable. A biologist in Anchorage claims that within two hours a mosquito swarm can drain half the blood from a man incapacitated and exposed on the tundra. In the Fairbanks airport I saw a cartoon in a local newspaper that reflected our perception of the Alaska mosquito: Two man-sized mosquitoes are in a tent perched atop a succumbed camper. One mosquito says to the other, "Should we drag him outside?" "No," says the second one, "then the big ones will get him." I resorted to a head net, gloves, parka, gaiters and copious amounts of repellent to keep the insects off my skin.

Mosquitoes notwithstanding, for each of us the observation of wildlife was among the most important reasons for making this backcountry trip. We had read *Arctic Wild*, by Lois Crisler, and agreed with her: "Wilderness without animals is dead—dead scenery. Animals without wilderness are a closed book."[1] If the weather permitted, one of the first things we did upon establishing camp was to set up Charlie's spotting scope. The high-power optics were ideal for studying the open countryside, a terrain which initially appeared lifeless, but after careful observation slowly revealed its secrets.

From a campsite overlooking the Sadlerochit River valley, we zeroed in on more bands of caribou, ground squirrels and another red fox. I didn't need a spotting scope, however, to see the black-brown hulk of a bull moose appear suddenly out of the nearby bushes. Although I knew that a considerable number of the animals thrive in the North Slope's more sheltered and vegetated valleys, I couldn't help wondering what a moose was doing 200 miles north of the Arctic Circle. This country of tundra, tussocks and waist-high willow thickets was far different from my idea of typical north-woods moose habitat.

Not quite as dramatic as moose but every bit as interesting were the birds. Although the refuge checklist contains a total of 140 bird species, not all of them are found on the North Slope. Several of the species that we might have seen earlier in the summer had completed nesting and migrated south to warmer climes across the Brooks Range. After a couple of days we had identified twenty-one species, about the same number as I routinely get at my backyard bird feeder in the winter.

Sooner or later we were bound to have a run-in with the king of the tundra. During dinner one sunlit evening, at our camp along a tributary creek of the Sadlerochit River, we spotted a dark hump moving through the brush below us, about fifty yards away. I thought it was another moose—we'd seen a cow and a calf trotting down the shallow creek bed a while earlier—but when the hump broke out into the open, it belonged to a grizzly sow with two small cubs. We set aside our food and crouched, ready for action. We had seen other grizzlies already without incident, but none were this close. The mother griz tensed when she saw us, skittered back a few feet, then stood up and sniffed the air. She undoubtedly smelled both us and our dinner, a strange combination of human aroma and freeze-dried chicken stew.

A relative newcomer to ursine behavior, Charlie was looking to

Judy and me to evaluate the situation. Prior to the trip, I had given him the standard briefing on what to do when approached by a bear: don't look it in the eye, yield the right of way, never run, move slowly away; any fast motion may excite the bear and it may interpret your presence as a hostile invasion of its territory. We remained frozen, waiting anxiously for the grizzly's next move.

After an interminably long time, the sow dropped on all fours and woofed with a clacking of jaws. She advanced, stopped, sniffed and snorted again before shuffling down the creek away from our camp. As I watched the griz family retreat, I finally stopped holding my breath.

We discussed the encounter in detail as we finished our luke-warm meal. We had been fortunate this time; a mother grizzly and cubs are a dangerous combination, particularly since we had no means to protect ourselves. It is legal in the refuge to carry firearms for self-protection, but although I am a gun owner, at this stage of my Alaska journeys I was philosophically opposed to toting a weapon. I felt it was a contradiction to arm myself against a species that I respected so much and that I so much wanted to see. Since Judy and Charlie agreed, our "firepower" consisted of metal pots and cups we could bang together and plastic whistles. From past experiences Judy and I had learned that noise is not the most reliable deterrent, but it helps.

Finally we reached the midsection of the Sadlerochit Mountains. Forty-five miles long and four to six miles wide, the 4,000-foot-high massif of frost-shattered limestone runs east-west between the Canning and Sadlerochit rivers. Its size was of no consequence to us, though, because by evening the mountains had vanished in a wet, dripping mist, followed by a bone-chilling fog that swept in from the Arctic Ocean. Visibility was limited to less than a hundred yards.

As we huddled around the stove sipping steaming powdered soup, our hoods pulled up against the drizzle, we reminded ourselves that the inclement weather was not without its benefits: at least the mosquitoes weren't bothering us. We had been monitoring their behavior, and our conclusion was that a temperature below forty-five degrees put them out of commission.

The weather next morning was more of the same: the fog had lifted somewhat, but apparently the Beaufort Sea cloud bank was not going to burn away. Packing up, we followed a U-shaped glacial valley that led deeper into the Sadlerochit Mountains. Well-worn trails, shed antlers and piles of pellet-sized dung suggested that this was one of the major caribou migration routes between the north and south slopes of the Brooks Range.

I thought how exciting it would be to observe the peak of caribou migration. After four trips to Alaska (this was my fifth), the closest I had ever been to a full migration was watching nature programs on public television.

We did witness a mini-migration, however, when thirty or so caribou materialized out of the fog across the creek. They stopped and stared; we stared back from a distance of only a few yards. The animals soon lost interest in us and trotted into the white mist. Long after I lost sight of them, I could hear the clop of their hooves splashing in the wet tundra.

Since leaving the cabins on Lake Schrader, we had seen no sign of people—no boot tracks on the gravel bars, no old campsites, no litter, not even a passing airplane. But when we reached the pass above the mountain valley, we discovered a stone ring about fifteen feet across. I knelt at the edge of the circle and felt the stones. Partly buried in the gravel, the whitish rocks were the size of a man's head, smooth to the touch except where adorned with black, ruffled lichens and red clots of moss. Part of an old Eskimo hunting camp, the stones had once been used to hold down a skin tent.

"They must have camped here, maybe centuries ago, waiting to ambush the caribou herd," I proposed.

"What a bleak place," Judy said, with a shiver. Persistent winds had scoured the pass clean: not a sprig of grass, not a flower.

We gathered at the edge of the ring, the fog swirling around our heads. I am a skeptic about most other-worldly phenomena, but I sensed that we were not alone. Spirits of unknown antiquity hovered off to the side, regarding us closely. Not wishing to offend the elders, we left the site exactly as we found it.

A few miles further on we made our own camp. We studied the topo map in an effort to pinpoint our location. The lusterless coastal mist obscured landmarks and made a shambles of our navigation attempts.

"I think we're a mile and a half west of Itkilyariak Creek," Charlie said, tracing his fingers over the blue and brown lines. "Judging from these contours, we're in a steep-sided valley with Mount Weller at its head."

I peered over his shoulder, trying to transpose the flat sheet of paper into three dimensions. "This must be a wild-looking place when the sun shines. Too bad we've come all this way, as far north as we're going to get, and can't see a thing."

There was another reason for my disappointment with the weather. This last day's march had put us in musk oxen habitat, but unless the fog lifted, we would have to bump into one of these Ice Age beasts to see it. I had never seen a musk ox; there are very few places in Alaska, or the world, where they survive in the wild. After being extirpated from the North Slope in the 1800s, in 1969 and 1970 sixty-nine of the shaggy-haired animals were reintroduced on the Arctic Refuge. Protected from hunting, the musk oxen population is now estimated to number between 400 and 500, and of these approximately 160 use the Sadlerochit River drainage year-round, feeding on forbs, tussock sedges and shrubby willows.

Unable to scan the valley for wildlife, and too chilly to sit still outside, I joined Charlie and Judy soon after dinner in the tent. I threw my sleeping bag over me and rummaged in my ditty-bag for my notebook. It was a cathartic activity, putting pen to paper, in between listening for critters outside and waiting for the fog to lift.

8 p.m.

Dark and gloomy outside the tent, damp and musty inside. This morning we started up the spur valley leading to Mount Weller, hoping that the fog would clear on the way, or possibly climb above it. Neither occurred. The ascent through the narrow gorge led us past many little waterfalls and cascades, and into some unexpectedly bizarre country. Late in the day, we entered a kind of amphitheater, floored with gravel and walled with eroded spires, parapets and battlements. It was as if we had stumbled upon the ruins of a lost civilization. The place would have been eerie enough in full sunlight, let alone in a mysterious, suffocating fog. Except for a few ptarmigan and wheatears, all we saw of wildlife was their sign. Dall sheep tracks and droppings were abundant—their trails traversed up the scree slopes out of sight. Bear spoor wasn't nearly as common, but bears were definitely there. We moved cautiously in the mist, the chance of a head-on collision with a griz adding immeasurably to our hike.

Pulling on stiff, wet, leather boots over ice-cold socks in the morning was only slightly more appealing than undergoing a root canal. The temperature was barely above freezing when we woke and there wasn't a glimmer of sunlight. The fog appeared to be unyielding, so we headed back toward Lake Schrader, following a new route to the Sadlerochit River.

We reached Sunset Pass about noon. Untrue to its name, there was no sun, and we were greeted with wet kisses of blowing snow. The only good thing about cresting the 2,100-foot saddle was that from here our route led mostly downhill. Four hours later, when we dropped to the hummocky, rolling meadows above the Sadlerochit River, the ground was entirely white. The snow was inches deep; it looked like early winter. Our feet were hurting. We tried to make light of our discomfort, but as the afternoon wore on the hike turned into a dismal march.

We dropped our packs and sat down on a pile of stones to take a break. Judy instantly curled up against the cold and closed her eyes. Charlie munched on a granola bar and studied the map. I took off soaked boots and socks and tried to revive my feet with bare hands. After a few minutes of massaging my numbed toes started to respond. I was about to slip the footwear back on when Charlie motioned me to be quiet. "Look, over there," he whispered, "topping that rise."

I followed the direction of his pointing arm for several seconds before focusing on a squat, black animal loping in our direction. In the diffused light, it was impossible to discern distance and size.

"Is it a bear?" Judy asked, suddenly wide awake.

"Not sure," Charlie answered, moving behind his pack.

I slapped on my socks and boots, oblivious to the cold.

We crouched and remained motionless as the animal began to take shape out of the opaque mist. It was dark and moved like a grizzly, only it was the size of a small cub. If it was a bear cub, where was the mother?

Detail started to emerge. "Hey," I realized at last, "It's a wolverine!"

The large weasel, about the size of a pit bull terrier and reputedly just as mean, was following a scent in the heath and wasn't aware of us. Soon it was so near it caught our smell and stopped dead. After rising on its hind legs to peer over the hummocks, it bounded closer to determine what we were. We were close enough to hear its raspy grunts, close enough to see the creamy-yellow chevron on its chest and its black fearless eyes. Close enough . . . I slowly stood up, ski pole in hand. What do you say to a wolverine? "Hey, get lost," I demanded. *Whirrr!* The thirty-pound weasel, pound for pound considered the most ferocious fighter in the arctic, spun around in one supple movement and disappeared into the fog in the direction from which it had come.

We were cold, wet and tired, but the wolverine encounter gave us a shot of adrenalin, which was what we needed to reach the

Conditions on the North Slope after an August snowstorm.

banks of the Sadlerochit River two miles away. The sight of the river bottom gave us another boost. The snowline hadn't reached this elevation. The ground was bare. We wasted no time in setting up camp. We pitched the tent on good level tundra, a precious commodity in a lumpy land. We unrolled our foam pads and fluffed up the sleeping bags. I could have fallen asleep immediately, but first we had to get drinking water and cook dinner.

The river water was clear and pure. Our meal of instant rice, noodles and freeze-dried green beans dabbed with margarine was simple and filling. In my insulated cup was eight ounces of throat-scalding tea. As we ate the fog lifted slightly, giving us tantalizing glimpses of the Sadlerochit Valley and the Brooks Range, endless open spaces beyond my means to gauge. The slopes a few hundred feet above us were white with snow. Beneath the snowline the tundra was a dull brown, with patches of brilliant oranges, yellows and scarlets. Summer's brief fling was over.

In the time it took us to finish dinner, we observed more animals than we had seen in the past few days. They, too, were drawn to the snow-free valley. Several moose, small bands of caribou, a golden eagle and flocks of plovers passed the fringes of our camp. We noticed fresh wolf tracks at the river's edge, but did not see the reclusive animals themselves.

Despite our desire to stay outside and watch wildlife, our

painfully cold feet forced us to retreat inside the tent. The temperature had plummeted to below freezing as we sat spooning out the last morsels of food from the plastic pouches. One by one, we closed our packs, took a last look around, and disappeared into the three-person geodesic dome.

"What's it like out there?" I asked Charlie the following morning. Closest to the door, he reluctantly left the warmth of his sleeping bag to take a peek.

"Not good, pretty crummy in fact," came his glum report. "It's sleeting."

"What about the temperature?

"Oh, it's above freezing—thirty-three degrees."

Judy rolled her eyes and turned over in her bag. Charlie closed the tent and burrowed back inside his sleeping bag. I lay there between them, wide awake, with no one to talk to and nothing to read; I had gone through all the paperbacks we had brought on this leg of the trip. Seeking solace, I returned to my journal.

Sadlerochit River Camp, 8 a.m.

> We have to move camp to Fire Creek, a distance of only five miles, but with stream crossings, terrible tussocks and sore feet I'm sure it will seem more like 15 miles. The clouds are scraping the ground now, meaning another day of cold mist and fog. I don't think our boots will ever dry out. I still have a pair of dry socks, but I'm saving them for an EMERGENCY. My spirits are still high considering the circumstances, however, I'm growing concerned about Charlie— he's been unusually sullen lately. I'd like to know what's bothering him, but when I ask he brushes me off, saying, "Nothing's wrong, I'm fine."

By the time we got done packing it was already past noon. By early afternoon a light rain had turned to a wet, sticky snow. The five-mile hike was a grind, a morass of tussocks and mucky sedge meadows. Upon reaching Fire Creek, we decided to hole up until the weather broke.

Fire Creek Camp, 6 p.m.

> Haven't been out of my sleeping bag since arriving here last night, not even to eat or pee. Reason: rain—incessant, dripping, cold, befuddling RAIN! The only good thing about it is that it washed off the snow sticking to the tent walls. We're each in our own little world, dozing, reading, writing,

map studying, taking occasional peeks outside to glare at the swirling fog. We're all growing concerned about our feet. Charlie says his are starting to peel and change color. After coming in from the cold and warming up my feet, my toes itch and tingle something fierce. Five straight days of freezing temps, rain and sleet is getting to be a bit monotonous. We'll keep on moving, of course. But what I'd like to know is, whatever happened to summer?

The morning ritual of putting on cold, wet socks and cold, squishy boots was always grim. Each time I did so, I admonished myself for not taking insulated, calf-high rubber boots as I had originally planned. I was assured by individuals who had visited the Arctic Refuge that leather hiking boots were the footwear of choice. Apparently these people had not mustered across the North Slope tundra during a long spell of snow and rain.

We broke camp in mid-morning and headed southwest along the Sadlerochit River. The Lake Schrader cabin was still fifteen miles away. We had four days of food left to cover the distance.

A few hours of hiking brought us to Gravel Creek. We waded in without taking off our socks or boots. By now it didn't matter. Immersed in slushy snow and tundra puddles for days on end, our footwear couldn't possibly get any wetter. After the stream crossing, we stuck our bare feet on each other's naked stomachs in an attempt to warm them. Wrinkled and discolored, our feet looked terrible. Worse, an anesthetic-like numbness was settling into our toes and heels.

We later learned that we were getting trenchfoot. Also called immersion foot, trenchfoot is a malady of the feet caused by long-term exposure to cold and wet. The affliction crippled thousands of soldiers in the Aleutian Islands during World War II, and more recently, Argentine troops in the Falklands War. There was nothing we could do to remedy the situation other than hope for dry weather or stay inside the tent nursing our feet. Neither solution was viable, so we trudged on, figuring that as long as we kept moving, we would be all right.

The continuing beauty of the North Slope terrain helped ease the discomfort we were experiencing from our feet. The upper Sadlerochit River slices through the permafrost, creating a small canyon with unusual rock formations and numerous ledges foaming with whitewater. To the north were more rolling hills and tussocked tundra, green when we arrived, now white with a dusting of snow, patterned in sweeping folds under an endless sky. On the west were the Shublik Mountains and the Third Range, which we would have only a day or two to explore. And to the south was the mighty Brooks Range, furrowed and wrinkled by the folding of the earth's crust, its higher slopes still concealed by clouds.

I stopped often to photograph. Dynamic subjects appeared in every direction, from late-blooming wildflowers, fluffy cottongrass and small ripe blueberries, to broad landscapes that even my 24mm wide-angle lens couldn't encompass. I hoped my photographs would capture some of the magic of the place so I could sprinkle it around when I got home.

I was absorbed in a photographic scene, trying to capture the expansiveness of the North Slope by placing my models in front of a striking panorama, when Judy interrupted my artistic creation. "Lar, behind you," she said urgently. "Turn around, slowly." Not a chance. I dropped the camera from my eye and spun around abruptly. Not thirty feet away, staring down at me from a small outcropping was a wolverine, bigger than the last one we saw and equally curious. I got my camera ready, certain that this would be my big break into wildlife photography, perhaps a cover shot for *Audubon* or *National Wildlife*. The animal had other ideas; it loped away before I squeezed the shutter. I scrambled up the rock pile as fast as I could. *Click.* My sole shot of the wolverine was of its bushy-tailed rear end.

We set up a short-term base camp at the east edge of the Shublik Mountains. After tromping across the North Slope for over a week, I embraced the opportunity of not having to hike with an alien burden on my back. It wasn't that I was tired of backpacking; it was just that hauling heavy loads over uneven terrain has a tendency to dull the senses. It's harder to study the smaller things that require close examination, scan for grizzlies and sheep in the distant tundra or even think with total clarity when deciding what route to take or where to pitch the tent. Like a sled dog, as soon as I'm strapped into a backpack harness, I've got to move.

Our day hike was up Snow Creek to its source, five miles from the Sadlerochit River. The creek was named in 1948 when a team of government geologists found deep snowdrifts there in late summer. The previous winter's drifts were still there when we arrived, but the view from the divide was worth the strenuous climb. On the other side was Ikiakpaurak Valley, brown and smooth, extending west between the Shublik Mountains and the Third Range. The valley was wild and tempting, and could have been the focus of a major trip in itself. With my eyes I followed the valley's watershed,

Cache Creek, to its mouth, and there saw the shining waters of the much wider Canning River. When I consulted the topo map, I learned that the Canning River formed the western boundary of the refuge and was twenty-three miles away.

We saw abundant bear and sheep sign at the edge of the Shubliks, and several small herds of caribou. They were probably members of the Central Arctic herd, which numbers about 12,000 to 14,000 animals. Smaller than the Porcupine herd, the Central Arctic herd's range is entirely north of the Arctic Divide from the Itkillik and Colville rivers on the west to the Sadlerochit River on the east. In late summer and fall, an estimated 2,000 to 3,000 Central Arctic caribou scatter among the foothills and uplands of the Sadlerochit and Shublik mountains, where they remain for the winter.

Far above the boot-sucking bogs we saw glorious flights of snow and white-fronted geese, joined by a few tundra swans, winging south in long wavering lines over the snag-toothed mountains. They were only a fraction of the millions of migratory birds that use the North Slope as a staging area before leaving for points as far away as the Chesapeake Bay, the Pacific Flyway, Asia, Africa and Antarctica. Urgent honking notes drifted down from the sky. The birds seemed in a hurry, and rightly so. The potholes and coastline of the North Slope were freezing over, and the birds needed open water.

Hammered by wind-driven sleet pellets the size of BBs, we headed back to camp. I was growing weary of looking at the plastic thermometer attached to my parka zipper; the mercury seemed to be permanently stuck at the freezing mark.

It was late when we arrived back at the tent, but we postponed dinner in order to doctor our feet. During the hike, I developed another podiatric problem as a result of continued immersion in icy, wet boots: bruised Achilles tendons, the connective tissue joining the calf muscles to the heelbone. I had never had problems with my feet prior to this trip, and was annoyed at this latest malady. Yet there was also humor in pathos. Sitting cross-legged in a circle, clutching, inspecting and kneading our pale wrinkled hoofers, we let out so many "oohs" and "aahs" that a by-passer would have thought a wild orgy was going on inside the tent.

Our next camp up the Sadlerochit River valley, five miles beyond the last one, was ringed with low mountains worn smooth by past glaciers. A layer of new snow coated the mountaintops; not enough, we hoped, to prevent us from reaching the 4,300-foot peak that we had chosen to climb.

Soon after breakfast the following morning, we swung on light daypacks and bounded up the talus- and tundra-covered slopes behind the tent. We were in good mood and stride. Our legs by now were strong, our stamina excellent. Proper equipment, nothing fancy—wool pants and shirt, polypro underwear, pile jacket, rain parka and pants, wool cap and gloves—kept us relatively comfortable even in the arctic summer blizzards. Except for our feet, I thought we had acclimated well to the North Slope.

It was a fairly easy walk-up, a 2,000-foot gain in elevation from the valley floor. Not exactly rarefied air, but high enough to attract the monarchs of the mountains, Dall sheep. We had previously spotted the sheep on far-off crags and inaccessible slopes, but because of poor visibility they were nearly indistinguishable from small patches of snow. Now we counted twenty-one ewes and lambs clinging to a steep ridge of scree and frost-shattered shale, warily watching our movements. On the ridge above them were a half-dozen mature rams, looking regal with their amber-colored, heavy curled horns. The sheep were uncertain about our intentions. The leader, probably the oldest ewe, nervously tapped her forefoot on the ground several times, then deftly clambered over the loose cobbles and slipped over the other side. One by one, the rest of the flock fell in line. Full of life a second ago, the ridgetop suddenly became barren.

When the clouds lifted a bit, I could see the dim, barely discernible white line of the Arctic Ocean, hazy and misty, marking the extent of the North Slope. This sight, from the mountains to the sea, more than anything emphasized how unique the coastal plain is. Described by the U.S. Fish and Wildlife Service as "the center of wildlife activity for the entire refuge," the coastal plain represents a portion of one of the largest remaining areas of undisturbed land in the world. Across this vista I couldn't identify a single human sign. The tundra loomed larger than life, timeless, verdant, exquisite . . . and now imperiled.

My emotions alternated between anger and glumness when I thought of how the Department of the Interior, the agency in charge of the National Wildlife Refuge System, had joined with the oil industry to open the fragile coastal plain to oil and gas development. For what experts predict might yield a few months' worth of oil at best, the North Slope of the Arctic National Wildlife Refuge will, if the demand for oil warrants, be transformed into another Prudhoe Bay industrial complex, which has all but obliterated the natural systems that once existed there. Only full wilderness designation will protect the 125-mile strip of coastal plain in the refuge, the only stretch of a 1,060-mile-long Arctic coastline not currently open to oil and gas interests. As I sat on my eagle's perch, gazing across the undefiled expanse, I could not understand the desire to rape such a national treasure for the sake of greed.

A recurrence of sleet drove us off the peak. During our descent it began to rain, then abruptly stopped. A beautiful double rainbow formed a prismatic bridge directly over our heads. We took it as a good omen, a sign of good weather to come. We reached camp under clearing skies, but when we started dinner it clouded over again. Rain began to fall.

When Judy withdrew to the tent after supper, Charlie and I discussed the trip: the ludicrous weather, the ever-present threat of grizzly bears, the monotonous tussocks and the deterioration of our feet were bugaboos affecting everyone's peace of mind. I was astonished, however, when Charlie said he was considering staying in the cabin for the next eight days while Judy and I continued the second leg of the trek.

I mulled over his discontent as I gazed across the blank tundra. A defeated attitude can be more crippling than bruised feet. I was disappointed and a little angry. I felt I was losing more than just a backpacking partner—I was losing a friend.

"Okay," I said. "I'm not staying at the cabin. But if you want to, we'll work something out."

The bitter weather broke the next day. The temperature at breakfast was still hovering around freezing, but the sun was out in full force. I was heartened to see Charlie's spirits and enthusiasm for the trip return almost to normal. Maybe that's all he needs, I thought, dry feet and a few days of sunshine. Well, I could use some of that myself.

We packed up and plodded southeast, following a looping stream that emptied into Lake Schrader near the cabins. There was no hurry. The snow at lower elevations had melted and ice no longer skimmed the surface of ponds. The sun made us lazy. Every half-hour or so we shed our packs and sprawled out on the hummocky carpet of moss and lichens, luxuriating in its dryness and warmth. We stripped down to T-shirts for the first time since we arrived.

At midday we passed through a divide that overlooked the twin lakes. Their glassy surfaces were tinted an inky blue, the same shade as the sky. Mount Chamberlin, the 9,000-footer towering above Lake Peters, glistened with glacial ice and shiny black rock. Still a couple hours' walk away, the cabins looked insignificant in this vast wilderness. We hurried down, eager to reach the cache of food, stove fuel, headlamp batteries, boot conditioner, paperbacks and dry socks waiting inside.

When we reached the cabin our excitement faded; the wire we had twisted around a nail to hold the door shut had been removed. Our first thought was that a grizzly had ravaged the interior and made off with our food. Charlie dropped his pack and ventured inside.

"Oh, no!" we heard him groan.

Judy and I rushed into the one-room shack. In the dim light, it took me a moment to comprehend exactly what had happened. I was stunned. Someone had tampered with our cache! The notes that had been taped on the sides of the plastic buckets were strewn about the floor, along with food wrappings that hadn't been there earlier. The lids to the buckets were still in place, but when we pried them off I became furious: only half our food remained. I had been ripped off before, but this was the worst. I would have felt much better if a grizzly had been the culprit rather than a member of our own species.

When the shock wore off, we tried to reconstruct what had happened. Apparently some people had flown to the lake during our absence, entered the cabin, seen the buckets and read the notes, then methodically went through our rations taking exactly what they wanted. About a fourth of our trail mix lunches was missing along with half the dinners; also gone were all our breakfasts, powdered soups, chocolate bars, fruit drink mixes, and three days' worth of emergency food we had brought in case the pick-up was delayed. They had even stolen nearly all our stove fuel, leaving us just enough to cook our remaining dehydrated dinners. Probably illiterate, the only items they didn't touch were the books.

"The slobs," Charlie said, picking up the litter the intruders had left.

"The bastards," I added.

"At least they could have left me my socks," Judy griped, rummaging through the buckets. The three coveted spare pairs she had cached were gone.

The most infuriating thing about this episode was that it could happen *here*—in one of North America's most isolated places. We wanted to think someone had really needed the food, but knew this was unlikely; the thief could have left a note of explanation with the spare pens and notebook paper that were in the buckets.

Speculating on this anonymous affront would provide us with hours of discussion during the ensuing days.

After sorting through the food bags, Judy and I decided we could still continue our trip into the Franklin Mountains if we reduced our rations to about one-half of normal. We would be hungry, but there was enough to take us through.

I wanted to leave the cabin site as soon as possible. While reorganizing my pack, I noticed that Charlie moved in kind of a funk. He hadn't come to grips with whether to accompany us or remain behind in the cabin. We had two camp stoves, one of which he could take if we separated, and the smaller of the shacks was weathertight so he wouldn't need the tent.

"Well, what are you going to do?" I asked. My voice had an edge to it that I couldn't hide. "You coming or staying?"

"I'm not sure. I haven't made up my mind."

Judy tends to avoid confrontations and stayed clear of the one that was developing. I didn't blame her, but something had to be done. I had no intention of moping around the cabin.

We were hoisting our packs, ready to depart, when Charlie apparently came to a decision: being alone for the next week and a half was less appealing than continuing the hike. He loaded his pack. "Okay, let's go."

The sun continued to shine as we followed the meandering Sadlerochit River deeper and deeper into the high country of the Franklin Mountains, a lesser offshoot of the Brooks Range. The grandeur of the sharp-edged peaks and picture-perfect river valley helped us forget about our groaning stomachs—and our recent discord.

The glacial, U-shaped trough seemed to be another major caribou migration corridor. A network of deep-worn ruts ran parallel to the river. The sphagnum moss had been grazed and trampled flat. As we leapfrogged our camps further from Lake Schrader, the hiking improved: dry boots and socks, no tussocks and bogs!

The higher elevations of the Franklins were covered with snow, but a few days into our journey we scouted a route that seemed reasonably clear to a minor summit approximately 3,000 feet above us. We chose to make camp near the river and spend the next day scrambling up the steep slopes.

When morning came it was cold and absolutely clear. I pulled my wool pants and shirt over long johns, and sighed in ecstasy as I slipped my feet into cushy wool socks and boots that didn't squish. As a last measure before leaving the tent, I put on my baseball cap and angled the visor to shield my eyes from the sun.

"Good morning," I cheerily warbled to my mates, who were just waking up. "It's a wonderful day for a climb."

Judy gave me one of her slothful, half-eyed stares. "Good morning, Mister Rogers," she intoned in a sarcastic high-pitched voice. "Do we have another wonderful breakfast to look forward to?"

She was indulging in a little self-pity because of our boring diet. Breakfast was a few spoonfuls of cold trail mix, the same high-energy concoction of nuts, raisins, M&Ms, sunflower seeds and dried figs we would have for lunch and part of dinner. The highlight of the meal was a cup of hot peppermint tea with a pinch of sugar.

After eating we zipped up the tent and further secured it with big rocks in case of sudden winds. We also left our food in different locations in case our camp was visited by bears; we had seen two grizzlies the previous evening far down the valley. Our chores done, we swung on our daypacks and aimed for the sky.

As is usually the case, the route up appeared much easier than it actually was. Six hours of scrambling up a staircase of rocks and rubble, often made treacherous by a covering of crusty snow, brought us to the unnamed peak. We had worked hard and savored the view. To the west we could see the Brooks Range melting into convoluted hills the color of adobe brick. Above us was the blue-and-white drooping tongue of a glacier sprawled between two shark-finned peaks.

On the cliffs and ridges across from us, beneath the snowline, was a large band of Dall ewes, young rams, yearlings and lambs. I wasn't sure what they were grazing on, since the alpine meadow consisted more of rock than grass and forbs. For the next hour we studied the white sheep through binoculars, trying to gain an insight into their mountaintop lives. For the most part, they nibbled at the tundra, chewed their cud and dozed. But occasionally we witnessed their amazing grace and sure-footedness as they frolicked on the precipitous talus slopes and easily leaped twelve- to fifteen-foot chasms.

Dall sheep do not migrate in the usual sense, but do often move considerable distances between winter and summer ranges. In a month or so, these sheep would begin to congregate on their winter range, usually a windblown slope free of snow where vegetation is exposed. Winter is a harsh time for the animals. Heavy, wet, freezing snow or rain may prevent the sheep from reaching necessary foods. The lambs, weighing from sixty to seventy pounds by their first winter, have it the worst. One study in Alaska revealed that only between 29 and 45 lambs per 100 ewes survive to be yearlings.

I took a final sweeping look—at the sheep, at the row upon row of mountains—before we headed down.

We moved camp the following day to a little knob overlooking the headwaters of the Sadlerochit River, now a fast-moving stream that we were able to skip across without getting our boots wet. The valley had narrowed as we closed the gap to the Brooks Range. We craned our necks to peer at the massive walls.

Dinner that evening consisted of meager portions of rice and mashed potatoes and freeze-dried carrots—tasty but not filling. Dangerous fantasies about food crept into our conversation.

"I'd *love* to have a Chicago deep-dish pepperoni pizza right now," I muttered.

"You would. Make that a cheeseburger with grilled onions and french fries for me," Charlie opted.

For Judy's part, she kept on complaining about not having those missing Hershey bars at the end of her meal. Lack of chocolate was putting her in a rotten mood. We feuded through dinner each night, oblivious to the fact that we must have annoyed Charlie tremendously.

After four days of clear, crisp weather we were dismayed when we observed a thick bank of evening fog slowly creeping up the Sadlerochit River valley to our ridge-top camp. We were ten miles west of Lake Schrader, and stoically awaited the ocean-born mist.

When the low, ominous clouds reached us, rain began falling in sheets out of a glacial gray sky, driven by gusty winds that rocked our heavily pegged tent. Within minutes the temperature dropped from fifty to thirty degrees. The cold rain gave way to twisted ribbons of snow. I cracked open the door from within the tent. We were drowning in fat swirling flakes. It was beautiful in a savage and disquieting way. The snow had begun to stick to the tundra so that the ground became indistinguishable from the leaden sky.

"What's it like out there?" Judy asked.

"Like Christmas," I answered full of false good cheer. I had seen a band of caribou heroically head into the stinging wind, antlered heads held low, faces and backs sheathed in icy concretions.

There was no point in moving camp, not in this renegade weather. During the next two days we stayed close to the tent except for brief forays into the neighboring valleys, now glazed over by ankle-deep snow. The hikes provided us with scattered wildlife sightings and visions of stark arctic country, but every afternoon the weather inched closer to winter. We hobbled back to camp with

Judy Bradford and Charlie Roger setting up camp overlooking the upper Sadlerochit River.

near-frozen feet and tumbled directly into the tent. Our boots, parkas, pants, hats, socks, gloves, everything, were piled in a big sodden mess near the door as far from our sleeping bags as possible.

The fog and unrelenting snow were still with us when we slogged to a new camp at Whistler Creek, four miles from the cabins. Tom was due to arrive in a couple of days and we wanted to give ourselves plenty of leeway to reach the rendezvous. The storms had been far too fickle, and being tentbound was a distinct possibility.

The following day the temperature again dropped well below the freezing mark. A howling North Pole wind lashed at the tent. Our backpacks, lying on the tundra mat, were neatly buried by a fresh dumping of snow.

Later it dawned on me that I hadn't seen a bird in awhile, not even a willow ptarmigan, which had been so common before. Had they all deserted us, fleeing to the other side of the Brooks Range, or were they trapped as we were, caught unaware by the weather like the stiff and frozen redpoll I had found earlier? I wanted someone to talk to, but Charlie and Judy were dozing. I was alone with my journal.

August 28, 8 p.m.

All in all, it's been a dull day. Spitting snow alternating with hail drumming on the tent have put us in a stupor. We've grown weary of reading, napping and playing Crazy Eights and Gin Rummy, our cards fashioned out of the pages of Judy's spiral notebook. Our sole excursions have been to grab a few bags of gorp for a cold lunch, thus breaking our cardinal rule in griz country to *never* eat inside the tent. For dinner we had some more trail mix washed down with snowmelt—another nutritionally unbalanced meal. The last hour I've been pouring over an Alaska state map, trying to decide where to go next. I can hardly believe it, but I'm leaning toward another trip north of the Brooks Range. Something about this place has grabbed me and won't let go.

It was more of the same when we awoke—a dark sky and a wet and cold arctic wind. After twenty consecutive nights of sharing a cramped tent, it was time to make our final push for the cabin.

We broke camp quickly, without discussion. We couldn't stand around too long or our feet would begin to freeze. I jogged in place to get the blood flowing. After a few minutes of this, I still couldn't wiggle my toes. Judy took off first. I helped Charlie with his pack; he lifted mine onto my back. Off we marched into the nightmarish tussocks. Each of us knew how pleasant it was going to be to get out of our wet, rock-hard boots and into dry socks and running shoes.

The cabins were only 300 yards away when Charlie suddenly halted. He fumbled for his binoculars with numb, shaking fingers. "I don't believe it," he stammered, peering through the lenses. "We're really stuck now."

I pulled my binoculars from underneath my parka. My fingers weren't working well either. I had a difficult time keeping the glasses steady, but near the cabins, half-hidden by a swale, were the unmistakable forms of a silver-tipped grizzly and two blond yearling cubs. They were investigating a small rubbish pile left behind by earlier, careless occupants. With the wind blowing hard in our direction, the bears hadn't caught our scent.

Normally we would have gone out of our way to avoid the animals, but we were growing desperate. Our feet hurt and the frigid wind was creating hypothermic conditions. We hurriedly discussed our options and reluctantly agreed to try and frighten the bears from the cabins, knowing full well it was stupid to irritate any bear, especially a mother grizzly with cubs.

We moved a hundred yards closer. The nearest person was probably forty miles away; nonetheless a tinge of embarrassment swept over me as I waved my arms, jumped up and down in a crane-like dance and shouted inane things. "Hello, bears! Time for you to leave, we've got reservations."

There was no response. In fact, the bears circled the cabins, dug furiously after a ground squirrel, then snuggled up next to each other in a big furry ball against one of the walls. We advanced several yards and repeated our demonstration. Again, nothing. Even closer, we howled, but the bears didn't lift their heads. The moan of the wind smothered our cacophony.

Judy had the idea of banging our metal cook pot and cups together. "Maybe the metallic noise will carry further," she suggested. We clanged away with our mess kits on the tundra plain.

The mother bear lurched to her feet. "Louder!" Judy ordered. "She hears it." I bashed the pot and cups together as hard as I could, unconcerned that I was putting big dents in the spun aluminum.

The sow stared across the creek at the aliens gathered on the other side. "She doesn't seem very frightened," I noted, stopping my racket for a moment. "If she starts walking toward us, drop your packs and back up fast."

The mother bear stretched and nuzzled her cubs, who slowly got to their feet. She then ambled on top of the swale to get a better look at us. Suddenly the 100-yard gap between us seemed totally inadequate; the bear could cover that distance in five seconds. When the sow turned broadside and gave a violent shake of her fur, I unfastened my pack belt and loosened the shoulder straps. Finally, the sow shuffled down the mound, and with a steady, rolling stride lumbered up the hill away from us. Abandoning the garbage, the cubs trotted behind to keep up.

"*All right*!" Charlie croaked. "It's about time they leave." His voice was hoarse from screaming, as was mine.

We waited until the bears were a half-mile away before we crossed Spawning Creek and made it to the cabins. We threw our packs inside and barred the plywood door, which was studded with nails on the outside to deter bears from leaning on it. The windowless interior was totally dark. Under the darting beams of our headlamps, we went to work on our feet. As we had done before, we formed a ring with each of us placing our feet on the next person's bare stomach. It took a while, quite a while, but finally our feet began to recover.

The afternoon passed slowly. We cracked the door to let in

some light. Outside the temperature was twenty-six degrees and seemed much colder because of the wind. The surface of Lake Schrader was whitecaps and foam; spindrift snow blurred the higher ridges and mountain slopes. The cabin was dirty and confining, about the size of a large closet, but we were glad to have it. We doubted the tent would have survived without damage in the open tundra. We also had doubts about an airplane landing on the lake in these conditions. Tom was due to arrive the next morning.

"I wonder how the weather is in Fairbanks right now," Judy said, voicing a concern we all had. The city was only a few hundred miles away, but at the moment it seemed to be in another world.

After a hasty dinner, we spread our sleeping bags on the rickety bunk beds; there were no mattresses, only bare rusty springs. Judy and I shared the lower platform. Wind shook the cabin's thin wooden walls and rattled the sheet metal roof. I reassured myself that the cabin had undoubtedly survived much worse than this as I drifted off to sleep.

The sound of clattering cans woke me. I hit the light button on my wristwatch—4 a.m. I held my breath. Heavy muffled footsteps and more sifting through cans; the scraping of a large furry body against the outside wall nearly sent me into a panic. It had to be a bear, and there was only a half-inch sheet of plywood separating us. I woke Judy and told her what was happening. I tried to wake Charlie, but either he didn't hear or chose to ignore me. Judy and I remained motionless. With hearts pumping wildly, we listened as the grizzly foraged through picked-over garbage inches from our heads.

Finally, after about ten or fifteen minutes, the noise ceased. Tiptoeing out of bed, I felt my way in the darkness to the door, carefully unfastened the latch, and peeked out. I was amazed at the beauty of the predawn tundra. Across the lake, the sky was awash with horizontal bands of pink and red. A three-quarter moon was about to sink below the other horizon. I took a step outside. Something was different: the wind had died down.

We were packed and ready for Tom to arrive by eight o'clock. Our concern about his arrival was growing. The earlier red sky was now the usual murky gray. The wind had returned to ruffle the lake. If the temperature dropped much lower, the floatplane's cables and rudder system could freeze up after landing. If the clouds dropped much lower, Tom might not even *find* the lake.

We waited patiently by the cabin. Small groups of caribou gamboled past, more intent on traveling than grazing. In the stillness of the arctic morning, we could hear the clicking of their hoofs. A red fox sniffed along the grassy banks of Spawning Creek, hunting for voles and lemmings. A golden eagle skimmed over the tundra in search of unwary ground squirrels. Out on the lake a pair of red-throated loons took turns diving, surfacing with silvery fish, which they fed to their nearly grown chicks.

In a few days the loons and other waterbirds would be moving south. We, too, felt an urgency in the air that warned us not to linger. The snowline had crept down the mountainsides to a few hundred feet above us. Skim ice was already forming on the edges of ponds and slow-moving creeks. Lake Schrader and Lake Peters wouldn't freeze solid for another month or so, but when they did, they wouldn't be ice-free again until July of next year.

As the minutes, then hours, ticked by with no sign of the airplane, we became increasingly fidgety. Judy and I were anticipating a warm motel room and a big feast in Fairbanks, but Charlie wanted to leave in the worst way. "This is my last trip to Alaska," he announced, as we waited outside, searching the sky for the overdue plane.

By one o'clock we figured we'd have to spend another night in the cabin. We were down to a day's worth of food and enough fuel to brew a few cups of tea. "No sense standing around being cold," I said resignedly. "I'm getting into my sleeping bag."

I was unstrapping the stuff sack from my backpack when I heard a faint hum. We dropped what we were doing and bolted for the door. Streaking overhead with a roar and a dip of its wings was Tom's cherry-red Cessna.

Within twenty minutes we were flying south fast and high over Lake Peters as we approached a notch in the Brooks Range. As the walls of the pass narrowed to a V, I watched in fascination as the wingtips practically brushed the sheer cliffs. A few downdrafts bucked the plane, then we shot through to the other side. I was stupefied. Across the Arctic Divide the ground was free of snow and visibility was excellent. The calendar had been turned back several months. Here it was green with few signs of the end of the arctic summer.

As I looked back toward the North Slope and its winter mantle, I recalled the words of explorer and wilderness advocate Bob Marshall, who had a hand in the creation of the Arctic Refuge. Upon the completion of an arduous month-long expedition to the Brooks Range in the 1930s, he said, "Adventure is wonderful, but there is no doubt that one of its joys is its end."[2]

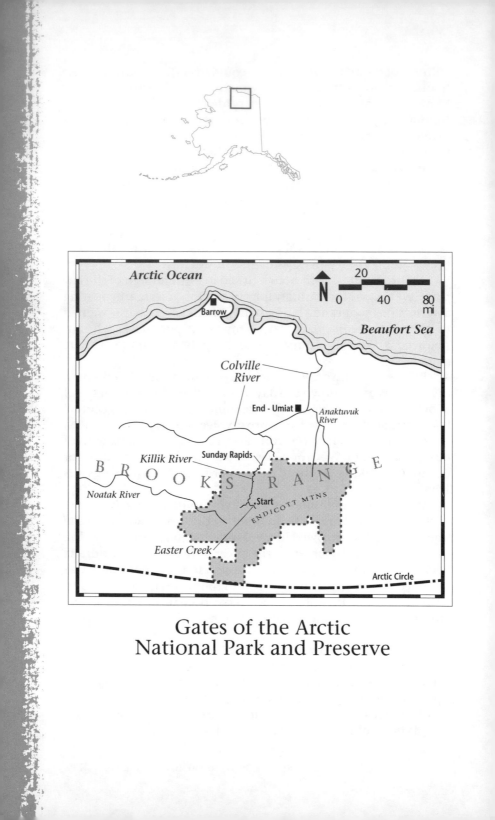

Gates of the Arctic
National Park and Preserve

KAYAK DOWN THE KILLIK

JUDY STIFFENED, HER PADDLE cradled on the kayak's deck. Although she was in the bow, and I could only see her back, I could tell from her body language that she was angry. A moment earlier, rounding a sharp bend in the Killik River, far to the north of the Brooks Range, we had spotted a grizzly sow and two yearlings swimming cross-current yards ahead. The bears had not yet noticed us. A sensible person, Judy wanted to do the sensible thing: pull ashore and wait for the grizzlies to pass. I countered by whispering that the current was too swift and it was too late to land. We both knew that I really wanted to get closer. She refused to paddle. Locked in a stalemate, we drifted downstream.

We were near enough to hear the bears' heavy breathing when the sow, seeing or smelling us, woofed an alarm. In a series of powerful lunges she scrambled ashore, dripping wet. Turning to face us, hackles raised, she coughed again, louder this time. Following their mother's lead, the cubs altered their course toward the gravel bar and hit the shore running. Gravel and dirt flew as flat-footed paws bit into the earth. Only when safely astride a willow-lined ridge did the bear family pause to look back.

Judy remained motionless, mute and tense. Ground down by her silent treatment, I finally tried to cajole her out of her anger. "We really couldn't do anything else," I stated, somewhat defensively. "It would have been stupid to get into shallow water and maybe get stuck. You see my point, don't you?"

"No, no I don't," she replied flatly. She wasn't ready to relax and think about the excitement of our close encounter. "What gets me is that you have all the control back there. You forget I'm the one in front, six feet ahead of you, sitting between you and a pissed-off bear. It looks different up here with nothing in front of me. Yeah, you're real daring with someone to hide behind."

She would cool off later, I was sure. But she had also made a point about taking unnecessary risks. Faced with the bears, a river we didn't know much about, the remoteness of the North Slope and Sunday Rapids ahead, she had every reason to feel edgy. "Okay, you're right," I apologized, weary of paddling solo. "I promise, no more shenanigans."

A week before (August 1) Judy and I had arrived at Fairbanks for our fifth trip together to Alaska. As usual, we were loaded down with a huge pile of gear. The folding kayak, waterproof bags, food bags, clothing, life jackets, stove and tent prompted our long-haired, bearded taxi driver to make a sarcastic remark about traveling light. We lied and told him we were spending three months in Alaska instead of three weeks.

During the ride to the motel, the taxi driver's comments made me wonder if we had taken too much gear. While not lightweight fanatics like some people I know, who go so far as to tear out labels in their clothes and drill holes in spoon handles, I wasn't thrilled about paddling a lumber wagon, either. We checked and double-checked everything at home, trying to anticipate precisely what we needed and what to leave behind. When in doubt about something, however, we brought it along.

Early the next morning we were met by Tom, our pilot on previous Alaska journeys. Tom said the weather was good for flying, "at least as far as the Brooks Range." That was good news, since weather-related delays are fairly common. By ten o'clock we were airborne, quickly gaining altitude in his Cessna floatplane. Threading between soft-edged cumulus clouds, we winged north toward the arctic circle at 150 miles per hour and 5,000 feet in elevation.

For two hours we swept across the vast *taiga*, or northern boreal forest of the Alaska interior, crossing rivers and lowlands where no roads exist and people live in enforced solitude in the bush. Then, on the horizon, wave after wave of charcoal-gray mountains appeared directly in our path.

I studied the airmap on my lap. Across the mountains, in bold black letters, were the words: Gates of the Arctic National Park. A knot of excitement tightened in my gut. Created by the 1980 Alaska Lands Bill, the Gates of the Arctic—a name coined by Bob Marshall, who explored the then-unmapped area in the 1920s and 1930s— is one of the largest wilderness areas in the United States. No roads or trails exist in the 8.5-million-acre park, but there are rivers for transportation, including the one which Judy and I were traveling.

"We're right there," Tom said a few minutes later, pointing his finger at a spot on the map marked "Helpmejack Hills" at the forefront of the Brooks Range. "We'll head up the Alatna River, then take this valley through the Endicott Mountains—I want to point out a few places I think you'll like. Then we'll veer across the divide to Tulilik Lake. It'll provide me with a landing strip and you with a campsite."

I was in no hurry to land, not with this view. With my forehead pressed against the aircraft's side window, I watched as the scraggly black spruce forest succumbed to velvety tundra and shrubs. This was the end of the line for what is commonly perceived as trees. From our mile-high aerie the stunted alders, willows and birch looked like olive-green snakes writhing along beside a network of shadowy creeks and ravines.

Of more significance to me, the rivers and streams were full from bank to bank. Tom confirmed that rains had been heavy here the last month, accounting for the high water levels. This was an enormous relief since the success of our trip hinged on whether or not the Killik was going to be deep enough to float our kayak.

I knew of only a handful of other parties who had made the same trip we wanted to do: a river journey that, broken into segments, included approximately five miles on Easter Creek, ninety miles on the Killik, and seventy miles on the Colville River, with a take-out at Umiat, a remote mining camp and gas station for airplanes in the middle of nowhere. A member of one of these groups told me about having to drag their boats a good part of the way on Easter Creek and the Killik River. The shallow streams had been full of rocks, resulting in badly battered folding kayaks and missed connections at Umiat.

Tom landed the plane in the center of Tulilik Lake, a tundra puddle not much larger than a duck pond in a city park. The motor stopped with a sputter and a growl. As I removed foam rubber plugs from my ears, I heard the wind whistle against the plane's struts, and wavelets lap against the aluminum pontoons.

With my feet on terra firma, I tried to take in everything with a single sweeping glance before the work began. We were in a spacious, glacial-carved valley near the northern edge of Gates of the Arctic National Park and Preserve. Surrounding us were the totally treeless north flanks of the Brooks Range, rising half a mile above the valley floor. To the north was the Killik River, carving a U-shaped trough which we would follow through the mountains and arctic foothills. And nestled in its own small valley, a half-mile to the east, was Easter Creek. This narrow, swift, rocky stream, named by a government geologist who explored its banks on Easter Sunday more than half a century ago, would be our entrance to the Killik River. There we would launch the Klepper in a couple of days.

I dug in my pack for my parka and stocking cap. A brisk wind was whipping up whitecaps on the lake. Oblivious to the chill, Judy breathed deeply, having been cramped in the back seat during the long ride. Her eyes told me what she was thinking. Her words confirmed it. "I wish we could stay here all summer."

Adding to our excitement at being on the North Slope again was the fact that we were in the precise area described by Lois Crisler in *Arctic Wild*. She and her husband had lived here for a year and a half, filming their surroundings and studying wolves. I could feel the Crislers' presence, the energy they had left behind. They, too, had landed on Tulilik Lake, on April 21, 1953.

After the plane was unloaded I noticed something amiss. Frantically I went through our gear a second time. "Oh, no!" I groaned. "We're short a stuff sack of food!" Tom searched the plane. Judy and I sorted again through the supplies, hoping I had made a mistake, but no, a bag was missing—a quarter of our rations for the trip.

Tom, normally unflappable, was more distraught than we were. "Gee, I'm sorry! I'm really sorry. I was sure I had all your stuff when I loaded the plane this morning. I must have left the bag in my garage. Are you going to be all right?"

"We'll be fine, Tom, really," Judy volunteered.

Speak for yourself, please, I thought. Memories of our final week in the Arctic Refuge made me feel suddenly hungry.

Tom rummaged through the Cessna's rear compartment for his emergency supplies. "Here, take this. It should help." He handed me a small plastic bag of goodies containing tropical chocolate bars, Jell-O mix, pudding mix, crackers, hard candies. "It's been in the plane awhile, but it's edible. Gee, I don't know how to apologize."

"Forget about it," Judy insisted. "We'll be okay. We eat too much on these trips anyway." I begged to differ, but there was no point making the man feel worse than he already did.

Six o'clock. Chores were done. We had lugged all our gear to a flat stony bench midway between Tulilik Lake and Easter Creek. We pitched the tent among a spattering of alder shrubs. We threw everything except the kayak bags and food inside. It had been a hectic two days since leaving home, and we were out of sync, hungry and bushed. But we could rest later, the urge to explore the neighborhood prevailed.

A mile away was a small knoll. From its crest we had a splendid view of our valley. Huddled out of the wind, munching Tom's crackers, I methodically scanned the open vistas through binoculars, trying to detect a blip of movement or anything out of the ordinary. Although the air was nippy, the sunny skies sent heat-waves rippling off the sparsely vegetated ground. Distant objects gyrated blurrily through the magnified lenses.

"Something's moving over there," I told Judy. We lay propped up on our elbows. I looked again. It was gone. Was it an animal or an illusionary dwarf willow I had seen?

There it was again, the half-seen outline of a black blur connected to a white chevron stripe. A wolverine! The powerfully built animal loped through a meadow of white-tufted cottongrass, then scurried over a ridge.

Although we had seen wolverines a few times before, each sighting of the big weasel was exciting. Along with the grizzly bear and the wolf, the wolverine is the ultimate symbol of healthy wilderness. A good supply of these top-of-the-food-chain animals suggested an ecosystem functioning as it should.

The next morning was clear, except for drooping, vaporous clouds in the mountains. The tent was stiff with frost, and ice tinkled in the water bottle when I lifted it to drink.

We choked down a couple of peanut butter granola bars. Most of our instant hot oatmeal breakfasts were somewhere in Fairbanks, along with the cocoa and tea. In a few minutes we were done. A meal of sweetened cardboard and teeth-jolting ice water was not something to dawdle over.

By seven o'clock the sun was already high overhead. We stuffed our daypacks and hiked up a moraine toward a large, isolated series of ridges southwest of camp. We planned to be away the entire day.

There was too much country of interest in these headwaters to rush off in the boat. We figured we could reach Umiat in about eight or nine days of paddling, leaving us the same number of days off the river. This was the type of paddle travel I enjoy most. Plenty of time to hike, photograph, read, wait out storms. No sense coming all this way to hurry out.

On this march and others from our Tulilik Lake base camp, we observed many more species of mammals and birds than I thought such an ecosystem could support. In addition to the wolverine, there were the sheep on the mountain ridges, a red fox that inspected our tent, scattered groups of caribou grazing in the valleys, inquisitive ground squirrels, several grizzly bears and some dozen moose. I was pleased that the birdlife seemed more prolific than that of the Arctic Refuge, which lay some 250 miles to the east at nearly the same latitude. A partial list for our first day included golden eagles, bald eagles, mew gulls, glaucous-winged gulls, long-tailed jaegers, a merlin, willow ptarmigan, horned larks, wheatears, northern shrikes and white-crowned sparrows.

The key to this amazing fecundity of variety and quantity was the tundra itself. With nothing but a thin veneer of topsoil clinging to rocks, sand and rubble, and with a cement-hard layer of permafrost a mere twelve inches below it, a web of vegetation ekes out a tenacious life. Forbs, grasses, sedges, lichens and reindeer mosses form tight, tough carpets that hug the ground out of the path of killing winds. Diminutive willows and alders, about waist-high yet full-grown, grow in spreading tangles in protected gullies and ravines. In three short months—the arctic growing season—enough raw fuel is manufactured to keep the warm-blooded animals sustained through the winter.

We remained at this base camp for four nights, every morning charting a new route over endless terrain. My biological clock gradually changed as a result of the nearly constant light. At home I'm a "morning person," usually going to bed by ten o'clock and waking up with the sun, but here I was sleeping late and sometimes not eating supper until nearly midnight. Judy—a "night owl"—was delighted with my altered state.

Our last morning in base camp began like all the rest. The sun shone into the tent; the daybreak temperature hovered at about fifty degrees. I hurried outside, seeking urgent relief. The first thing I noticed were the two cow moose—regulars around here—browsing in the willows about 100 yards away. The first few mornings they had trotted off at the sight of my bright blue long johns and disheveled countenance, but now they ignored me completely. A half-dozen bull caribou were more curious. They formed a neat row of voyeurs on a nearby hillside and watched intently as I went through my morning rituals.

To augment our dwindling food stores, after breakfast I tried something I hadn't done since grade school, a diversion I'm sure I was better at then than now. Breaking out a spool of monofilament fishing line and a few all-purpose lures from our emergency kit, I approached Easter Creek with the idea that later we would be stuffing our faces and stomachs with grilled fish for dinner. Several hours and uncounted casts later I had one undersized, highly illegal silver-skinned fish on shore: an arctic grayling. I had foul-hooked it, and there was no sense throwing the fish back. Wrapped in aluminum foil with a pat of margarine, and baked in willow coals on the gravel bar, the grayling's firm, pink meat made a superb snack.

A westerly breeze was keeping the mosquitoes under control, so we decided to trek up Easter Creek, toward the Arctic Divide. We carefully selected the items we would need: first-aid kit, rain gear, wind gear, hat and gloves, insect repellent and headnet, a bag of gorp, water bottles and a .357 Magnum Smith & Wesson stainless steel revolver.

The gun was a new addition to our Alaska outfit. Our trip to the Arctic Refuge had shown us that we needed a more effective deterrent to bears than screaming, pot-banging and whistling. After much soul-searching and a review of all the available literature on bear deterrents, we decided to pack the revolver to augment our lines of defense.

The pros and cons of carrying firearms into grizzly country are guaranteed to spark heated debate, particularly in Alaska where it is legal to do so except in certain national parks. Both pro- and anti-gun camps have valid points, but ultimately, the decision is a personal thing. Taking a gun into grizzly country brings with it a terrific responsibility. By virtue of its awesome power, a firearm encourages a person to be overconfident and lazy about bear-avoidance procedures. Worse, in careless hands, a firearm can injure or kill a bear that in reality posed no threat. There are, at last count, only between 24,000 and 33,000 grizzly bears surviving in North America; of that number, less than half reside in Alaska. The death of a few dozen bears in certain locations can eradicate an entire population. To kill a grizzly bear for sport or defense of live-stock or property is to me unacceptable. But then there is that nagging matter of self-preservation.

We rehearsed how we would act in hypothetical situations. We would fire the revolver in the air after all other bear-scare methods failed to work. Only in a worst-case scenario, in case of an actual attack, would we attempt to shoot the animal. I have been around weapons long enough to realize that even a well-placed slug from this caliber is inadequate to drop a grizzly in its tracks. The gun made us no less cautious or forgetful that in Alaska's bush the grizzly demands extreme caution and abiding respect.

We strapped on our packs and followed a fairly open gravel bar along the creek. Hiking was easy until we reached a high cut-bank. Crawling up the loose clay was nothing compared to the difficulty of crossing the tussocky green abundance we next faced. The lumpy, teetering pedestals of grass, encircled by moats of ankle-deep water, were hell on earth for any flightless creature with two legs.

Tussocks aside, there were benefits to being on top of the creek bed. Our view was limited only by the power of our binoculars and the acuity of our vision. Gazing across the valley, I saw a pair of bull moose browsing in the floodplain willows. We also saw a solitary grizzly across the creek a half-mile away, ambling along in an unhurried manner in our direction. We kept an eye on the griz as we continued toward the spine of an open ridge.

We were hot and grimy when we reached the crest of a minor summit, nearly 2,000 feet above the valley floor. I pulled off my sweat-soaked shirt and plopped down on the soft, cushiony tundra. A raven croaked as it passed overhead. Otherwise I could hear nothing but the singing of blood in my ears.

I cleaned the sweat streaks from my glasses and squinted. The sun was still bright and steady in the late afternoon. Beneath the clouds, cast in a lavender glow, was a land that had not changed much since its rebirth after the last Ice Age. At every compass point were tundra-coated ridges and creased valleys, brushy gravel bars and blue-green ponds, sensuously winding creeks and streams. Most tantalizing, only because we were unable to see the other side, were two saddle-shaped passes about twelve miles to the south. Survey and Kutuk passes lay directly on the Arctic Divide, the watershed that dictates whether raindrops flow north to the Arctic Ocean or south and west to the Bering and Chukchi seas. The 6,000-foot mountains that couch the passes are small by Alaska standards, yet imposing and full of mystery.

I unfolded our topographic maps. Four 1:250,000-scale sheets, taped together, covered our entire route. The topos were the most detailed available but were not really detailed at all: one inch equals four miles. The maps were only one-dimensional sheets of heavy-stock paper, but studying them was like opening a book of dreams. The contour lines and place names, hidden valleys and unclimbed peaks—thousands of square miles of undisturbed, uninhabited country—was paradise for anyone with the least bit of wanderlust. We got a kick out of pronouncing the names on the map. Some were familiar and descriptive—Marker, Shivering, Lonely; while others—Kaviktit, Enekalikruak, Nigaktoviakvik, Silalinigun, Egiklak, Mayukuit—were tongue-twisters. Scores of other high points and streams remained nameless, which is as it should be in a land of untamed beauty.

As a river runner, I soon became entranced with the blue lines— pencil-thin squiggles that represented rivers and streams I yearned to follow. Directly across the divide was the source of the Alatna River, a premier float trip that winds southeast through the taiga, toward the Koyukuk River, for 145 miles. A day's hike west of the Alatna were the granite cliffs and spires of the brooding Arrigetch Peaks. They jumped off the map with their tightly spaced contours and hanging blue glaciers, not surprising since *Arrigetch* is derived from the native term meaning "fingers of the hand extended." About sixty miles southwest was Mount Igipak, the highest point in the western Brooks Range at 8,510 feet. Its glacial waters are the birthplace of the Noatak River, arguably the best long-distance paddle trip in Alaska, flowing through the 6.6-million-acre Noatak National Preserve. A little further south of Mount Igipak, also on our maps, was Walker Lake, and at its outlet the gentle Kobuk River. And only twenty miles west of where we sat was the Nigu River watershed, one of the least-paddled rivers on the North Slope, one which I have every intention some day of running. Rivers; journeys. So many. All on a single map.

Tired and hungry, we were anxious to get back to camp before twilight. On the return march we saw animals we had missed from above. A gathering of caribou—five magnificently antlered bulls— passed like shadows through the streamside brush. They snorted in alarm and clattered down the pebbly creek bed when a silver-tipped grizzly emerged from a jungle of willows. The backlighting of the sun created a halo effect on its blonde fur. We climbed quickly up the bank and hid behind a pile of boulders. The bear didn't appear to know we were there, which was not particularly reassuring. The animal shuffled lethargically to a row of blueberry bushes and in no particular haste raked them clean with paws and muzzle. Suddenly, the grizzly lost interest in berries and galloped up the hillside in a frantic attempt to nab a startled ground squirrel. When the dust cleared, the grizzly stood empty-mouthed and panting. The ground squirrel had made good its escape, but griz didn't know that. Frustrated, the husky bear shuffled a few more paces, then sprinted in the opposite direction, running as only a grizzly can when it goes all out. The bear flattened a cluster of willows in its path.

The twilight thickened as we neared camp. I collapsed as soon as we reached the tent, spent from our twelve-hour hike across broken ground. Judy suggested we try some evening fishing, but considering my past lack of success, I politely declined. Instead, I pulled out a roll of duct tape and worked on repairing one of our waterproof bags that a ground squirrel had chewed open during our absence. As if that weren't cruel enough, the rodent also had managed to make off with a bag of oatmeal. Our food was disappearing fast.

The buzz of mosquitoes was the first thing I heard upon awaking the next morning. Yawning widely, I checked my digital watch. It flashed 7:30. Really exhausted, I had slept late again. Feeling magnanimous, I let Judy sleep for a few more minutes, then, after a gentle nudge and a good-morning kiss, whispered in her ear: itslaterthanhelltimetogetup!

After my partner began to stir, I slipped into my filthy clothes and stepped outside into blazing sunlight. Oddly, the mosquitoes weren't a problem away from the tent. I scanned the sky. Pale blue skies again. But what was this? A new weather system, in the shape of ebony, sullen clouds, was poised to the north like a colossal battering ram. I guessed that the front would take a day to get here, and by then we would be well down the river.

We broke camp and assembled the boat. The Klepper went together without a hitch, all the parts well-worn and molded from past trips. This, though, was to be our kayak's maiden voyage down a river, notwithstanding our short stint on Katmai's Grosvenor and Savonoski rivers. There is a large gulf between lake/ocean touring and river running. The twisting, fast-moving, rocky stream would be a challenge for the straight-tracking, fabric-hulled craft. I carefully checked the gray, Hypalon hull, and as a precaution layered on strips of duct tape over any signs of wear.

Under increasingly threatening skies, we portaged the kayak and gear over the final quarter-mile that separated our camp from the creek. The three carries took most of the morning, but finally, under a steady drizzle, we were perched at the edge of the stream.

Of all the chores involved in camping and kayak touring,

Judy Bradford setting up the Klepper kayak at camp near Easter Creek by the headwaters of the Killik River.

packing the Klepper is my least favorite. If I hadn't done it before, I wouldn't have believed that we and all our gear would fit inside the slender boat. While Judy put the finishing touches on our seating arrangements, I nervously paced the bank. Although Easter Creek had dropped a few inches since we arrived, the feisty mountain torrent was still several feet deep and moving faster than I liked.

"Make sure your life jacket is zipped up," I cautioned Judy. "Yell 'rock' if you see any in our way. And when I yell 'paddle,' give me all the power you've got. We've got to have more forward speed than the current for the rudder to be effective. We won't be able to draw and sweep this thing like we do with our canoe."

Judy curled her lip. "Right," she said sardonically, indicating that my patronizing instructions were really not necessary. She was, after all, no stranger to river running.

"Sorry," I acknowledged. "I'm hyper myself." If our boat was irreparably damaged we would be stranded. We had no radio or means of contact with the outside world. We would have to wait for Tom—the only human being who knew our specific itinerary—to mount an air search. Our credo was simple: No Mistakes!

Judy going first, we wiggled into the open cockpit among the assortment of waterproof bags. As soon as we were firmly in place with the sprayskirt attached, I released the willow branch I was hanging onto, our last link to land. The boat shot downstream. Bouncing from bank to bank, we tried to maintain control as we skidded between boulders and over short rapids, past walled mud-banks and gravel bars. Whenever possible we hugged the outside bends with the deeper water, threading the line between running into an undercut wall and spinning into a foam-specked eddy. My thoughts were centered on keeping the craft intact until we reached the Killik River five miles away. Our bullet-fast descent didn't take long.

The Killik appeared suddenly. Easter Creek merged with the river at an intricately braided gravel bar that camouflaged the confluence. Only when the stream grew wider and deeper, the valley more spacious, were we absolutely certain we had entered the Killik.

A lot of water was still draining into the valley from the surrounding mountains and hills and the current was swift. Without even paddling, we cruised at about the same speed as a cantering caribou. A few waves curled aboard, but with the sprayskirt snapped and tightly drawn the water rolled harmlessly off the deck.

We were floating through an elongated land between mountain ranges. Full-bodied green and gold hillsides, their tops sheared off by scuddy clouds, overshadowed our tiny kayak far below. Lining the river were verdant grassy meadows and marshes, highlighted with white, shining tufts of cottongrass. Tributaries from adjoining valleys gushed in from both sides.

"This is definitely the best," I chortled, mesmerized by the untouched vastness passing by. "Trippin' down a spectacular arctic valley, letting the river do most of the work. Sure beats struggling over the same ground on foot."

A few miles after the confluence, the valley narrowed and the river slowed. Side creeks dumping their gravel loads into the Killik had dammed the river into long, bulging pools connected by stretches of lively riffles. We looked forward to the fast water for the thrills it brought, but the aquamarine, pellucid pools were perfect for animal watching and relaxing.

In the afternoon we beached the kayak in the lee of a high sand dune, glad for the screen it provided from the cold, upstream winds. We had on adequate clothing, but still felt a chill from the damp air and steadily dropping temperatures.

Judy stepped out first and dragged the bow on shore. I unclipped the sprayskirt and stood up, and nearly fell down. My legs were numb. Too much sitting, not enough circulation. Shakily, I hobbled to shore, grimacing from needlelike pinpricks as the blood tingled back down to my feet.

"How far have we come?" Judy mumbled, her face buried in a bag of trail mix in quest of the elusive M&Ms. I examined the plastic-wrapped map velcroed to the spraydeck. "About seven miles, I guess. Not bad considering our late start and the headwind we've been fighting most of the day." Judy looked up; no more M&Ms. "I wonder if we'll go this whole trip without seeing anyone."

That thought had been crossing my mind too. The only sign of humanity so far had been a high-flying jet airplane headed toward the North Pole. This lack of human contact suited me fine. It's not that I'm reclusive, just selfish. The fewer people I have to share wilderness with the better. Thus, when a single-engine floatplane came buzzing over the river, I hoped it was merely sightseeing and wasn't going to stick around.

"Probably some hunters," I grumbled, perturbed that our space had been invaded. Hunting season for sheep and caribou was set to open in a week. We knew of at least one guide licensed by the state to operate out of the Killik area.

The aircraft droned directly over us, banked sharply and circled low. "What a jerk," I snarled. I became even more irritated when the plane passed low enough for me to identify the lone figure in the cockpit. The figure—a man—waved. "I don't believe it," I yelled. "It's Tom! What's he doing here?"

Judy turned pale. "Oh no," she groaned, always assuming the worst. "It must be our parents. Something must be wrong."

"No way," I replied. "He wouldn't fly all the way up here to tell us if one of our parents croaked."

Judy glared. "You don't know that! Come on, let's see if he's landing."

In a short while we were a half-mile downstream, pulling the boat ashore where we thought the plane would be. I was bending over when I heard a familiar voice: "Well, hello down there!" Tom, a wide grin on his face, appeared up on the bank. "I think you may want this," he said, holding up a fat red stuff sack at arm's length.

He slid nimbly down the bank and told us what had brought him north again so soon. "This morning I dropped off a pair of kayakers on the John River, about fifty miles to the southeast. Since it was only a short detour to swing on up here, I brought the food bag, knowing you must be pretty tired of being on a diet."

I noticed that a long coil of bright orange surveyor's ribbon was tied to the stuff sack. "Oh, that's for an airdrop," Tom explained, "in case I wasn't able to set down. The ribbon would have made it easier for you to find the bag."

Fifteen minutes later the little floatplane was hedge-hopping across the tundra, quickly gaining altitude as it angled south to the distant mountains near Kobuk National Monument. We waved as Tom passed overhead, still dazed by his abrupt appearance and welcome surprise.

It was a struggle crunching twenty additional pounds of food in the already cramped boat, but somehow we got it all in. "I was just getting used to being hungry," Judy said, stuffing a couple of high-energy Granola Grabbers in our ditty bag for a late snack.

"Not me," I answered emphatically. "In fact, I was hoping Tom was going to surprise us by giving us a few extra goodies from the supermarket. Oreo cookies and a bag of taco chips and salsa would have been nice."

A few miles further on we pulled over to a grass-covered dune to make camp. There was plenty of light left for travel, but we didn't want to rush out of the mountains just yet. After pitching the tent and organizing our gear, we devoted the rest of the afternoon to an uphill hike toward an unnamed mountain a mile away. Our rubber calf-high boots sunk in the wet, spongy muck, making us recall the days of misery we'd spent trudging through similar stuff in the Arctic Refuge, with soaked leather boots and frozen feet.

"No wonder (squish) Charlie (squish) gave up backpacking," I grunted. Not a day went by that we didn't feel appreciative of our new waterproof footwear.

It didn't take long to reach the base of the foothills, nor to locate a band of Dall sheep on the naked slopes. With their superb eyesight—there may be none better among Alaska's mammals—the white sheep had undoubtedly seen us well before we saw them. Since we posed no threat far below in the valley, the animals continued grazing on the sparse lichens and forbs interspersed among the loose rocks.

We plodded on. We intercepted a small herd of caribou striding across the hoof-sucking muck; it appeared as if their broad cloven hooves never touched ground. I snapped a few pictures as they passed. The racks on the bulls were enormous, polished to a glossy sheen; the smaller females were adorned with simple spikes. In a span of five minutes these "deer" of the north traversed a distance that it would have taken us an hour to cross.

The prospect of a marvelous sumptuous dinner encouraged us to return to camp. I was salivating at the thought of rich gooey lasagna, my favorite freeze-dried entree, slathered over half a rye bagel and a slice of Gouda cheese. I would wash this down with spring vegetable soup and a nightcap of peppermint herbal tea. A Hershey's almond chocolate bar would be dessert right before bed.

My food fantasy evaporated when, nearing camp, we intersected an abundance of fresh grizzly tracks along a rivulet that emptied into the river. The autographs in the mud hadn't been there when we left. We climbed a small rise to scan the surroundings. The griz was out of sight, but I knew it was there—somewhere. It didn't really matter as long as our camp wasn't molested. With some relief, we found everything exactly as we had left it.

We have been fortunate that our camps have never been ransacked by a grizzly. We had met a party of four California men in Fairbanks a year earlier who told us of their adventure. They were a few days into a three-week kayak trip down the Alatna River when they stopped to make an overnight backpack into the Arrigetch Peaks. While they were away, their camp was demolished by bears. All of their cached food was eaten or dragged off, and their inflatable kayaks were badly torn and punctured. After patching the boats, they continued down the river. For four days they subsisted on berries and a few fish until chancing upon a family of native Alaskans on a hunting trip. The family gave them enough food to make it out of the wilderness.

The next day was an R&R break, filled with tundra walks, eating, loafing, eating, wildlife watching and delving into our small library of paperback books. Throughout the day the air was humid, but the rain didn't start to fall until after we went to bed.

The following morning our planned early departure was weather delayed. I lay on my back—the tent's awning kept out the rain—and watched the billows of foaming vapor churn past our camp. The mist swirled over the valley and collided into ridges and peaks, giving the place a moody, mystical atmosphere. The only problem was that the rain was certain to raise the creeks and rivers even higher.

A few hours later, when the downpour turned into a trickle, we packed up and launched the boat. The weather was doing crazy things. The Killik's current would have provided us with a swift journey, but our progress was hindered by the buffeting wind. It pressed against our faces as we pushed downstream. As Judy picked the tempo and I followed, our wooden eight-foot touring paddles swung in unison. I was glad to have a streamlined, low-riding kayak. An open canoe would have been satisfactory, but a rubber raft would be hopeless in these winds. The Klepper was proving to

Along the shore of the Killik River, Judy Bradford examines a map.

be a dependable river runner after all.

Distances were deceiving in this expansive land. A mountain that seemed to be a mile away was in reality five times that far when I checked it on the map. Mile after meandering mile slipped under the hull as we floated down wide pools and through easy whitewater. The riffles were fun, short little runs, a prelude to the much larger and more serious Sunday Rapids, a day or two's journey away.

A string of low, wavy dunes rose to our left, an odd sight in this arctic landscape. We pulled ashore to investigate. Piled up by centuries of strong winds and abundant sand, the dunes' undulations were softened by a creeping mat of willows, alders and wildflowers (especially wildflowers) hugging together for warmth and protection between the grasses. Mountain avens, yellow buttercups, bright-magenta dwarf fireweed, lupines, gentians, mountain heather and heliotropic arctic poppies made a splash of color across the palette of the land. Much more interested in botany than I, Judy knelt by the delicate flowers, admiring them, trying to identify them positively with the aid of a field guide. She pointed to a few that she wanted me to photograph. After I shot half a roll on the sweeping landscapes—the "big picture" I was more interested in—I was happy to oblige. We had some botanist friends at home who would be perturbed if our slide show didn't have any macro shots.

Beyond the dunes, off to the side of the Killik, was a wide valley hemmed in by gradually diminishing mountains remote from the main upthrust of the Brooks Range. To the east was Kaikshak Hill, a 1,600-foot-high rocky seam sliced through by several creeks with native names: Silalinigun, Nigaktoviakvik, Aniakvik, Togoyuk. To the northwest, on the north bank of Akmalik Creek, loomed 4,126-foot Kikiktat (meaning "like an island") Mountain. Primitive country, this. As far as we could see—thirty, fifty, eighty miles?—there was not a single alien object (except us) in this arctic tapestry.

This first impression, however, was deceiving. Another day of paddling brought us to a campsite near Kikiktat Mountain. We were now beyond the northern boundary of Gates of the Arctic National Park and Preserve, and in country owned by the Arctic Slope Regional Corporation (ASRC), native Alaskan selected lands that include almost the entire lower Killik River drainage north to the Colville River. A mere dozen miles west of camp were the Kurupa Hills, once an unsullied, wildlife-rich region, presently a colony of rumbling oil rigs. Because it was hidden by the foothills we couldn't see the development, and it wasn't on our U. S. Geological Survey map printed in 1955, but for an hour or so as we floated downriver to Kikiktat Mountain, we heard the faint hum of electrical motors over the horizon. It was another sobering reminder, if one is needed these days, that no wilderness, no matter how small or how large or how inaccessible, is sacred in an environmentally up-for-grabs world.

There's a saying by the late Edward Abbey, maverick environmentalist and author, "that wilderness belongs to all, and belongs to no one." In reality, of course, people do own wilderness. I tried not to dwell on what I thought might happen in these vast ASRC lands, nearly all of which are still as wild as anyplace in Gates of the Arctic National Park. The image of drilling pads, airfields, oil processing facilities, roads and pipelines in this pristine country made me sick. It was depressing to be aware, to know what is being lost.

Leaving our camp at Kikiktat Mountain, we proceeded north from pool to pool, around oxbows and bends, toward Sunday Rapids. I calculated the distance to our next campsite, and the start of the major whitewater, to be about fifteen miles as the raven flies.

Despite the miles we still had to cover, I was growing concerned that we were moving down the river too fast. We didn't want to end up at Umiat prematurely, especially when one of the pleasures in floating the Killik had been the abundance of wildlife we could see from our movable blind. The open valley, for the most part, provided meager concealment for large mammals. Moose and bears were visible as much as a mile away. Caribou also stood out because of their white rumps, creamy brown coats and restless actvity.

However, it was the winged creatures that we found ourselves studying the most. The Killik is blessed with an abundance of nesting habitats that attract a wide variety of avian species. We approached to within a boat-length of a red-throated loon; it submerged, leaving only a tiny stream of bubbles. A family of tundra swans pattered across the water and with strident bugling lifted heavily into the air. A V-formation of red-breasted mergansers whistled overhead. A snowy owl fanned back and forth above the tuft-grass looking for rodents. And high in the sky, a young gyrfalcon, the color of dull ivory, learned how to spin and dive under the tutelage of soaring parents. With the sightings of other new birds—northern harriers, rough-legged hawks, arctic terns, bank swallows, redpolls, longspurs, robins, sparrows and shorebirds—our bird list was up to forty-four species.

We paddled apprehensively down a mile-long glassy channel girdled by lonely tundra and thousand-foot bluffs. At the end of the pool, immediately past the spot where we had converged with the swimming mother grizzly and twin cubs, was the start of Sunday Rapids. This Class II-III, fifteen-mile stretch was so named by government geologists because a field party swamped several boats while going through the rapids on Sunday, June 3, 1945. With an average drop of twenty feet per mile, we figured Sunday Rapids was going to be the crux of our trip.

As the pull of the current intensified, I heard a faint sound: a dull, continuous murmur that caused my pulse to rise. "This is it, Sunday Rapids," I announced, trying to maintain a semblance of calm with my even, deliberate words. Who was I kidding? I was hyperventilating. With shaky hands I scaled my binoculars and camera in their waterproof case. There was time for a quick, final glance back toward the mountains. The sun was barely visible behind a pall of haze, but a slanting radiance broke through and set the tundra ablaze with a golden hue, the color of early autumn.

Low bluffs pinched the river. We raced through sunlight and shadow. I guided the boat onto a bubble line of foam that led to the center of a V-chute. We were suddenly looking down an incline, a waterslide, with haystacks and partially submerged boulders lying in ambush downstream. "We're in it now!" I hollered above the din as we slipped down a glassy accelerating tongue. "No chance to scout." I yelled "power" and Judy doubled her paddle strokes.

Waves lapped at the side of the kayak. Cold water curled over the deck and splashed our chests. I gulped down my nervousness and dug deep with my double-bladed paddle. The Killik's surface was a madcap blend of dancing whitecaps and dark, abrupt troughs. Breakers smashed over the boat, sending icy rivulets down our necks and sleeves and through chinks in the sprayskirt. Our seats were awash in water.

I labored to keep the boat on keel with the current. The kayak flexed and creaked as it rode over the waves, its flexibility one of the reasons the Klepper is so strong. My confidence in the boat and ourselves was increasing. We were charging over and through hazards I would feel nervous tackling in my trusty, seventeen-foot deep-hulled tripping canoe. The Klepper's seaworthiness was enhanced because of the heavy payload under its deck. The ballast kept us low in the water and provided greater stability.

It was late afternoon before we found a gentle eddy to pull into for the night. After miles of demanding whitewater we had to rest.

We dragged our gear to a site well above the rising river and began the hour-long task of making camp, made more urgent by the simultaneous appearance of mosquito swarms and rain. Instead of a time-consuming hot dinner exposed to the elements, we wolfed down part of the next day's trail lunch, then scrambled into the tent.

Sheltered by the taut nylon dome, we were dry and bug-free, cozy. Over the patter of rain and the whine of mosquitoes we heard the caroling of red-throated loons and the music of turbulent water. We watched through the door as an energetic red fox sprang into the river and dog-paddled across, somehow managing to keep its long bushy tail dry. Scurrying out on a gravel bar, the animal shook briskly, then plunged into the willow thickets. When a shift in wind blew rain into the tent, I zipped up the door, shutting out the view, sealing us in.

The morning ushered in more rain. My breath vaporized when I exhaled, turning to ice crystals on the inside walls of the tent. There was no urgency to get out of our warm sleeping bags since this was a designated rest day. We stayed put until ten o'clock, totally content to read, doze and catch up on our notes. Finally our hunger got the best of us. Being in grizzly country, we had to leave the tent in order to eat.

A breakfast of freeze-dried scrambled eggs mixed in with a crumbled bacon bar and crackers was better than anything I've ever had at a roadside Denny's. Our cup of hot tea turned cold, however, when our attention was distracted by three wolverines loping by directly in front of camp. The big tawny weasels, probably a mother with full-grown young, stopped, sniffed and reared up on their hind legs when they spotted us, then dropped back down and bounded into the riverside bushes. I had been watching the animals with hypnotic fascination. After they vanished, I looked down. I had been holding a camera body in one hand, a telephoto lens in the other, but I never quite managed to put them together.

The remainder of the day we spent hiking the ridges behind camp. From the highest slopes we had outstanding views of the Killik valley and the Brooks Range, where our trip began. Great footloose country, this, but when on a river trip my thoughts never stray far from the river itself: is the water level rising or falling, what's around the next bend, is the wind at my back or in my face, what about rapids or obstructions, where is the next good campsite, how many miles do I want to paddle today? The tug of the river was stronger than the lure of the hills.

I had shoved a stick into the ground at the river's edge the night before, and examining it upon our return to camp, I discovered the river had risen a foot in the past twenty-four hours. Gravel bars exposed earlier were now flooded, and turbid rivulets were flowing in the willows and alders on the bank. The wind was rising and it looked like more rain. We pulled the kayak up to higher ground and tied it to the tent and some woody shrubs. That evening I read *People of the Deer*, a Farley Mowat book, as long as I could stay awake. The last thing I remember before falling asleep was the sound of a breeze whipping through the willows and water gurgling past our tundra ledge.

Soon after waking the next day we shoved the kayak into the swollen river. For most of the morning the rough water continued. The fast current, steep banks and willow jungles on either side offered us no place to land. At our pace it was impossible to stop and observe anything along shore. Although our concentration was directed downstream, there were still minor accidents. I cringed whenever we scraped a boulder or slithered over an unseen gravel bar, hoping that there was no damage to the rubber skin.

All was not whitewater, of course. While cruising under a steep cut-bank we chanced to look up. A paddle length away and a few feet above a buff colored grizzly returned our stare. It was part frightening apparition, part comic relief. For a long time after that briefest of encounters I chuckled at the image of that bear's stupefied face. It undoubtedly would have been even funnier if I could have seen my own.

Late in the afternoon the rapids diminished. We pulled out for the night on the first high ground we could find. From our maps, it appeared that the Colville River was a day's journey away. To celebrate our safe deliverance through Sunday Rapids, we opted to lay over the next day—no packing, no paddling, just loafing and hiking. We would devote ourselves to enjoying the neighboring ridges and vast emptiness of the valley floor.

Hiking was arduous over the tussocks, but we were rewarded for our efforts. From a low rise behind camp we were able to see forever across the rolling North Slope. The rest of the world seemed utterly distant. I relished the feeling that we were totally out of contact with the clutter, confusion and cacophony of civilization. I heard nothing but my own breathing. The silence was a million years thick, flowing breathlessly across the land.

Caribou trails crisscrossed the tundra everywhere. Across from us we spotted fifty to sixty caribou; they seemed numerous until a herd of several hundred poured over the ridge. They were soon joined by scores of other grunting, jostling animals that merged on the valley floor. The restless wanderers formed a swollen river as they trekked southward toward well-used passes in the Brooks Range to their forested wintering grounds hundreds of miles away. With the hoof clicking and snorting, the chaos of calves trying to keep up with cows, the tentative sparring between rival bulls, the pulse of life was palpable. The caribou passing below were the most we had ever seen at one time, but they represented only a small segment of the populous western arctic caribou herd, more than 200,000 strong.

The caribou drifted up the valley in a steady, determined gait, pausing only briefly to graze. After they left we turned our attention elsewhere. Three bull moose dunked for water plants in a tundra pond a half-mile away. Even from this distance their outlandishly massive antlers were conspicuous. Across the river, between us and the moose, was the warm, quiet scene of a sow grizzly teaching her two young cubs how to harvest blueberries. The cubs mimicked their mother's actions by grabbing the ripe, juicy berries, but they were not sure what to do with them.

Because of a wilting breeze, things were not as peaceful where we sat. In spite of the dropping temperatures, we were attacked by fierce clouds of mosquitoes. I was starting to feel less kindly toward the arctic. "The caribou leave and we attract every bug for hundreds of square miles that's looking for blood," I complained. I scratched my neck and behind my ears, already a cluster of red, rising welts. We tried hiking the ridgetops to catch the wind, but these were big, powerful Alaskan mosquitoes, not about to surrender to anything less than a hurricane. We were outnumbered and outgunned, and they won in the end. We looped back to camp to pick up the head-nets we had left behind.

We were in for a surprise more disturbing than the mosquitoes when we arrived at camp. The grizzly sow and cubs we had watched earlier were about a quarter-mile away, intent on crossing the river. Without hesitation, the sow plunged in and emerged on our bank 200 yards upstream. The cubs balked—the river was swift and wide—but finally they stepped into the rushing current. They were instantly swept downstream. After a minute the two shaggy bundles weren't even at midstream. The mother didn't seem concerned, but we were. As our anxiety mounted, we cheered them on.

"C'mon, get going!" Judy cried. "You can do it."

"Move it! Move it!" I found myself chanting. "C'mon, just a little bit more."

The cubs struggled heroically while their mother ambled toward our camp. Bear cubs are natural swimmers, but these tiny guys were at the limit of their abilities. Finally, after what must have been an exhausting, terrifying ride, they struggled up on shore. We were worn out, but they were apparently fine. The plump cubs gave a quick shake, then scrambled toward their mother, who was still, to our dismay, shuffling closer to camp.

They walked to within a few yards of our food bags—the boat and tent were further on—when the sow stopped. Her shovel-shaped head arched right and left, her keen nose sniffed the air.

We were concealed partway up a small rise, having retreated when the bears swam the river. I was beginning to cold sweat, certain that we were about to have a serious encounter.

"Don't you think we'd better do something, try and frighten her away?" Judy proposed.

My mind worked slowly, trying to dredge up a useful answer. I recalled that Bob Marshall, the inveterate explorer of the Brooks Range, was once confronted with a similar situation. "About 150 feet ahead were three grizzlies," Marshall wrote. "This may seem like a long distance to a catcher trying to throw a man out stealing second, but not to a man faced by three bears, eleven miles from the closest gun, one hundred and six from the first potential stretcher bearer, and three hundred miles from the nearest hospital."[1]

I was mulling this over—where was the nearest hospital, anyway?—when the mother grizzly surprised us by veering away from the bags. Her new course was directly toward the kayak stashed alongside some waist high willows.

"This could be bad," I sighed. "I'd rather lose the food than the Klepper. We can go hungry for a couple of days, but we can't walk out of here."

I dug into my daypack and removed the revolver from its leather holster. We had brought the gun for just such an emergency, but I felt it was sacrilegious to fire it—even as a warning shot—unless there was no alternative.

We went for the alternative. Instead of firing, we whooped and hollered, blew whistles and waved our arms over our heads. The sow whirled and faced us. Rising on her hind legs, the bear see-sawed her head back and forth, attempting to pick up the scent. We intensified the hullabaloo, but, unbelievably, our efforts were not enough to make her leave.

The sow dropped, lumbered toward the river, and with the cubs at her side, lay down about a hundred feet away. We tried everything except popping off a .357 round, but the trio refused to budge. Even my college fight song (I'm amazed I remembered it) was lost in the wind. It was nearly 11:30 p.m., under a chilling twilight, when the bears finally departed of their own volition. Stiff-jointed and cold, we retired cautiously to the tent, too tired and adrenalized to eat dinner. I zipped shut the tent flaps and placed the revolver near my head within easy reach. Then, without undressing, I slipped into my sleeping bag, pulled the hood of the bag above my ears and drew my stocking cap over my eyes. The nylon walls may keep out a stiff breeze and bugs, but against grizzlies they do nothing.

Daybreak was a long time coming. At first light I crawled outside. The boat was untouched, and the two food bags, "hidden" under bushes fifty yards from the tent in opposite directions, also were unmolested. That was the good news. The bad news was that a short distance from the tent was an unmistakable example of what a bear does in the woods, a memento that wasn't there when I went to bed.

As we were preparing to leave, I gave my navigator's report. "This afternoon we should be near the Killik's mouth. That'll leave us only eighty more miles on the Colville with seven days to do it. Umiat's in the bag."

Judy, who does not believe in tempting fate, cringed in exasperation. "Did you have to say that? Now we're jinxed!"

Jinxed or not, we set the boat in the water, squirmed in among our dwindling supplies and pushed off for parts unknown. The Killik was a different river in these lower reaches. Although still swift, it lacked the big waves of previous days. Our main problem now was choosing the correct channel among many braids. Fortunately, the river level was much higher than normal, as evidenced by the flooded shoreside willows. As careful as we were, however, we ran into a couple of hidden gravel bars. It was during these hit-and-run collisions that the Klepper received the most abuse. Grinding to a jerky halt over the submerged rocks, we had to jump out, push the boat to deeper water, then hop back in before the water went over our boot-tops. An inspection of the boat later on revealed that despite the crunching, the only significant damage was a broken wooden rib, easily splinted with a willow branch and tape.

Maybe it was because we were preoccupied, but we saw only a few animals along the way, mostly birds that drifted in the water ahead of us. Canada geese, black and gray and white with flotillas of downy goslings, gabbled at our approach. Many of the adults were flightless with the late-summer molt. The geese were joined by a scattering of tundra swans, loons, gulls and ducks, familiar species we'd already seen. We kept searching the banks for grizzlies and wolf, caribou and moose, but all we saw were empty willow thickets up close and empty tundra far off.

Stormy weather raked our camp. We were holed up within sight of the Colville, Alaska's largest river north of the arctic divide. With no tarp and no cover, we dined in the rain. For entertainment there was a wet and bedraggled marsh hawk coursing the sodden tundra, its owlish gray head pointed downward to detect a lemming or vole, and a pair of snowy owls, their creamy-white bodies in sharp contrast to the pale green and russet land.

We turned in at 10 p.m., damp and chilled. As soon as I was settled, I flipped to page one of *Gipsy Moth Circles the World*, an account of Sir Frances Chichester's 226-day solo circumnavigation of the world, completed in 1967 when Chichester was a spry sixty-five years old. Chichester served as an inspiration for me, a forceful reminder that age was no barrier when it came to taking risks, to a long life of challenge and adventure. His *Gipsy Moth* voyage established several sailing firsts, including the fastest voyage round the world by any small vessel and the longest passage that had been made by a sailing vessel without a port of call (15,500 miles). The plopping of raindrops on our snug little shelter, enhanced by the wind moaning about the tent flaps, was the perfect accompaniment to a superb seafaring story.

Morning ushered in more wet and wind. "Let's sit it out," I offered. "We've got plenty of time and some good books. No sense paddling in stuff like this."

Judy wasn't eager to venture forth either. Using her pile jacket as a pillow, she contentedly opened a James Herriot book about the peculiar and hilarious life of a country veterinarian in prewar England. Comfortably ensconced myself, I, too, was actually glad to be tentbound.

But only up to a point. Later in the day, feeling guilty because of our inactivity, we put down our books and crawled outside. The rain had let up and we munched on some leftover gorp while walking down to the river to stretch our legs. At the stream's edge, I tossed a stick into the current and watched it float downstream. The cove where we had beached the boat the previous day, formerly a dry sandbar, was now inundated with six inches of water.

I was on my way back to the tent when I heard Judy yell. I spun around, expecting to see a grizzly bear; instead, I saw her pointing upstream. "Kayakers! Across the river."

With binoculars I could make out three blue single-seat Kleppers, unmistakable even in the fading light. The tiny flotilla was shooting down a braided channel along the Killik's opposite shore.

"It's awfully late to be out paddling," I remarked, running back to the bank. "But they don't seem to be in any trouble."

The kayakers saw us and we waved. Three flashing paddles acknowledged our greeting. Then they were gone, swept around the bend and onto the Colville. Their abrupt appearance and departure left us wondering about them: where did they come from, how long had they been out, what wildlife had they seen, where were they going? Excluding Tom, these were the first human beings we had seen in two weeks.

Our questions were answered the next day as we pulled ashore on the Colville for a noontime snack. While we were slicing up our last chunk of cheese, the flotilla bobbed up, paddled by two men and a woman. I invited them to share a bite of food with us. "Thanks," the man closest to the bank replied, "but we had a late breakfast and still have a long way to go today." They remained in their kayaks, sprayskirts sealed, as we exchanged information about what we had seen and where we had been.

A month into their five-week trip, they had been dropped off by floatplane near the Arrigetch Peaks. For ten days they backpacked over the Brooks Range divide, following the Alatna River. Their kayaks had been cached at Easter Creek by the pilot. They were planning to float the Colville all the way to the Arctic Ocean.

"How'd you like Sunday Rapids?" one guy asked. "We had a pretty hairy ride in these singles; your double must have been even worse." When I told him we didn't experience anything overly threatening, he was impressed. Having never paddled a single Klepper, I was interested in his opinion that the smaller boats are considerably more maneuverable, hence better, for river running.

"There's another reason I prefer the singles," he continued. "She (he nodded toward the woman) and I used to paddle a Klepper double, but we always ended up quarrelling. When she wanted to go right, I wanted to go left. Our marriage was saved when we got these solo boats."

"He's right," the woman added, laughing. "Now we're separate but equal."

"Separate but equal, I like that," Judy said, giving me a wry smile.

We were getting cold just sitting there in the wind. With the weather turning more blustery by the minute, we agreed that this open gravel bar was no place to linger. After wishing each other well, they peeled into the current and spun downstream, following the Colville to the ocean.

During our brief conversation, we had all expressed an appreciation of the Colville as a paddling stream. Formed by Thunder and Storm creeks in the De Long Mountains far to the west, the Colville etches an irregular east-northeast course for 350 miles to Harrison Bay on the Beaufort Sea. For three-quarters of its length the river flows through the treeless Arctic Foothills, a rolling, desolate terrain of bluffs, ridges and rock strata folds. Most of this upper stretch offers an easy float with no major hazards. Beyond Umiat, however, where our fellow travelers were going, the Colville meanders through the flat Arctic Coastal Plain, a windy, wet, often fog-bound region.

There were many facets of this big river that I liked: the prairie-like immensity of the valley, an open sky without walls; the subtle colors on the hillsides, blushing or fading in the slanting sunlight of the far north; the storm clouds we could see so far away; and the river itself, appreciably wider than the Killik, with longer, deeper pools between riffles, but still providing a steady five or six mile per hour flow.

Others have undoubtedly been affected similarly by the river. The Colville was named in 1837 to honor Andrew Colville, an officer of the Hudson's Bay Company; however, native Alaskans, residents of the region prior to the arrival of the European travelers, had other names for this arctic river. To them, the upper sections were *Kang'-e-a-nok*, the Eskimo name meaning "headwaters" and *Nig'-a-lek Kok* or "Goose River." The name *Kupik*, "Big River," was used to describe the Colville's broad lower stretches. As we followed the forking river east, my only regret was the many miles of wild river we were missing upstream.

Although we were within a bureaucratic no-man's-land, squeezed between native holdings on the south and the enormous Naval Petroleum Reserve on the north, Umiat, with a population of five, was the only development. Consequently, wildlife populations have been relatively unaffected by man. An abundance of small lakes, ponds, marshes and lagoons adjacent to the river provides splendid habitat for a variety of birds. The highlight of our birding came when, in a single morning, we sighted all four species of loons that inhabit North America, three species of falcons riding the thermals, and a squadron of bugling sandhill cranes.

Our last morning in the backcountry was still and cold, threatening rain, or maybe snow. During our final days on the river, the temperature had plummeted into the thirty- to forty-degree range, with frequent squally storms and nightly frosts. If those chirping songbirds had any sense they would be hurrying south. Winter was on the way.

We were in somewhat of a hurry ourselves. We couldn't risk arriving late at Umiat. Tom was scheduled to meet us at a specific date and time and we were timing our arrival for the night before. Any delay could be not only inconvenient for us and Tom, but awfully expensive.

The temperature dipped below freezing while we headed north, the sun merely a diffused, uniform gray lighting overhead. We balled our hands inside wet-suit mitts in an effort to keep them warm. I steered the kayak with the foot-controlled rudder as the current pushed us along.

We glided past a dozen caribou loafing on a gravel bar. A fleeting image passed through my mind, an image anchored in the mists of time. I imagined I was a Nunamiut, an inland Eskimo hunter, armed with a bone-tipped spear. Every muscle of my body was poised to fling the deadly projectile into the caribou's chest. It seemed easy to kill one of these magnificent bulls, with their thick white neck ruffs and sweeping upthrust antlers. I looked deeply into the animal's eyes. They revealed nothing, no fear. I put away the imaginary spear.

Slushy snow blanketed the ground when we pulled up to a rocky shore. By following the river's loops and bends on the map, I knew we were close to Umiat. We were unable to see any development because of the lay of the land, but above the wind we heard the hum of electric generators and the sound of a truck.

We found a better place to unload the boat—on a gravel bar marked with knobby tire tracks and strewn with the usual assortment of river landing litter. I was emotionally torn by this sudden intrusion into the wilderness. I was glad to be here, glad that our journey had gone so well. Still, I found it upsetting that this pocket of civilization existed at all. Judy climbed the bank and reported that the buildings were a half-mile away. "Let's leave everything here," I suggested. "Maybe we can talk someone with a truck into carting our stuff to the airstrip." Might as well take advantage of the development. . . .

Walking into Umiat after having been in the bush for three weeks was the next closest thing to entering the Twilight Zone. The base resembled an installation from a science fiction film: modular-style trailers, graveyards of otherworldly machines, gravel roads going nowhere, oil drums and pumps. And in the background was that steady mechanical drone, an alien, preternatural presence.

"This place gives me the creeps," Judy said in a hushed voice. "Where is everyone?"

I, too, felt as if something sinister were watching us. I felt better when I saw a fellow human being walking up ahead. "C'mon, let's catch up to that guy. Maybe he knows where we can find a truck."

The worker, a cheerless, middle-aged man dressed in oily coveralls and grease-stained pac-boots, was not surprised to see two people appear out of nowhere, and he was uninterested in our request. Motioning us over to a white trailer, his only utterance was a cryptic message: "Talk to O.J."

Other human beings were nowhere in sight as we hiked down the heavily rutted and pot-holed gravel lane. At the front of the white trailer, nailed above the door, was a crudely painted wooden sign, "Umiat Hilton." We laughed at the irony, knocked the mud off our boots and stepped inside.

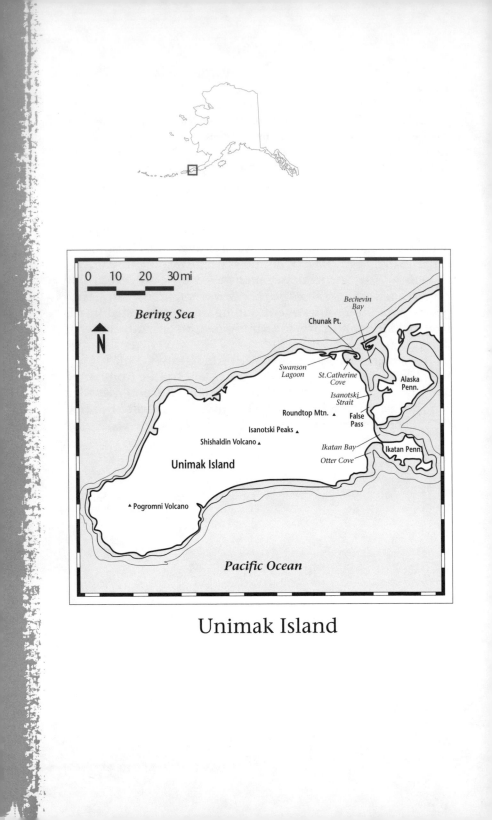

Unimak Island

Unimak Island: The First Aleutian

"CAN YOU GUYS BE READY IN five minutes?" the pilot asked, startling us out of our lethargy in the airport waiting room. "The clouds have lifted enough for a minimum clearance take-off."

Judy and I had been stranded at the tip of the Alaska Peninsula for half the day, waiting to leave Cold Bay for a backpacking trip on the Aleutian Island of Unimak. With the squally Bering Sea a few miles to the north and the less-than-peaceful Pacific Ocean just to the south, Cold Bay's weather is suitable more for ducks than for humans. Approximately 300 people reside here, employed mostly in commercial operations that support various airlines en route to the Aleutian Islands and Asia. Accessible only by air and water, the town is literally at the end of the line on the Alaska mainland, 650 air miles southwest of Anchorage.

We were ready. We put on our parkas and laced up our rubber boots. As I grabbed my gear, I looked out the window again. Nothing had changed: still plenty of low gray clouds and spitting rain. At that moment, even this drab, drafty Quonset hut terminal was hard to leave.

Within minutes we were squeezed in alongside our bulging

backpacks in the cockpit of the single-engine Piper Cherokee. The pilot fiddled with the controls, received clearance from the tower, then slowly powered the aircraft down the rain-slickened runway. Pointing the plane into the stiff wind, he gunned the motor and we rose into the air. The land soon gave way to the whitecaps of Izembek Lagoon, then the heaving rollers of the Bering Sea. I looked behind me. Cold Bay, with its cluster of houses, was swallowed in the mist.

Thirty minutes later our destination came into view. Unimak Island looked dark and forbidding. Swirling fog covered the island's steep slopes almost to the water's edge, masking the lofty volcanic peaks that I knew were here.

The plane banked sharply and hugged the beach of black, glistening rocks. A few frightened gulls flapped madly out of our way; otherwise, the irregular shoreline was lifeless and bleak. Judy and I studied the coast for possible hiking routes along the maze of small boulders lining the beach. It was disconcerting to note that the high tide had submerged some sections we planned to traverse.

"False Pass ahead," announced the pilot over the engine's drone. Through the streaked windscreen I saw a tiny village nestled at the edge of a dark green channel of the sea. "The weather's getting worse, so get ready to unload in a hurry."

After touchdown, we taxied over to a cluster of clapboard buildings at the far end of the gravel strip. As we unloaded our packs, two Aleut women and a small child took our places on the plane. "See you in three weeks!" the pilot yelled to us and was off again.

We picked up our gear and hiked to the village's small general store. Bill Bright, the superintendent of the False Pass Salmon Cannery, welcomed us inside. Over a cup of hot coffee, he explained that the cannery owns most of the buildings in False Pass, but the cannery complex had burned to the ground the year before our visit and only he and a few assistants remained as caretakers. The bunkhouses, mess hall, store, office and fuel supply weren't damaged in the blaze. "Our only business now," he said wistfully, "comes from the sixty or so Aleut natives who reside in False Pass and passing commercial fishermen in need of foodstuffs, dry goods and other supplies."

False Pass is the only village site on the sixty-seven-by-twenty-two-mile-wide island. The town owns 61,000 acres adjacent to the Isanotski Strait on the island's east side. The rest of the million-acre island is owned and managed by the U.S. Fish and Wildlife Service as part of the Alaska Maritime National Wildlife Refuge. We were told that initially there was some resentment about "locking up" the land by classifying nearly all of Unimak as a federal wilderness area. Now, however, some have come to realize that having a protected wilderness area in their backyard can be a good thing.

We asked Bright if we would be likely to see anyone else in the backcountry during our visit. "I doubt it," he answered. "The people here are fishermen. They don't have much use for hiking into the mountains. I've been working here for a long time. As far as I know you two will be the first backpackers to this place."

Judy and I already knew, however, of someone who had preceded us into Unimak's interior. In the early 1930s, Father Bernard Rosecrans Hubbard, nicknamed the Glacier Priest, led two expeditions to the island. He said his purpose was exploration and photography, much as it had been when he documented Katmai's volcanic explosion for *National Geographic* a few years earlier. But his main objective on Unimak was to climb Shishaldin Volcano, the highest peak in the Aleutians. Very little was known about it because it is almost continually obscured by clouds. Thwarted on his first attempt by terrific winds, rain and snow, Hubbard pressed on and eventually led the first ascent of "the sentinel of the North Pacific."

We had no desire to imitate the Glacier Priest's mountain-climbing route; we had our own plans. We decided to spend the first twelve days exploring the Bering Sea side of the island to the north, and the last seven days on the Pacific Ocean side to the south. The superintendent let us leave a cache of food and fuel for the second part of our outing in his store. Even so we still had trouble fitting everything inside our packs.

Before we left, a new acquaintance in town advised us to look for a cabin near a creek in the area we intended to hike. It was built during the old fox trapping days in the 1920s. Although we figured the cabin would be a mess, we appreciated the information. If the weather continued to be blustery, the use of a cabin, messy or not, would be pretty good for a few days. We hoisted our packs and headed northward along the shingle beach, glad to finally get started and a little nervous about the uncertainties that lay ahead.

Because we started so late, we only covered about two miles before setting up camp for the night. We pitched the tent on a dry tundra bench overlooking the narrow end of the funnel-shaped Bechevin Bay. Directly across from us, no more than a couple of miles away, were the mountains of the Alaska Peninsula, giving us the sensation that we were actually on the mainland rather than an

Aleutian island. And in essence we were. As the largest and eastern-most island of the Aleutian Chain, Unimak is an ecological extension of the Alaska Peninsula. Separated from the mainland by the half-mile wide Isanotski Strait, Unimak is the only island in the 1,100-mile archipelago with mammals similar to those found on the peninsula. Brown bear, wolf, wolverine, river otter, ground squirrel and natural populations of caribou are well represented on Unimak, but are totally absent on the remainder of the 279 or so maritime islands to the west.

The next morning the weather was cloudy, but there was no wind or rain. After breakfast we were ready to start following the narrow shoreline along Bechevin Bay. The shingle beach, which we had thought excellent for hiking, soon turned into a rough obstacle course. Slippery algae- and barnacle-encrusted rocks the size of pumpkins and larger forced us to hop from stone to stone, a less-than-graceful technique when lugging a heavy frame pack. We were never sure which rocks would roll underfoot. More than once our ski poles saved us from a misplaced step that easily could have resulted in a tumble or a sprained ankle. At other times we had to go up and down the steep clay bank to avoid boulder piles that blocked our path. Hiking over the tundra for these short spells, I wasn't sure which terrain was worse: the shoreline or the upland tussocks. Either way we were faced with a long, slow haul to the north side of the island.

In the afternoon we caught our first glimpse of Unimak's abundant wildlife. I hadn't seen a sea otter since wandering the northern California coast some ten years before. About a dozen of the sleek, dark weasels floated on their backs in the swells, drifting, resting, feeding on urchins. A few of the females had half-grown pups nursing on their bellies or riding clasped to their chests. Occasionally one of the mothers rolled over and corkscrewed smoothly beneath the waves, leaving her pup floating on the surface for a minute while she foraged for food on the bottom of the sea. Through binoculars we could identify the whitish-silvery heads of some of the older otters. Their heads and prominent white whiskers have earned them the nickname "Old Man of the Sea."

Further on we saw a sea otter on the beach, which surprised me since I thought these marine mammals rarely came ashore. Unlike its cousin the river otter (*Lutra canadensis*), the considerably larger sea otter (*Enhydra lutris*) is awkward out of the water and avoids long travels afoot. Their hind feet, huge and webbed—almost flippers— are quite useless on land. Carrying only my camera, I crept to within a few feet of the snoozing animal. I easily could have caught it if I wanted, and I wondered if it was sick, injured or even dead. I threw a pebble near its nose. The otter's black, moist eyes snapped open. Its broad head turned and we stared at each other, but only for a second. Traveling no faster than I could walk, the startled animal slithered into the surf, where it rolled on its back and looked us over. Then with a graceful kick and backflip, the otter rippled out to deeper water to join its fellows bobbing in the kelp.

Sea otters became a routine sight. Whenever we stopped for a break, we could usually spot a group of them between the breaking waves, enjoying the wind and the leaping water. Other marine mammals were far less common. We knew the channel between Unimak Island and the mainland is used by sea lions, walrus, orcas and giant whales, but whenever we heard a "whoosh" it was always the same story: another harbor seal had surfaced to breathe. The only time we saw the animals on shore was at low tide, lounging on flat offshore rocks.

The further we got from False Pass, the more frequent became the animal signs. At intervals among the boulder beaches were narrow strips of sand or fine gravel washed down by creeks. Generally at each one of these fan-shaped deltas we saw the tracks of wolf, caribou, otter and, more often than not, bear.

At Rocky Point, a headland jutting into Bechevin Bay, we left the shore for tundra meadows, a treeless landscape of emerald-green grass, sedges and forbs. Looking back south, toward the center of the island, the knee-high vegetation eventually faded into bands of alders on the foothills and ground-hugging mats on the alpine ridges. Then came Unimak's spectacular range of volcanoes—Shishaldin Volcano (9,372 feet), Isanotski Peaks (8,025 feet); and Roundtop Mountain (6,140 feet)—rising abruptly toward the sky. All but their lower slopes had been obscured by clouds since we arrived. The profusion of beauty at our feet, however, more than made up for the shrouded distant vistas. In early August, wildflowers were at their peak. White bog orchids, lupine, yellow monkey flower, wild geranium, iris, monkshood, cow parsnip and Indian paintbrush were just a few of the species we were able to identify.

Since there were no windbreaks, we hoped for a calm night and staked our dome-shaped tent tightly to the ground. Around midnight I bolted upright, wide awake. A violent, rain-laden wind was blowing across the unobstructed heath. The tent snapped one way then another like the mainsail of a boat caught in a squall. We quickly dressed in our foul-weather clothes and organized our gear.

Judy Bradford examining large grizzly/brown bear tracks on the beach; wolf tracks are nearby.

"This is how it was before Charlie and I had our tent flip in Denali!" I shouted over the howl. The geodesic dome shelter is designed to handle an enormous amount of punishment, but in fifty- to sixty-knot winds on the open tundra, there's always the possibility that something will give.

The tent shuddered and strained. The nylon side panels ballooned in and out, bending the lightweight aluminum poles until it seemed they would break. The sand did not hold the tent pegs well, and I began to fear that if one peg pulled out the whole tent might go. We sat with our backs against the walls to give them extra support, and spread our gear bags out to help hold down the floor. I considered collapsing the tent and huddling inside, but Judy wanted to stick it out.

Together we remained with our backs to the tent walls, staring at the darkness and waiting for dawn. We were irked with ourselves for being a little lazy about picking a campsite and for underrating typical Aleutian weather. We would be more careful from now on.

The gale finally passed. The awful racket of the flailing tent subsided about 9 a.m. We were exhausted, but anxious to break camp, unwilling to spend another night in this exposed location. Besides, the weather was fairly good considering where we were: broken overcast skies, a temperature in the mid-fifties and a slight breeze. Suddenly the island's north shore, still six miles away, didn't seem so far.

Our newfound enthusiasm faded as the morning advanced. We tried staying on top of the bank to avoid the treacherous shoreline, but because of the numerous deep, alder-choked ravines running perpendicular to our route, we always ended up back down at the beach. It was tough going, more so for Judy because I was able to doff my pack and rest while she caught up. "How you doing?" I asked her repeatedly when she arrived alongside. Each time her answer was the same: "Fine, don't ask me again!"

Not everything was bad while we were hiking the shoreline. We couldn't look up often when hop-scotching over the slimy boulders, but when we did there were always new and interesting seabirds to observe. The bird life here was different from that of other Alaska peninsula wildlife refuges I had visited. The biggest difference was the lack of geese. We hadn't spotted one so far, despite the fact that nearly the entire North American population of black brant and emperor geese would be congregating in nearby Izembek Refuge in a couple of weeks. I noted that Isanotski Strait and Bechevin Bay were well-used corridors for many species that weren't common in Izembek. A continuous stream of oceanic birds—pelagic and red-faced cormorants, black-legged kittiwakes, Aleutian terns, horned and tufted puffins, common and thick-billed murres, pigeon guillemots and tiny murrelets and auklets—skimmed over the waves, winging back and forth from feeding grounds in the Pacific Ocean and the Bering Sea.

At midday we reached a small rise and saw a hook-shaped cove directly ahead. Unlike the tumultuous and expansive Bering Sea across its northern neck, St. Catherine Cove's waters were sheltered and relatively tranquil. I could see why the Russian ship *St. Catherine* chose to winter here in 1768.

The cabin we had been told about was somewhere in this area. Since only one stream entered the cove and the cabin would have been built near drinking water, we figured it would be easy to find. An hour later we saw the cabin, perched on a knoll overlooking a small salmon stream. "Doesn't look too bad," I said, studying the simple hut through binoculars. "The windows are broken and there's the usual junk outside, but the roof and walls seem okay."

To reach the cabin we had to wade across the stream. We took off our pants and boots and gingerly stepped into the thigh-deep channel. The water was ice-cold and clear and swarming with sea-run salmon. Silvery schools of fish surged out of our way as we crossed. Some headed back toward the cove, others continued upstream to ancestral spawning grounds miles from the sea. A few of the hook-mouthed males—I think they were chum salmon—were far too busy to notice us. Locked in combat with their sharp-toothed jaws clamped tightly over each other's faces, the fish were physically spent and would have made easy pickings for a hungry bear or a human with a club or spear.

On the other side of the stream we sat in some flattened rye grass to dry our feet. I should have realized immediately that the flattened grass was a danger sign. With my boots back on I began to look around. A few yards down the bank, on a soft stretch of mud, were long-clawed tracks, half-eaten fish and cow-sized droppings.

As we approached the weathered wooden shack, I recalled tales of people entering a wilderness shelter only to find a grizzly rummaging inside. To our relief, when we peered through a window all we saw was a long-tailed weasel scurrying over the floorboards. Surprised to see us, the small cream-colored animal, long and slender with a white belly and black-tipped tail, disappeared under a loose plank. The weasel reappeared a second later, leaving its hideout suddenly and bouncing from one side of the cabin to the other. Finally the weasel stood up on its hind legs with its tiny feet dangling in the air, then vanished through a mouse-sized hole in the wall.

It was our turn to appropriate the cabin. The door was already open so we walked right in. Up close, the cabin was in better shape than I had originally thought. The interior was slightly messy—discarded old clothes, newspapers, a Collier's magazine dating from 1948, scraps of wood, dirty dishes and mouse droppings littered the floor. But at least the structure appeared to be weather-tight and there were two plywood bunks for our sleeping bags. With a little creative rearranging, the cabin might even be relatively secure from bears. Grabbing a broom and shovel that some previous occupant had left behind, we set our packs in the corner and went to work cleaning up the place.

By the time we were ready for dinner, the cabin was more than livable, it was downright homey. I felt a bit decadent having so much room to move around in and a metal roof over our heads. But as I listened to the wind rustle outside and rain drops tap on the ceiling, I found myself quickly adjusting to this new style of camping. This sure beat having to worry about our tent getting flattened or having to bolt down dinner in a brewing storm.

I went for a walk by myself that evening. A light rain was falling, the sky was dark and menacing. In the distance to the west and south were the broad green bases of Unimak's volcanoes. Their snow-cone peaks, as usual, were lost in a varying layer of low-hanging clouds that never looked the same twice.

I spotted a lone bull caribou about a half-mile away, or more accurately, it spotted me. Reacting in typical caribou fashion, this one was immensely curious. It moved closer and closer in quick jerky gallops until it was a mere 100 feet from me. The animal studied me for a few moments, snorted, then ran off. A minute later it was back for another look. This odd behavior was repeated several more times. Finally the caribou wheeled about and trotted away. Soon all I could see was its long legs flying over the soft tundra and its white stubby tail sticking up defiantly.

Fortunately for me, the husky brown bear I spotted on the way back didn't have the same fascination for human beings that the caribou had. We saw each other at precisely the same time: the bear was down at the stream with a chum salmon flopping in its great predacious jaws. I was across the stream, not sure if I should stand my ground or flee. The grizzly growled and swayed with slow, deliberate movements like those of a Chinese boxer, its heavy fur jiggling and its rump twitching. Carrying the salmon, the bear scrambled up the bank and bounded away with an agility and grace that belied its mammoth size.

"How was your walk?" Judy asked upon my return. She was lying on top of her sleeping bag with her headlight on, reading the paperback *Glacier Pilot: The Story of Bob Reeve and the Flyers Who Pioneered Alaska's Skies in Single-Engine Planes.* Our food bags were hanging from a rafter above her head.

"I'll tell you all about it," I said brusquely, "right after I barricade the windows and doorway." I dragged some odd pieces of corrugated metal roofing material in front of the two windows, and made sure the vestibule door was securely jammed and roped in place. "There. Not exactly bear-proof but better than it was before."

"Sightings close by?" Judy asked.

"Yeah. I almost bumped into a grizzly at the stream. It ran off, but I'm sure there are others. . . ."

As it turned out, we were too tired and the cabin was too comfortable for us to worry about marauding bears. We slept from ten that night until nine in the morning. Strong winds careened over the tundra during the night, but inside the one-room hut we were cozy. While eating breakfast, listening to the cold breeze whistle harmlessly outside, we talked about how nice it would be to spend a summer in this cabin: no tent to pitch and pack soaking wet, no winds to blow out the stove, no having to crawl over each other to go out at night.

Well, we didn't have the whole summer, but we had a few days. After studying the map we decided that the area afforded plenty of interesting day hikes using the cabin as a base. Such luxury was new in our wilderness travels.

Judy feigned disappointment at not having to carry her sixty-pound pack again. It might be true that I have a masochistic streak, because I really did feel a tinge of guilt about opting for ease.

We stuffed lunches and a few essentials into daypacks, barred the door behind us, and randomly picked our first destination for a day hike: the foothills beneath Roundtop Mountain and Isanotski Peaks about five miles away. Persistent low clouds still obscured the bulk of the mighty mountains, but at least a portion of their slopes was visible. Above the vegetation line was a wasteland of jet-black cinder and lava flows. Higher yet were white crevassed glaciers that trundled downward until finally reaching their melting point at about the 2,000-foot contour.

Gazing toward the mountains, I thought about what a remarkable man Father Hubbard was. What could be stranger than a chubby, forty-two-year-old Jesuit priest/geologist/educator/author/explorer leading a handful of brawny Santa Clara University football players and a native Aleut on expeditions to climb the highest peak in the Aleutians—nearly a two-mile ascent—using dog-teams to pull heavily laden sleds equipped with bicycle tires for passage over the summer tundra? Hubbard's stamina, both physical and mental, was legendary. He commonly carried eighty- or ninety-pound packs. He didn't mind pushing himself and his companions to the limit across vast distances and over unspeakable terrain. He regularly held mass out on the open tundra (the mass kit alone weighed nearly 100 pounds); compiled motion pictures and photographs of all his expeditions, which later were shown on a hectic lecture circuit from Washington, D.C., to California; and wrote numerous internationally published articles and books. Two of his more popular titles, *Mush, You Malemutes* (1932) and *Cradle of the Storms* (1935), describe his far-flung adventures to Unimak Island, Aniakchak Caldera, Katmai, Kodiak Island and other remote locations in the Aleutians and the Alaska Peninsula. Hubbard's enthusiasm for the region, perhaps more than anything else, sparked my interest in seeing this part of Alaska for myself. I wish I had had a chance to meet the man, but he died in 1962 at the age of seventy-three. At the time he was in the process of cataloging his huge film collection, said to be the largest film library on Alaska in the world.

Judy was skeptical. "Dog sleds on the tundra? Twenty-five mile foot marches with heavy packs over stuff like this? Get real! Either Hubbard must have been divinely inspired or we don't have the Right Stuff, or . . . someone's not telling the truth."

Her opinions, at least about us, were reinforced after we had hiked only a few miles. Backpacking long distances over Unimak's spongy tundra, as we had originally planned, required more effort than we were willing to put out. More and more I liked our idea of making lightly loaded day-hikes on this section of the trip. There was no point in moving camp every day to trudge off somewhere that wasn't necessarily any better than our cabin location.

For wilderness lovers and wildlife watchers, it is virtually impossible to have a dull moment while hiking Unimak's grasslands. Several bands of caribou grazed over the tundra on ridges and meadows to our right. They were part of the large Alaska Peninsula herd, though only about 2,500 caribou reside on Unimak Island. To our left a red fox kept pace with us for a few hundred yards before veering off to meet its mate on the brow of a hill. I got out my camera, took a few steps closer to the duo, and was immediately confronted by an angry willow ptarmigan. In a bold attempt to protect her half-grown fuzzball chicks, the mother grouse charged me, screeching to a halt a step away. She didn't care how big I was. With a defiant stare, she spread her wings wide to make herself appear larger than life, and pranced back and forth to give her youngsters time to escape. Judy and I retreated. Only then did the ptarmigan leave her post. Hugging the ground, she crawled over the tundra in the opposite direction from her chicks until she disappeared from sight.

The mother grouse's hysterics were understandable. A lot of animals out here, including opportunistic bears, would enjoy snacking on a plump young ptarmigan. Figuring we'd detour up a small rise, we hadn't gone more than a hundred yards before we spotted a huge brown bear—the Lord of the Valley—watching us from on top of a big sloping rock. We waited, not daring to move, for what seemed a very long time. Finally the bear strolled off. Not sure of his direction, we decided to backtrack. We had come only four miles, but it was already getting late. Besides, the weather was changing again. Only the bottoms of the mountains were now showing, and it looked like rain.

The cabin was exactly as we had left it. We had taken care to close and wire up the door so that we would know instantly if anyone had entered. We weren't expecting an intruder—so far we hadn't seen any other people or boats or airplanes—but we hadn't forgotten what happened when we last stored supplies in a remote Alaska hut.

It was my turn to get drinking water. I grabbed the two-gallon water bag and walked down to the stream. Noisy, flitting gulls were already there, attracted by a few spent salmon on shore. I found a clear-flowing riffle and dunked the bag, wondering if the water was as pure as it looked. On all my Alaskan trips I have never treated the water in any way—no filtration, iodine or precautionary boiling. I knew that I had been fortunate not to have been stricken with intestinal ailments, as even in Alaska's wilds the frequency of giardia disorders from contaminated water is on the rise. I studied the clear liquid again, thinking of all the wildlife that was using this stream—from defecating brown bears to fungus-ridden salmon floating belly-up. I filled a metal cup and took a long, deep, unfiltered swig. The stream water was sweet and cold; it sure tasted good.

I snapped the rubber cap on the water bag and stood up. A female mallard who had been hiding in the tall grass suddenly paddled out to mid-channel. Her cluck brought out five downy ducklings who followed her downstream. The mallard hen had reason to be concerned, and not just because of me. Upstream, a river otter ran humpbacked through the grass and slid down the bank into the water. Although otters can and do kill birds and small mammals at times, their principal diet consists of fish, which was what this individual was interested in. With a loud splash followed by a struggle, the otter dragged a foot-long, lean and racy silver salmon up the bank and into the vegetation. Only then did I realize that the animal had young of her own. A pair of otters half her size scrambled out of the grass and nudged against her. Their chirruping chatter and antics were amusing and I stayed to watch them until they moved out of sight.

In the morning I peered outside the vestibule doorway and was greeted by rain and a chilling wind that made the cold more acute. Pretending to be a gentleman, I served Judy hot tea and granola bars in bed. Then fixing myself a drink, I crawled back into my own warm sleeping bag. The inside of the cabin was only a few degrees warmer than the temperature outside, but we couldn't have been more at ease. All our gear was dry, we were out of the wind, and we had plenty of good reading material.

Some time later we stirred out of bed and went for a short hike along the beach to the north. The wind and rain still beat across the tundra, making for a wild and invigorating day. We relished this type of weather. It was the humid ninety-plus degree heat wave that was scorching the Midwest when we left for Alaska that we abhorred. The ground was dry and dusty in Illinois, the air sticky to the touch. Sweat beaded on my forehead at work even while taking it easy in the shade. Judy and I appreciated escaping to the far north for the summer as much as snowbirds did migrating to Florida or Arizona for the winter. A little sun would be appreciated now and then during our Unimak trek, but as long as we stayed clear of knock-down williwaws the Aleutian weather suited us fine.

There was no leisurely breakfast in bed the following morning. When I peeked outside at 5:30 and found patches of blue and no breeze, I prodded Judy awake and fired up the stove for a quick hot drink.

"Let's get going! Move it, move it!" I bellowed, trying to sound like a Marine drill sergeant. "We're getting soft sitting around the cabin, too soft. It's time for some serious hiking."

Judy rolled over to face the wall. "Why don't you go see if there are any bears down near the stream?" she beseeched from under the cover of her sleeping bag. "If you don't come back in a half-hour, I promise I'll get out of bed and go looking for you."

Rather than go bear hunting, I sat down on my bunk with a mug of tea and studied the topographic map. The scale was one inch to four miles, not very detailed, but adequate for our purposes. The oblong-shaped island's most notable features were the blue-white concentric circles representing Shishaldin, Isanotski Peaks and Roundtop volcanoes. From east to west, the three volcanoes form a continuous barrier of ice- and snow-covered lava fields for upward of twenty miles. I could see why Shishaldin's white cone has long been a landmark for passing mariners on the days that it is visible. Isanotski Peaks and Roundtop Mountain lack the symmetry of their taller neighbor, but judging from the map, they seemed just as rugged and spectacular. On the far side of the island were more volcanoes, caldera lakes, tonguelike glaciers, mountain ranges, rivers, lagoons, ponds, tundra meadows and grasslands, enough wild country for countless expeditions.

Judy was finally out of bed; at least one of her legs was firmly planted on the floor. I quit dreaming of other places on the island and concentrated on where we could go today. Four miles to the northwest was Swanson Lagoon, a shallow inlet separated from the Bering Sea by a strip of low-lying dunes. I took a compass heading off the map in case we got fogged in, then cleared off the table. Judy had reminded me that this was a hot breakfast day—oatmeal and cocoa.

Soon after eating we were headed cross-country over the divide that separates St. Catherine Cove from Swanson Lagoon. We made good time over the usual assortment of wet mattressy meadows and drier undulating swells. By ten o'clock we were perched atop a little hill with the lagoon spread out before us. We flopped down to give our legs a rest.

During the break we watched caribou and birds. Paddling on the calm waters of the lagoon were several red-throated loons, tundra swans, gulls and some ducks—mallards, green-winged teal and harlequins. A bald eagle drifted slowly down to roost. And at the far side of the lagoon, stalking the sandbars on their long, skinny legs, were a dozen or so grayish-brown sandhill cranes. We could hear them bugling back and forth, a forlorn, haunting rattle that epitomizes all that is wild.

Hiking past the lagoon's muddy shore, we broke through a tangle of shrubs and climbed another low rise that commanded a view of the coastal plain. Down at the creek we saw two beefy grizzlies ambling along a tundra stream a quarter-mile from the lagoon. Another brownie was in the water up to its chest trying to snag salmon. After watching them for awhile, we slipped discreetly away and made a wide detour so we could continue to the west.

I felt I was in an episode of Marlin Perkin's *Wild Kingdom* television show. At the next knobby hill were more caribou, heads up and alert, gazing over the tundra in the direction of the seashore. They were visibly agitated, stomping their hooves and leaping in the air. Finally they had had enough. With great antlers and snowy white necks held high, the animals bolted and within seconds were galloping off at full speed over the brow of a hill. About five minutes later we discovered what had caused the caribou to flee: wolves! A pack of five materialized from a crease in the rolling moorlands. These were the first wolves Judy had ever seen, and they were only my second sighting.

We flattened ourselves on the tussock-grass and watched the wolves come closer. The animals moved effortlessly over the hummocks, ignoring the caribou and heading in our direction. We knew there had never been a documented case of a healthy wolf attacking a human. We felt only excitement, not fear, at this encounter.

The lead animal was nearly white, in stark contrast to the other members of the pack, who were varying shades of grey. It skirted the hillock we were on, eventually reaching the precise spot where we had been hiking. The leader stopped in mid-stride, one foot poised in the air; the rest of the pack bunched up at the rear. The white wolf sniffed the ground, following our scent back and forth along the trail. Suddenly pandemonium erupted. The wolf leaped in the air and spun around. When its feet hit the ground, it dashed toward the mountains. Equally startled, the others sprinted along behind.

Only when about a mile away did the wolves cease running. We could barely make out the sight of their regrouping as they greeted each other with wagging tails, face licks and an abundance of body contact. Then, with the white wolf again in the lead, the pack headed west in search of new country that didn't reek of human beings.

After the wolf incident we returned to our home on the tundra, for that was how we were beginning to feel about the cabin. It was all right with us that the cabin didn't have a stove; after all, there was no wood to burn. We didn't even mind the small rodents that scurried over the floor at night, since they would be food for the long-tailed weasel when we left. We did, however, gripe that evening about the open windows, which were covered partly with clear plastic visqueen. Mosquito netting would have been a nice addition. Up to now the weather had been sufficiently inclement to keep the bugs from swarming. During the night the temperature began to rise, ultimately reaching sixty-two degrees, the high for our trip. The heat wave brought forth tiny creatures thirsty for blood. Mosquitoes entered through cracks in the door and windows, alighting on my arms and buzzing around my head while I tried to sleep. Worse was some unknown pest that laid claim to my wrists. When I awoke early the next morning, both my hands were swollen and tender. There was no pain, only intense itching. A couple of matched pinpricks of blood marked where some small bug, probably a spider, had nailed me.

On the last day that we stayed at the cabin we hiked to Chunak Point, about five miles away, at the far eastern tip of St. Catherine Cove. We felt great joy in our isolation as we roamed the deserted wide and sandy beach facing the Bering Sea. A brisk wind blew onshore, bringing with it the pungent odor of saltspray and kelp. For two landlubbers from central Illinois, this was a novelty. Offshore a long string of sea otters rocked and rolled in the swells. Above the otters were thousands of seabirds, mostly puffins, flying west. The flocks were part of an incredible population of seabirds, numbering in the millions, that uses the isolated, rocky cliffs of the Aleutian Islands to nest.

The hook-shaped sandpit surrounding the cove receives the brunt of frequent Bering Sea storms. As a result, the peninsula offers superb beachcombing. We came across an exotic array of flotsam that had been washed far up the beach, even into the grass-covered dunes on higher ground. The most conspicuous finds were of Japanese origin. Japanese fishing fleets routinely haunt the Bering Sea and North Pacific, and like so many ships across the world, they use the ocean to dump their garbage in. Rubber sandals, fishing nets (deathtraps for sea birds and marine mammals), wooden crates, glass liquor bottles, plastic jugs and more provided interesting beachcombing, but we were perturbed that so much foreign trash was washing up on the island's shore. We took only one item as a souvenir: a frosted-green glass globe, about the size of a baseball, used by the Japanese as floats to hold up fishing nets.

We returned to the cabin in early evening, glad to get out of the wind. I was feeling good. The swelling on my wrists had gone down and mosquitoes were no longer a problem; the temperature had been dropping all day.

While fixing dinner, we fantasized again about spending the summer in the cabin and being part of the landscape as the season unfolds.

I said: "We could get dropped off by boat with three months' worth of food and fuel. Use the cabin as a base of operations, and take week-long backpacking trips from here. Maybe bring the Klepper for some kayak touring. And we could even try climbing Shishaldin Volcano."

"Always the planner," Judy joked. "Here I was thinking of a nice relaxing summer along the Bering Sea, and you go filling it up with all kinds of mini-expeditions."

After putting away another meal of doctored minute rice and freeze-dried peas, we sat around organizing things while there was still some natural light. We gradually realized that a sunbeam was coming through the window, spotlighting what had been a gloomy cabin wall, and we raced outside.

The tundra was awash with soft golden light. For one of the few times during our visit the sweeping clouds and the towering cumulus above parted, exposing a line of snowclad summits. First Roundtop, then Isanotski, and finally cone-shaped Shishaldin Volcano emerged out of the tattered, dark, charcoal-gray mass, giving a scale to the scenery that was absent before. Roundtop and Isanotski appeared higher because they were closer, but it was their distant neighbor that I focused my camera on. Shishaldin's ashy peak stood clear above the lowland tundra, soft feathers of bluish smoke curling out of its conical vent. Like many Aleutian volcanoes, Shishaldin's fires still rumble. Father Hubbard had written that the warmth and fumes exuding from Shishaldin's vent had almost overcome him and his companions. I hurried to a nearby rise, snapping pictures of the volcano as I went. The oblique light was reaching a zenith. Shishaldin turned from white to pale pink to roseate. Then, as if a switch had been flicked, the mountain was gone. Fast-moving clouds settled back down.

The next morning I awoke early, anxious to see if the sun's brief appearance foretold clearing weather. It was a glorious dawn, with Shishaldin rose-pink against a clear blue sky and hoarfrost sparkling on the grasses like blue gems. I shivered. It was cold out here. I tiptoed back to get properly dressed and grab my camera and binoculars.

"Where you going?" Judy's head appeared from under her sleeping bag.

"Sorry, I didn't mean to wake you." I leaned over and kissed her.

Judy Bradford looking back at Shishaldin Volcano, the highest peak in the Aleutian Islands.

"It's a beautiful morning. I'm going out for a short walk. I'll be back in a half-hour."

"Okay. What time is it, anyway?"

"Five o'clock."

"Oh, in that case, take an hour."

The sun felt good on my face. I checked the thermometer dangling from a nail on the outside cabin wall. In the shade it registered twenty-eight degrees Fahrenheit. I climbed the nearby rise to gain a better perspective of the surrounding country. "Amazing!" I said to myself out loud. The views were superb all around. Shishaldin and the rest of Unimak's peaks glowed from the rising sun. In the foreground, the undulating tundra grasslands and meadows were predominantly green, but splotches of russet and withered brown— the colors of fall—were starting to appear. Across Bechevin Bay, in Izembeck National Wildlife Refuge, Frosty Peak shimmered with a new dusting of snow. And further in the distance—I checked and rechecked the map, unable to believe they were fifty miles away!— rose the weird, needlelike Aghileen Pinnacles, mountainous landmarks that I knew well from my visit to Izembek the previous year.

When I returned to the cabin, Judy was already up and was hanging out our damp clothes and sleeping bags to dry. An hour later we were ready to go and had braced the creaky wooden door shut. A tinge of melancholy swept over me as we left the cabin and St. Catherine Cove behind. "Remember," I said, as we topped the rise and looked back at the tranquil scene, "if we ever get the whole summer off, we're coming back."

Following a looping tundra stream, we began our inland trek, headed for a long and narrow valley flanked by Roundtop Mountain and a high parallel ridge. We had food for six days, time enough for us to poke leisurely back to False Pass, making a few two-night camps along the way.

The knee-high grass was damp from past rains. The easiest hiking was along double-tracked bear trails, which cut a convenient swath through the vegetation. Despite generations of grizzlies walking the same paths, the ground concealed deep clefts and it was hard to tell what was firm and what was not. Our rubber boots often sank in the soft muck to above the ankle. After a couple of hundred yards I was clammy and hot from the condensation of sweat inside my rain parka and pants. I stopped and changed into quick-drying windgear over my polypropylene long underwear and felt better immediately.

After a few hours of hiking we had encountered several bears and were confronted with another bear-induced dilemma. According to the topographic map, the stream we were following meandered between sharp ridges for about seven more miles before reaching its source on the slopes of Roundtop Mountain. Our plan had been to hike this distance in two days, loiter near the volcano for a day or so, then trek on toward False Pass through a gap in the mountains. Wilderness itineraries, though, are always subject to change; when we saw a sow grizzly and two yearling cubs walking the creek directly in our proposed line of travel, we decided to change our plans. Because the valley was so narrow, there was little chance to detour safely around them, and with a veritable fish market at their feet, they seemed in no hurry to move.

We made a hasty decision to alter our route. The high country would be the best place to avoid bumping into bears as long as the salmon were running. "We could follow that ridge back part of the way to False Pass," I said, pointing to a steep grass- and brush-covered slope to the east, which according to the map was some 2,000 feet above the stream. "Then we'll cross over the divide and drop down to the coast. It should be pretty easy."

Judy looked at the bluff, then looked at me. "Pretty easy, huh? With those alders? I remember having this same conversation before."

The climb only took a few hours, but about half that time we spent tearing and clawing our way through tall grass and a thick belt of alders. In situations where barging into a bear is a distinct possibility, I usually adopt a fatalistic attitude to help me overcome my dread: what was going to happen would happen, and there was nothing I could do to change it. Still, the dry-mouthed fear persisted. I had come across several places where bears had recently bedded down among the alders, their fibrous droppings still loose and moist.

I had been plodding uphill, thinking Judy was behind me. But when I looked back she was nowhere in sight. A brief moment of panic ensued. I was ready to ditch my pack and start searching for my companion, when I saw a red wool hat about a hundred feet downhill and to my right. The hat was poised on top of a ski pole poking above a dark, jungly little draw. "What are you doing down there?" I laughed.

A disembodied voice replied. "I must have taken the wrong turn. Keep talking, I'll follow your voice out of this mess."

Finally we reached the ridge top. The alpine scenery made the ascent worthwhile. The windswept crest was rocky and open, covered with crusty lichens and velvety sphagnum moss. In sheltered swales and behind the protection of boulders grew blue and red and yellow wildflowers. We imitated the flowers by setting up a comfortable camp at the foot of a rock slide to avoid the heavy winds that gusted overhead. The ground was flat and dry, perfect for pitching and pegging out the tent. The only inconvenience at our new site was the lack of potable water nearby. While Judy organized our gear, I slipped and floundered back down into the alders, and found a pencil-thin trickle issuing out of a miniature sylvan glen. The air was quiet in the crevice. The only sound came from the steady drips of the clear, cold water falling on a moss and fern bed, and an errant mosquito, which I silenced with a swat of my hand.

It took a long time to fill the water bag and plastic bottles, but I didn't mind the wait. About 500 feet beneath me, pacing the edge of the stream, was another mama brown bear with two infant cubs. While the youngsters roughhoused on shore, their mother waded into the stream for a bedtime snack. The cubs followed after her, crossing and recrossing the stream, stopping to rest only when mom lay belly-down on the bank to eat.

Later that evening, after eating our own dinner in the shelter of the rock slide, we strolled to a sheer cliff face overlooking the shallow, grassy valley. The sun was setting over the Bering Sea, giving us time for a final lingering look at the wilderness sprawled out below. Judy and I watched the valley with binoculars. At first glance we saw nothing more interesting than a raven, but as we searched methodically up and down the stream, large brown shapes began to materialize. Closest to us were the grizzly sow and cubs I had seen earlier fishing and playing, then other grizzlies came into focus. Within a half-mile stretch we counted four more adult bears.

It was pleasant to sit half-hidden on the knoll with a commanding view of the whole valley, watching the bears, noticing how dusk changed the colors in the mountains and valley. "I'm really glad we decided to camp up here," I mused, as I locked on yet another grizzly lumbering into the picture from downstream. "I know," Judy uttered. "I'd be a nervous wreck by now if we were down there."

The fading light finally forced us to abandon our roost. I checked the time: ten o'clock, a late night for me. Judy and I didn't say much on the way back to the tent. For that matter, sleep didn't come easily because we were thinking about the bears.

The weather was also restless that night, taking a turn for the worse. The next day around noon the rain squalls ceased and the low streaky clouds blew north to the Bering Sea. The high peaks were concealed, but at least our ridge and the surrounding slopes were clear. I didn't need much convincing when Judy suggested we stay another night at this camp and spend the day hiking the uplands. Packing a trail lunch, rain gear, camera and binoculars, we traced the rock-strewn crest higher into the mountain realm.

The hiking was excellent over the matted tundra. The higher we climbed, though, the spottier the low-growing vegetation became. Eventually all that remained underfoot was mustard-colored gravel, stained from oxidation, black lava rock and a smattering of dirty snowfields left over from last winter. I was surprised that so many caribou trails ran through these high, narrow mountain ridges. But studying the map, it became apparent that if the caribou didn't cross to the other side of the island here, their next available path would be fifteen miles to the west on the far side of Shishaldin Volcano.

The sky became clearer the closer we got to it. A few random rays of sunlight poked through the clouds. Then the dusky scud moved from the island's peaks and we were left squinting into a dazzling sun. A curtain had been pulled back, revealing unknown marvels. We couldn't see Shishaldin Volcano from our position, but the close presence of Roundtop Mountain and its big neighbor, Isanotski Peaks, more than made up for it. A thin white cascade fell hundreds of feet from a deep notch cut in top of a cliff that faced us. Above it reared 4,000 feet of ice and rock, half-veiled in cloud. The two volcanoes are connected by a saddle of glaciers and permanent snowfields. I hadn't heard of anyone reaching the summit of either mountain, and in a selfish moment hoped that no one ever would. Let the mystery remain.

To the east, across Bechevin Bay, was Trader's Mountain, and nestled in its fold, Trader's Cove. According to our topographic map printed over thirty years ago, a small Aleut settlement (population seventeen) called *Morzhovoi*, meaning "walrus village" in Russian, lay on the south shore of the cove, but from our position we couldn't see the handful of cabins that the map indicated was there. Further south, beyond Isanotski Strait, was the green upthrust of the Ikatan Peninsula, a part of Unimak Island we planned to visit after resupplying at False Pass. All was blue-green as I looked at the north Pacific, one of the stormiest oceans on earth. I harbored a desire to circumnavigate Unimak Island by kayak some day, a trip I estimated might take as long as six weeks, allowing for frequent storms. Judy wasn't too intrigued by the idea, but that was all right. We already had our next two trips to Alaska planned.

A mile or so from camp we paused to look over the narrow valley that we had almost followed to False Pass. There were ten grizzlies in view at the same time—four alone and two sows with a pair of cubs apiece. Certainly a few more were out of sight in the brush. While the adults wandered back and forth along the stream, the cubs tussled near their mothers. Only once did we observe a potential conflict. A huge blond individual with dark brown legs ambled up to one of the sows. The sow watched the interloper closely, as adult boars commonly kill cubs when they have the opportunity or when the mother is not near. She let the boar approach to within thirty or forty yards before she gathered her cubs and took off running into the tundra.

Around 6 p.m., while returning to camp, we saw a dark, low-slung animal loping across the open ridge. I fixed it within the circle of my binoculars. A wolverine, headed our way! We crouched to conceal ourselves behind a modest pile of lichen-encrusted stones. While Judy kept an eye on the big weasel, I frantically rummaged through my daypack trying to dredge out a telephoto lens. "Hurry up, Lar! It's going to run right past us," she urged. Exasperated, I dumped the contents on the ground, found the lens case, and snapped on the telephoto. Too late. The wolverine was already fifty yards away, traveling faster than I thought possible for such a bow-legged animal. I snapped off a few pictures anyway.

As satisfying as our ridgetop camp was, the time came to leave. The following morning we were back on the move. By 2 p.m. we were at a new campsite on the side of a deep, treeless gully that led down to Isanotski Strait. At least we thought it led down to Isanotski Strait. We couldn't see more than a hundred feet ahead when a heavy fog rolled in from the north.

We hunkered next to the stove, sipping soup and munching on leftover nuts, raisins and M&Ms. There wasn't a breath of wind; the air was dead calm. My beard was soaking wet from the enveloping mist. Suddenly I snapped to attention.

"What's wrong?" Judy asked, her body rigid.

I put my finger to my lips. "Ssshhh . . . listen."

Dog-like yelps coming from the grey void startled us. They grew louder and closer, until out of the gauzy haze appeared the mysterious creature: a red fox. It sat at the edge of camp, watching us and barking repeatedly: one quick yip, a pause, then another yip. I had never heard a fox bark and was intrigued by its peculiar behavior. The fox yawned, scratched its ear with its hind leg and laid down. This unusually friendly behavior made me wonder if it was sick. Judy was thankful that the bears we had seen were not so friendly.

A solid layer of the white stuff hung over our heads the next morning, pressing down on the treeless landscape. Even though it hadn't rained, the outside of the tent and our pack covers were wet from heavy condensation. Breaking camp, we followed a ridge adjacent to the ravine, confident that it would lead us down to Bechevin Bay. From there it would be a half-day's hike to False Pass over familiar terrain.

The descent over the alpine tundra was carefree until we hit a 300-yard-wide strand of alders, which were about ten feet tall. I attempted to force my way through the compact mass of low, crooked trees contorted by the wind but could not. We slithered slowly ahead by literally walking in the trees, with unsure footholds on springy horizontal branches or teetering on the hummocks between them. Floundering, one minute we would disappear to our waists and the next we would have to step as high as our chins. Branches slapped our faces and hooked our packs and rootwads snared our feet. Worse than the physical abuse, however, was the thought of tramping up on a slumbering grizzly in this dwarf forest of nightmarish proportions.

"This isn't working," I announced in disgust. "There must be an easier way to get to the beach."

We trudged back uphill, past the alders and through the tall grass to the neighboring ridge. We slid back down through the tall grass and into a new alder thicket, its dull green tentacles waiting patiently to embrace us. This time there was no turning back. It took two hours of tripping, cursing and panting to reach the shore. On the brighter side, though, there were no biting bugs, the temperature was cool, and underneath the alder canopy was the best salmonberry picking we've ever had.

Our trip changed radically when we arrived at False Pass the day after we hit the beach. Enjoying the amenities of civilization, if only briefly, we shared hot blueberry muffins, apple pie, orange juice and coffee in the warm cannery mess hall with some False Pass residents and visitors.

By noon we were repacked and ready for the second part of our trip. Our destination was the Ikatan Peninsula, about eight miles south of False Pass, connected to the island by a tapering, storm-washed sandbar. Dominated by Dora Peak, an 1,800-foot green-swathed horn, the peninsula is reputedly a wild place, creased by rugged gullies and tumbling waterfalls. The fishermen said that a small fishing village used to operate there and that we might find an old cabin or two for protection if we needed it. The thought of another cabin interlude was tempting, but as was the case with our first outing, we had no definite itinerary and planned to stop and camp anywhere that caught our fancy.

The wide sandy beach, unlike the rocky shoreline north of False Pass, allowed us to make good time. We made frequent stops, however, to identify an assortment of bird life inshore. Plovers, turnstones and sandpipers scurried along the water's edge like wind-up mechanical toys. In deeper water were red-throated loons, cormorants, harlequin ducks, glaucous-winged gulls, pigeon guillemots and puffins. Patrolling the kelp, diving for small fish, were hundreds of shrieking terns. It was unbelievable that these sleek bundles of feathers should fly the length of two American continents twice a year. I could only guess the number of storms they would encounter during their six-month journey from Alaska to Antarctica. Buoyant threads of gossamer, the terns seemed to delight in teasing a slowly flapping bald eagle who had the audacity to fly in the same airspace.

About a mile from the Ikatan Peninsula, within sight of the

abandoned village, we encountered a swift-flowing river whose origin was the glaciers of Roundtop Mountain. On the map, the river looked more like a stream we could wade or even jump across. We tried crossing at its mouth, but even at low tide the river was too fast, too deep and too wide. "If only we had a small raft," Judy lamented, noting the many miles of good beach-walking on the other side. We considered floating our packs across on foam pads and swimming over, as Colin Fletcher, the well-known author of *The Complete Walker*, did when crossing the Colorado River in the Grand Canyon, but one dip of my hand in the icy water convinced me not to try.

We followed the river inland for about a mile, searching for a sheltered campsite. The terrain was open and rolling. Grassy dunes alternated with pockmarked craters, the pits giving the tundra a look of having been bombed. We chose the deepest of these bowls as a site for setting up the tent. At the bottom of the depression all we could see was a sparsely grassed wall and the sky. I didn't like being shut out from the rest of the world, but at least we were below the main force of the wind. As soon as everything was straightened away, we scrambled up to the crater's rim to cook dinner. The view was impressive: Roundtop Mountain and the east face of Isanotski Peaks brooded above; wide-mouthed Otter Cove and the Pacific Ocean shone turquoise and infinite a mile to the south.

Before we left Cold Bay, John Sarvis, manager of Izembek National Wildlife Refuge and custodian of the federal refuge on Unimak Island, had told me that the island's south side is much less productive for wildlife viewing. Hemmed in by volcanoes and mountains glazed over with fields of lava and ice, there is far less grazing ground for caribou and fewer salmon streams to attract bears. Except for birds, a long-tailed weasel and a few harbor seals, we hadn't spotted any animals since leaving False Pass.

One of the great things about Alaska's backcountry is that there is always the unexpected, the *truly* unexpected. While fixing dinner that night, we spotted a red fox sprinting over the tundra followed by a large tawny wolf. Twisting and turning at breakneck speed, the fox kept a few feet ahead of its pursuer, which was snapping at the bushy, white-tipped tail floating in the fox's wake. I was certain that at any second the chase would be over, but somehow the much smaller fox was able to zig when its pursuer zagged.

The animals ran behind a rise. I thought we had lost them when they came spilling out of a swale just thirty yards from us, their chests heaving, running all out. They were far too busy to notice us as they raced by. The wolf was a few feet behind the fox as they hurdled toward the river. Without a moment's hesitation, the fox leaped into the rushing current and swam to the other side. The wolf plunged in as well, but lagged behind. Scampering up on the far bank, the fox gave a quick shake of its fur and glanced at the wolf struggling in midstream. Not content with a meager lead, the wily fox dashed down the bank, and when certain the wolf was ashore, plunged back into the river and recrossed to our side.

The wolf halfheartedly gave chase, but wasn't about to swim the river a second time. About ten minutes later we got our last look at *Canis lupus*. Stalking a clump of tussock-grass on the tundra flats, the wolf jumped high in the air and landed hard on its front feet. It tore at the turf with its paws and jaws, but this wasn't the wolf's day. Even the bite-sized lemmings and voles were getting away.

The water was boiling when we refocused our attention on the stove. We didn't know it then, but that dinner of pasty rice and cardboard peas in a bag was the last hot meal we would have for some time. During the night a front came in from the south, bringing with it winds and driving rain. We huddled inside the tent the entire day, our only forays being to relieve ourselves and get drinking water from a nearby creek. We considered heating up a meal by bringing the stove inside the tent, but when we weighed the fire hazard and the potential of attracting bears, we decided on trail mix for a main course with a chocolate bar for dessert.

The next two days were repeats of the first, except that the storm had increased in ferocity. Listening to the wind howl over our campsite, I guessed the gusts were reaching eighty miles per hour. Inside the bowl the tent swayed when violent eddies swooped down, but the worst that happened was that a couple of pegs pulled loose.

The booming of the North Pacific surf was as disconcerting as the concert of wind and rain drumming off the tent fly. I tried not to think about the tidal wave that had washed over Unimak Island on April 1, 1946. Generated by a massive earthquake deep in the Aleutian Trench, the wave—eyewitnesses say it was over 100 feet high—demolished Scotch Cap Light, a now-abandoned lighthouse on the island's southwest side, killing five Coast Guardsmen stationed there. The waves swept the Pacific at over 500 miles per hour, killing 159 in the Hawaiian Islands less than five hours later. While hiking the beach, we had already witnessed how high run-of-the-mill storm waves could get. Strands of kelp and driftwood were washed up hundreds of yards from shore. We read our paperbacks, wrote listless garble in our journals, talked until there was nothing left to say and dozed until even our dreams were having dreams.

The violent weather seemed destined to stick around. A brief look at the river coming off Roundtop Mountain made us glad we had chosen not to cross it. The recent deluge had caused it to swell to twice its size and rise several feet. The river's previously clear, aqua-blue water was now the color of cement.

At 5:30 a.m. on the fourth day, the gale diminished somewhat. There was no sunrise, just a gradual lightening of the sky to a somber gray. Low clouds and wreaths of swirling mist suggested the weather could go either way. At least we could go for a short walk to clear our brains and stretch our legs without being battered by horizontal sheets of rain. We were stir-crazy. Another day of staring at yellow nylon walls and eating cold squirrel food might put us over the edge.

We zipped up the tent and pulled on our daypacks. Slogging through the wet, foamy tundra, we jumped over a succession of rivulets as we headed for a thousand-foot high isolated ridge a few miles north of camp. We felt exhilarated by the fresh air, tangy with saltspray. The birds seemed as happy with the change of weather as we were. Parasitic jaegers, enviably buoyant on long, pointed wings, cruised overhead in the crosswinds, their sharp beaks pointed straight down as they looked for prey. Also on the hunt were bald eagles and rough-legged hawks, big birds that had no trouble riding the gusts with their much broader wings, and a lone peregrine falcon, built strictly for speed, that flew steadily from its mountain aerie to the sea.

The ridgetop was breezy, grassy and unremarkable except for a single huge boulder, perhaps fifteen feet high and thirty feet wide. Judging from the conglomeration of rounded rocks embedded in the matrix, the boulder was a piece of volcanic vomitus that one of the nearby peaks had coughed up in some past eruption. Coating the monolith was a thick growth of moss and lichens, streaked with white from perching birds of prey. While Judy roamed the hillside gathering blueberries for our oatmeal breakfast, I climbed to the top of the boulder to scout for wildlife. A lone grizzly appeared about a mile upriver. I don't know why, but for the first time, I found myself wondering how a brown bear keeps its fur from becoming mildewed.

We returned to camp and fixed ourselves a hot meal just before the wind freshened and the sky ripped open with another drencher.

We put away our stuff and quickly retreated inside the tent. Usually I enjoy inclement weather, the moodiness, the grayness; it's far better to mix things up than have a constant diet of blue skies and sun. Still, when I looked outside before zipping shut the door, I saw an ominous cauldron of black crud rolling in which I could have done without. The clouds were low and showed no sign of lifting. I was sick and tired of wind and rain. There was so much more to see on Unimak Island, and we were stuck in the tent.

Despite severe weather the following morning, we packed our gear and began the journey back to False Pass. There was a chance, albeit a slim one, that the bush pilot would pick us up the next day as planned.

It was cold and invigorating hiking into the storm. This was just another of Unimak's many sides. For each moment of discomfort during the past three weeks, there had been countless more that were a delight. As we approached False Pass late in the day, we were each in our own little world, cocooned by the sound of the wind and surf, our heads encapsulated in wool hats and parka hoods. We were not returning from a grand adventure in the tradition of Father Hubbard. Even better, I thought, we have our own tradition.

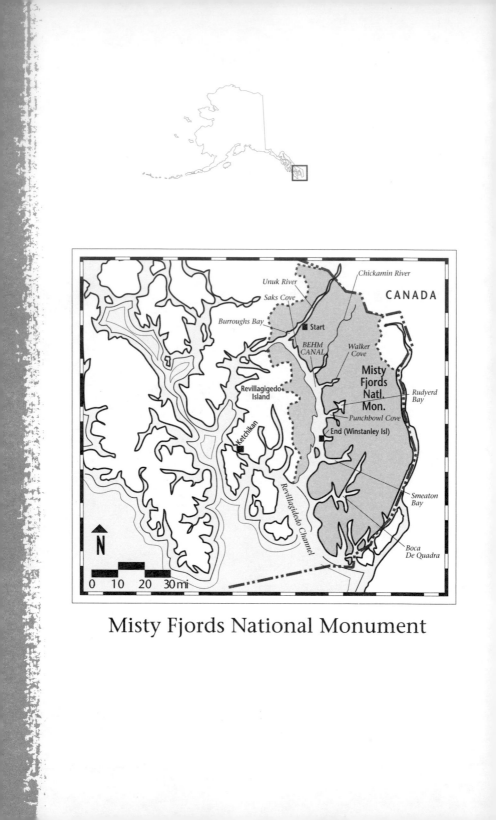

Misty Fjords National Monument

Coves, Bays and Misty Fjords

IT WAS EERIE NAVIGATING against the mild current, snaking past ancient moss-draped trees and underbrush so thick it was impossible to see more than a few feet past shore. The creek narrowed as we paddled farther, eventually becoming about as wide as our kayak was long. Schools of salmon and trout splashed the surface, and with a dull thump occasionally bumped the rubber hull.

"It's spooky in here," Judy said softly from the bow.

"Yeah, I know. Let's go a little further, to that logjam, before we head back to the fjord."

We were a quarter-mile from our camp at Walker Cove, afloat in a foot of water, when the sounds of snapping branches and heavy padded feet broke the silence. I heard a deep, gravelly cough, the measured tread of an animal. Whatever was making the noise was nearby, and big. Many large species of mammals are found in Misty Fjords. Was it moose? Grizzly bear? Black bear? Wolf? Blacktailed deer? This enormous parkland at the southernmost tip of the Alaska Panhandle has them all.

I was just about to spin the boat around when the streamside bushes parted. Grizzly! I swallowed hard when the she-bear walked out with two half-grown cubs at her side. The bears were so close I could have touched the big sow with my paddle if I had been stupid enough to try. For a fleeting second I fantasized about taking a quick photograph, but sanity prevailed. The click of my camera might have been all it took to make the bear charge.

With her back to us the mother grizzly rooted around in the undergrowth. Suddenly she sniffed the air, rose on her hind legs and dropped down. Her stiletto-like claws scraped the ground. My scalp tightened as I imagined it being ripped from my head.

Inexplicably, the bears didn't notice us. While the little ones tussled on the muddy bank, their mother shuffled along the shoreline and grabbed a few bites of grass. Then the grizzlies took a few steps into the forest and vanished as dramatically as they had appeared.

A week earlier bears had been far from our minds as we sat in a Cessna 185 floatplane on the way to Misty Fjords National Monument, a 2.3-million-acre unit within southeast Alaska's Tongass National Forest. Clouds hung low over the mountains, steady winds whipped up waves on the water and a light rain dribbled from a leaden sky. With my face pressed against the vibrating Plexiglass window, I strained for a sight of some recognizable feature. A thousand feet below lay a mind-boggling combination of wild cliffs and verdant forests that stood sentinel over sheltered arms of the sea. It was another Alaska extravaganza.

The pilot's voice brought me out of my thoughts. He pointed earthward. "Great kayaking country down there," he yelled over the Cessna's drone. "That is if you enjoy that kind of thing." The airplane suddenly banked sharply. "There's Burroughs Bay," he said, nodding toward a wide fjord flanked by steep mountains. "You see that hook-shaped inlet on the right? That's where we'll try to land."

After a quick, low-level pass to check for obstructions, the single-engine craft splashed down and skidded to a halt near a broad mudflat. "Wish I could get you closer to shore," he apologized, "but as you can see the tide is out."

Our bush pilot was in a hurry to unload and get back in the air. Bags came flying out faster than we could catch them. "Before the ceiling drops," he explained between tosses, "I want to be back in Ketchikan."

When the plane was empty, the pilot waded into the water and pushed it around. "Sit tight if I'm late," he called from the cockpit door. "Even if it's clear here, the weather may be rotten over the next range. See you folks in a couple of weeks."

Silence settled over the bay as the mustard-colored airplane faded into the distance. We weren't able to contemplate our surroundings because the sea would soon be surging in, leaving the mudflat under twenty-five feet of briny water. We hastily hauled our gear up the beach into the climax forest, a hundred-yard haul over slippery rocks and slimy seaweed. Only when we had safely stashed the supplies under the towering conifers did we rest. I sat on a duffel bag and sipped from a canteen. Judy munched on leftover bits of a chocolate bar. We began to hear familiar sounds, accentuated by the silence. A climax forest is usually a quiet place where life goes on unheard and unseen, but from a distance came the shrill rattle of a bald eagle, the soft exhalation of a harbor seal, the trill of a winter wren; I could discern the sound of a waterfall tumbling over a cliff face hidden by fog. That's when it really sank in that we were entirely alone, immersed in thousands of square miles of wilderness.

Once described by the U.S. Forest Service as "the most spectacular and inspiring scenic portion of Alaska," Misty Fjords National Monument embraces a myriad of environments from mountaintop glaciers bordering Canada to large marine estuaries of the Pacific Ocean. When President Jimmy Carter declared the area a national monument in 1980, he stated that Misty Fjords was "unparalleled" in regard to natural resources. Nearly every animal species common to southeast Alaska finds a niche here; its waters support Alaska's second-richest commercial fishing industry and populations of seals and endangered whales.

Except for its highest peaks, Misty Fjords has been unglaciated for hundreds of years. Proof of this is in the impressive old-growth trees that compete for space from shoreline to timberline several thousand feet above sea level. Yet past glacial activity has made Misty Fjords what it is today. Deep, narrow saltwater bays and inlets and sheer cliffs jutting more than a half-mile up from sea level are just some of the signs of successive Ice Ages.

Despite being one of the largest parklands in the United States—about half the size of New Jersey—Misty Fjords remains off the beaten track. It is accessible only by boat or aircraft. No permanent roads exist. The fjords usually visited by travelers from the lower forty-eight and Canada, we had been told, are those further north in Glacier Bay.

After a short break, we searched for a campsite above high tide.

The only problem with this ordinarily simple task was the difficulty of walking in the primeval forest, let alone setting up a tent. Thick wet underbrush, mossy hummocks, devilsclub shrubs and countless downed trees transformed the floor into an obstacle course. The fallen trunks made any progress, except up and down the slope in the direction the trees fall, very difficult. We finally settled on a lumpy matlike patch no larger than our tent, surrounded by twisted logs that leaned over beds of delicate ferns and white orchids. As we set up the tent, Judy pointed out that this was our first wilderness camp together since our marriage earlier that year. At the moment I couldn't be too sentimental. I was too preoccupied with the God-awful bugs.

From the moment we walked into the forest, swarms of blackflies congregated around every square inch of my exposed flesh. Fresh out of the airplane, it took me awhile to figure out what was happening. By the time I got my gloves and headnet on, my hands and neck were riddled with raised, itching bites.

We did have another salvation, though, besides disappearing under headnets or sealing ourselves in the tent. After quickly assembling the Klepper, we carried the boat to the water and paddled away from land. The flies followed us valiantly, but those hitchhikers that I didn't massacre eventually abandoned ship and returned to shore.

I took a deep breath and tried to unwind. I was still suffering from the throes of last-minute packing and jet lag. It had been a long, tiring two days: flying into Ketchikan after a night curled up on a couch in the Seattle airport, and today the anxious vigil in the bush pilot's cramped office waiting for a break in the weather. But now, with camp squared away and the bugs temporarily vanquished, I delighted in the pristine countryside. I was feeling better, much better, snuggled in our boat, the light mist soothing my itching skin. For an hour we paddled, not going anywhere in particular, just investigating our new environs. As darkness approached, we turned around and headed back for camp, now much closer to the water because of the flooding tide. I tucked my gloves over my parka sleeves and cinched the headnet straps. I was ready for the flies.

Early the following morning we huddled under a tarp and sipped hot cocoa, waiting for another pot of water to boil so we could have our breakfast of instant oatmeal spiked with Grape-nuts and raisins. It was still raining, which came as no surprise since we were, after all, in a temperate rain forest. A thin stream of water trickled off the blue nylon canopy and disappeared into the green sphagnum moss at our feet. Saturated, oozy clouds rested a hundred feet above the bay, obscuring most of the other shore. I couldn't imagine how a place could be much wetter.

The pint of steaming oatmeal in my belly produced beads of perspiration on my forehead. I was tempted to shed a layer of clothes, but as the flies were active I left on my armor: a long-sleeved polypro shirt, hat and bug net and wool pants under a full waterproof suit. Out of curiosity I checked the thermometer hanging from the tent awning. The temperature was a sultry sixty-four degrees. "Too hot for Alaska," I complained. "We'd be having a real scorcher if there were any sun."

Between bites of breakfast we discussed our objectives for the days ahead. Starting on Burroughs Bay at the monument's northern boundary, we intended to take two weeks to paddle sixty miles to the south. The actual paddling mileage would be more than that, though, since we planned to explore a number of coves, bays and fjords along the way. At the end of our journey we would meet our chartered floatplane at an island on Behm Canal, the major waterway of Misty Fjords. Then it was a short flight back to Ketchikan, the Panhandle's largest and southernmost city, fifty miles away.

This was our first trip with the Klepper since our Killik River excursion two years previously. It felt good to be using the boat again, and we were excited at the prospect of ocean touring. Our last spell of sea kayaking was when we journeyed to Glacier Bay. There is something about traveling by folding kayak that provokes a dichotomous feeling of homeyness and wanderlust. In its simplest form the folding kayak is a hodgepodge of unrelated parts, but when assembled it becomes a synergistic vessel capable of transporting us virtually anywhere along the coastline. Much more than a conglomerate of rubber, canvas and wood, the Klepper protects us and becomes our home in the water: a movable, seaworthy home. Without it we would be trapped, stranded in the impenetrable forest, prey to the blackflies and bears. With it, we can seek the horizon, in the open, with nothing blocking our path.

Our plan for the first few days was to explore the vicinity around our camp rather than rushing out of the bay. We were more interested in what Thoreau called the "tonic of wilderness" than in covering miles, which was good, because there was plenty of Thoreau's elixir in this place.

To prepare for the outing, I put away the food while Judy zipped up the tent and readied the kayak. Putting away food on this trip meant hanging it from a tree limb, a novel procedure for me in Alaska since on all my previous journeys there had been no large trees and I simply laid the bags on the ground. To be of any benefit, the supplies have to be beyond the reach of a grizzly bear standing on its hind legs, and far enough from the main trunk to dissuade a black bear, a species more adept at climbing. I tried to remember the last time I was obliged to hang food as I uncoiled the line and missed my first toss over the limb. I think it was when I backpacked regularly in Yellowstone National Park. If my memory was correct, hanging food was a hassle then despite the park's straight, tall lodgepole pines; it was even more of a hassle now to hoist a pair of heavy bags twenty feet up a crooked, bending branch using only stretchy nylon parachute cord.

It was low tide when we were ready to go. We lugged the boat across the mudflats to the water's edge, reminding ourselves to check the tide table first next time. Our movement attracted the attention of a number of harbor seals, the most common coastal marine mammal from southeastern Alaska to the Bering Sea. Scores of the whiskered, dog-faced animals lurked offshore like U-boats on patrol, watching our every move. Constantly submerging and slowly reappearing, the curious seals poked their earless, pear-shaped heads above the surface to inspect the recent arrivals about to invade their realm.

Seals weren't the only creatures giving us the eye. All around were bald eagles, so many that we finally quit counting. They perched on treetops, snags or mudflats, or soared overhead. Their numbers meant that a good salmon river was nearby. In this case it was the Unuk, the largest river in Misty Fjords. With its headwaters high in Canada's Coast Mountains, the Unuk would offer a different paddling experience if we could get inside. Its proximity was the main reason we began our voyage at the head of Burroughs Bay.

Ignoring the seals, we launched the kayak and quickly paddled to deeper water to escape the flies. The Unuk's mouth, actually a wide, braided delta, was about three miles away. Our slow approach allowed us to study the river and choose a route up its silt-heavy flow.

An hour of paddling put us near the river's mouth, a confusing scene of narrow channels, small islands, willow-lined sandbars and giant rootwads and stumps flushed downstream from the interior and settled in the mudflats. The ebb tide had sucked the delta dry. We nosed the kayak forward a little at a time until becoming

Judy Bradford in a tidal creek estuary near Burroughs Bay and the Unuk River.

grounded, then waited patiently for the incoming tide to lift us up.

The in-rushing sea was as dramatic as any flash flood. I was re-minded of a nature program on television that showed a cracked and bleached Arizona wash being quickly transformed into a raging river after a thunderstorm. This wasn't a rip-roaring torrent, but the effects were the same. Sandbars dry one moment were covered with a foot of gurgling water the next. We didn't dare stray far from the boat for fear of losing it when our backs were turned. Within an hour or two all the tidal flats were inundated. We paddled upriver as the sea water continued to gush in. There were two opposing cur-rents to deal with: one going downstream from the river, the other pushing upstream from the tide. Beyond the Unuk's mouth, we were forced to ferry from bank to bank to catch the right flow.

Remote and mysterious, ringed by snowy peaks and an im-penetrable, fog-draped forest, a mass of mountains swallowed us in their folds as we nosed up the river. Pink salmon and cutthroat trout streaked under our hull, their quicksilver flashes monitored by bald eagles roosting in the upper branches of spruce and black cotton-wood. We spotted an elusive blacktail deer skulking through the woods and a family of hyperactive river otters prowling the bank. But other wildlife—bear, moose, wolf, mink, beaver—were repre-sented solely by their tracks on shore.

The day turned grayer and wetter, and the river more narrow and shallow as we moved further from the influence of the tide. The urge to learn what was around the next bend was strong; however, when the kayak's hull began to scrape bottom, we took it as a sign to turn back. A hard right rudder and left forward sweeps pushed the nose of the boat around. We covered the few miles in a fraction of the time it had taken us to paddle up.

When we arrived at the river's mouth, the bay was no longer calm. Light gusts blew in from Behm Canal, sending ripples over the water. I crammed my sou'wester hat tightly onto my head to ward off the drizzle, then, matching Judy's paddle cadence, beat through the swells toward camp.

I had nearly forgotten about the blackflies during our day on the water. A few minutes on land showed me how bad they still were. I shuddered at the thought of being without a headnet. The flimsy piece of netting was the only thing that kept the pests from chewing up my neck and face; insect repellent, even the 100 percent DEET stuff, had no effect. The only time I absolutely deplore using a headnet is while I'm eating. Shoveling food under a headnet is a sloppy and rather unsatisfactory arrangement at best.

The technique I use is to lift a corner of the shroud with one hand and quickly jam the spoon into my mouth with the other. More than once during dinner, I missed the bullseye. Judy disgustedly pointed out the lumps of swill dribbling down my bearded chin.

When we awoke the next morning, we were tempted not to move. The tent felt secure and warm and it was drizzling outside. June and July are supposed to be the driest months in this part of Alaska, each with seven inches of rain. Since it was already mid-July, there was a chance the quota had almost been met. I checked the tide table booklet. A very low tide—minus 4.4 feet—was due to peak in an hour. I opened the tent flap and peered out. A wide band of mudflats separated us from the water. Since we planned to do another exploratory paddle across Burroughs Bay, we chose to wait for flood tide so that we could launch the boat without a long carry

In the intervening couple of hours, we lost ourselves in other people's adventures. Judy was reading *Snow Leopard* by Peter Matthiessen, a tale of the author's search for the elusive cat, and the philosophy of life itself, in the mountains of Nepal. I was engrossed in Kenneth Brower's *The Starship and the Canoe*, which among other things follows the journey of a *baidarka* (an Aleut kayak-like boat) down the Alaska coast. The boat was paddled by George Dyson, the son of the brilliant physicist, Freeman Dyson. After reading, we wrote in our journals and talked.

Judy's administrative job in health care was taking its toll on her health and a plan to rescue her from burnout began to emerge. A career track that had started immediately upon graduation from college was going to be intentionally, temporarily, derailed. She wanted to take a year-and-a-half off—"midlife retirement" she called it—to see the world; I wholeheartedly agreed.

In January she would be off on a tour of the globe. A few of the highlights were to be two-and-a-half months in East Africa with a wilderness educational program, six weeks in Mexico studying Spanish, and a tour of France and Spain by bicycle. She was also going to accompany me on my three-month leave of absence to the mountains and fjords of South America's Patagonia.

I wished I was going with her to Africa—I had gone there when we first met, and the place beckoned still, but I wasn't prepared to give up my sojourns to Alaska with its solitude and grizzly bears, not yet. As John Muir wrote a century ago, "To the lover of pure wilderness, Alaska is one of the most wonderful countries in the world." It still is. I planned to keep coming back as long as I could journey beyond the high hills.

After we had eaten breakfast and tidied up camp, we carried the kayak to the water and stepped in. I said good morning to the cadre of harbor seals offshore, patiently watching us as usual to see what we were about to do. By cutting diagonally across Burroughs Bay, a journey of about three miles, we and the seals reached the mouth of Grant Creek. Once past the funnel-shaped tidal inlet, however, we lost our escorts when the stream became just deep enough to float our boat. "The seals are missing the best scenery," I joked as we eased into the enchanting chasm. Thundering cascades, fed by some of the thousands of small highland lakes that help absorb the more than fourteen feet of annual rainfall in Misty Fjords, plunged through narrow clefts to become mountain torrents, which in turn rushed down through great, rounded granite boulders. Thickly grown forests covered the steep slopes. The green strand provided some respite from the chiseled lines of the landscape.

Our journey up the creek was cut short by the incessant rain and a steadily lowering fog. The fog gave the country a mystical aspect, creating a dreamscape that seemed appropriate in a place called Misty Fjords, but there was no point in paddling if we couldn't see anything. We turned the boat around and reentered the bay. The seals were there, waiting to escort us back.

Leaving on an ebb tide, we packed up and paddled toward the mouth of Burroughs Bay, ready to see a new section of the monument. An hour or so later we entered Behm Canal. More than 100 miles long and unusually deep, this glacier-scoured trench, named in 1793 by Captain George Vancouver for a major in the U.S. Army, divides Revillagigedo Island on the west from the mainland on the east. As long as the canal was calm we gave little thought to the fact that the passageway offered little shelter. But when the weather changed around mid-morning, alternating between patches of sun and wind-driven rain, we became aware of the unbroken cliffs on our left and the two to three miles of open water on our right. Whitecaps were building; waves curled over the deck. Because of our limited sea kayaking experience, each protected inlet was a relief.

We reached the next inlet along our route, Saks Cove, around three o'clock. I was pleased with our first day's paddle; we had covered about twelve miles.

"Are you sure we should camp here?" Judy asked after we landed. Although there appeared to be few places to set up a tent, I was unperturbed. After nosing around the shore, I finally settled for a patch of soaking wet ground carved out among the fallen trees and waxy undergrowth. It was only after we pitched the tent that we found driftwood and fronds of kelp in the nearby bushes, irrefutable evidence that the site had recently been flooded. Before Judy could give me her "I told you so" spiel, I checked the tide table. Twice. By my calculations, we were okay. The fluctuation of the tides would be less pronounced this week; there would be a foot to spare between midnight's high water and our camp. Judy wasn't taking any chances. "I think I'll set my watch alarm for 11:30 tonight," she said matter-of-factly, "merely as a precaution."

As soon as we had our camp arranged, we set up our kitchen area under the tarp and brewed some tea. While I fiddled with the stove, Judy cut a few wedges of Gouda cheese to go with our whole wheat bagels. We would have dinner later. With nothing more important to do than wait for the water to boil, I stretched out my legs, leaned against the overturned kayak and gazed across the cove. Judy had her back against a mossy tree and was jotting something in her notes. It felt nice to have our chores done with nothing left to do but relax.

Suddenly it dawned on me: there was something different about this campsite. "Hey, there are no bugs! Do you realize we've been here over an hour and I haven't seen a single blackfly?" My meager knowledge of blackfly biology yielded only one plausible explanation: because blackflies breed in freshwater streams, the Unuk River acts as a major hatching ground. There are countless other creeks and streams within Misty Fjords, but none with the Unuk's tremendous flow.

Encouraged by the absence of six-legged pests, we went for a short walk in the forest behind our camp. It turned out to be a very short walk because we were boxed in by downed timber and thickets of alder, willow, huckleberry and spiny devilsclub. Everything dripped with moisture. Nourished by the abundant precipitation from air masses lifting over the coastal mountains as well as temperatures moderated by the adjacent seas, Misty Fjords' vegetation has run amok. The ferns, mushrooms, trees and forbs were so leafy green, oozing wet and ancient, that I half-expected a scaly armored dinosaur to come stomping out of the Mesozoic growth.

Although a few rays of sunlight stabbed through the clouds, their illumination never reached the forest floor. The Sitka spruce, cedar and hemlock rose to the height of a twenty-story building. The bases of the trees were swollen with massive, moss-covered buttresses, and great beards of gray club moss dangled from the canopy. The trees sighed and murmured, or at least I thought they did.

Judy didn't mean to, but she broke the spell by lamenting that such forests are still being cut on national forest lands. Her words hung heavy in the thick air. I merely nodded my head, knowing that if I thought about it, I would become surly and depressed.

The woodlands of Misty Fjords are a segment of the coastal temperate rain forest that parallels the Pacific Rim from northern California to Cook Inlet in Alaska. Although the vast majority of the monument's forest is protected within a congressionally designated wilderness area, elsewhere much of that great coniferous arc has been logged, including the majority of California's venerable redwoods and large tracts within Alaska's two national forests. Ironically, the bulk of the timber harvested on public land is shipped directly to Japan and sold for a price below market value.

While the fight to preserve old-growth forest in the United States is a necessary and ongoing skirmish that continues to concern several major conservation groups, there is another environmental wrecking ball loose in Misty Fjords that, by all accounts, will cause even more havoc than the denuding of forests. Only fifteen miles south of Rudyerd Bay, the fjord where we planned to spend the last days of our trip, is the long, Y-shaped Smeaton Bay, an important habitat for fish and wildlife. On a small knoll at the head of Smeaton Bay is one of the world's richest deposits of molybdenum, a hard, gray, relatively rare metallic element used to toughen steel alloy and to soften tungsten alloy. In the rush to pass the Alaska Lands Bill before Ronald Reagan became president in 1981 (it was thought, with good cause, that Reagan would not approve the legislation creating new and enlarged Alaska parklands and refuges), conservationists had to make certain concessions to prodevelopment lobbies. Among the most pronounced of these giveaways was a nonwilderness "mining exclusion" of 156,210 acres in the Smeaton Bay area. The mining rights to the Quartz Hill molybdenum deposit were granted to U.S. Borax and Chemical Corporation.

Borax's proposed mine—they have dubbed it the "Ultimate Pit"—could prove to be the largest mining development in Alaska, not to mention the world's largest open-pit mine. Over its expected 70- to 100-year operation, the mine will produce up to 80,000 tons of tailings, mixed with processing chemicals and other wastes, *each day*. The open pit, at completion, will measure two miles across and be 1,800 feet deep, with little hope for reclamation. A crew of 1,000 will construct the mine, and when and if it begins full production, 800 employees with their families will be stationed there. The temporary work camp at Smeaton Bay will be transformed into Alaska's ninth largest city; heretofore, no one has lived permanently in Misty Fjords National Monument, not even the rangers who have their headquarters at Ketchikan. For its efforts, Borax expects to accrue some $25 *billion* in yields.

Standing under the swaying trees, wondering how such a travesty could be allowed on public land, I tried to convince myself that a major miracle would force Borax to pull out. Maybe an alternative to molybdenum would be found; maybe world prices for molybdenum would remain as low as they are now, making it economically unfeasible to extract it from the ground; maybe conservation groups—the Sierra Club Legal Defense Fund, the Wilderness Society and others, who are appealing the latest environmental impact statement decision that authorizes Borax to begin work—would pull a major upset victory out of federal court.

We launched the kayak after a late evening meal, seduced by the long Alaska summer days when the sun hovers in the sky for twenty hours. The topographic map showed a strip of flat beach at the far end of Saks Cove. It looked like a good place to stretch our legs, since our hiking opportunities had been minimal because of the steep, forested terrain.

The cove was green and clear, unlike silt-charged Burroughs Bay. As well as the ubiquitous bald eagles, we saw ducks—mallards, teal, white-winged and surf scoters—gulls, auklets, red-throated loons and chunky tufted puffins with parrotlike beaks. Our bird-watching didn't end when we dragged the kayak up the sandy beach. Sandpipers and sanderlings dashed along the tide line, in perfect synchronization with the lapping waves. Flitting from branch to branch at the forest's edge were small, secretive birds—thrushes, a rufous hummingbird, kinglits, golden-crowned sparrows, a winter wren. And at a purling stream entering the cove from a mountainous ravine, we saw a pair of slate-gray dippers scouring the stony bottom for tasty morsels.

To our surprise, only one set of tracks was evident on the strand. The rear print was like that of a child, and the foreprint resembled a large cat's. I squatted on my haunches. "Black bear," I said, pointing to the short, uncurved claw marks perfectly preserved in the wet sand. "If this was from a griz, there'd be much longer, curved claws."

As I stood up and looked down the beach, my identification of the tracks was confirmed. A black bear was shuffling toward our Klepper. It was a small bear, weighing perhaps 150 pounds. Its size, lack of a distinct shoulder hump, and smaller, more pointed head with a straight-faced profile easily distinguished it from a grizzly. We kept a wary eye on the bruin as we eased toward the kayak. The bear was languidly grazing on the lush beach grass and hadn't noticed us yet. Clods of dirt and long stalks drooped from the animal's mouth, a comical sight that helped perpetuate the black bear's image as a generally harmless, bumbling clown. *Ursus americanus* can be a dangerous foe, however. In Alaska and elsewhere, the black bear has killed and mauled many more humans than the feared grizzly. Part of the reason, of course, is that far more black bears than grizzlies inhabit North America, but as one Alaska wildlife biologist put it: "Even a small black bear is potentially lethal, for the strength and quickness of these animals is surprising."

I cupped my hands and bellowed a couple of war whoops; upon hearing my shout, the near-sighted animal pricked up its ears, stood at attention, then lumbered toward us, bobbing and weaving its head.

"Oh, great, Lar, that's just great," hissed Judy. "What do you have planned for an encore?"

As I increased the din, the bruin finally got the message that two human beings were sharing the same beach. It stopped, shuffled from foot to foot, briefly pawed at a piece of driftwood, then ambled up a brush-choked little creek. We waited a few minutes to make certain the bear wasn't merely lying in ambush, then hurried to the kayak and under cover of darkness made our way back to camp.

That night I tried to update my journal. Events from that morning already seemed days old. If I didn't record my impressions right away I might forget them. Lying on my sleeping bag, the tent aglow from both our headlamps, I noted in my spiral pad the animals we'd seen, the vagaries of the weather, the terrain we had paddled through, some personal reflections. Though my words were clumsy in this rough form, lacking any type of cohesiveness and eloquence, I knew they would spark a multitude of memories when I reread them at a later date.

During the night the rain stopped, and for the first time during our trip there were blue skies overhead. With another twelve-mile paddle facing us, we got on the water without delay while the weather was good.

We made good progress for the first few miles after leaving Saks Cove, our paddling aided by the tide surging out of Behm Canal. I estimated our speed at three knots, using elapsed time between known landmarks on the map. However, a rising tailwind and steepening swells put an end to our tranquil travel. The sun created chaotic air currents that whisked down the mountaintops to rake Behm Canal. Foaming whitecaps rushed underneath the Klepper's flexing hull. We tightened our sprayskirts and dug deep with our paddles, ready to make the most of the windy ride. Solid and dependable, the beamy Klepper plowed on. By timing our sprints, we were able to surf off the tops of the waves. Only when the wind altered direction, causing the waves to pound at us from right angles to the boat's keel, did kayak surfing become less of a thrill. I didn't like the wind blowing in this direction because the next safe harbor was at the mouth of the Chickamin River, where we planned to spend a couple of nights. Until then the shoreline was a continuous cliff with absolutely nowhere to land.

It was about 4 p.m. when we passed Fish Point and entered the Chickamin River estuary. The shallow, mile-wide bay, shielded by rugged 4,000-foot mountains, was placid compared to Behm Canal. We drew in our paddles and rested near the protected shore. The boat lapped against a boulder spangled with stringy green algae, helmetlike barnacles and blue-black limpets; fastened to a ledge beneath the sloshing waterline were a couple of bright orange starfish. Above the boulder was a real neck bender: a 2,000-foot-high slope bristling with a phalanx of conifers that rose almost straight up from the sea.

Scores of bald eagles soared overhead or perched on tree boughs. We counted twenty-two of the fish-eating birds at a single time, more than we saw on the Unuk. A big fellow on a nearby snag tilted his head back and croaked a rattling cry. Beneath the bird was a fish skeleton picked clean.

Studying our national bird, I was reminded of the time when most fishermen would shoot bald eagles on sight (a few still do) in the mistaken belief that eagles reduced their harvest of salmon. Alaska even had a bounty on bald eagles as recently as 1953, when state authorities paid two dollars for a set of claws. Recent studies, however, show that the birds dine mostly on dead or dying salmon and are no threat to Alaska's fisheries. Legally protected under the federal Endangered Species Act, Alaska's breeding season population now numbers about 30,000—more than in all the rest of the states combined.

Easing further up the estuary, we hardly gave a second look to the seals loafing on a sandbar exposed at low tide. Plump, hairless and cadaver-gray, they reminded me of undercooked Polish sausages. The seals were busy doing whatever seals do when undisturbed on land: some dozed; some scuffled with their neighbors; a few, totally at ease on their backs, scratched their taut bellies with stubby front flippers. They filled the air with their dolorous cacophony, which sounded like dog barks and lion roars.

Fatigue and terrain dictated our choice of campsite that night. Once again the selection was limited. Thick forests and unapproachable cliffs swept upward toward bare-rocked mountaintops, but we eventually came upon a protected harbor large enough to berth a single kayak. We drew against the rocks. While Judy stayed with the boat, I probed the woods for a place to spend the night.

Fifteen minutes later I returned, spouting a tired cliche: "The good news is I found a campsite; the bad news is it's about 75 yards from here, up this embankment and into the forest."

"Let's do it," Judy urged, sliding out of the boat. "It doesn't look like there's anything else around. And I don't really want to paddle any more today."

Storing the kayak at the edge of the woods, we carried the rest of our gear to the campsite in two more trips. The ground was covered with a spongy carpet of tightly rooted low plants. Overhead loomed enormous, shadowy conifers. The trunks of both living and fallen trees were jacketed in moss and the upper boughs supported clusters of mistletoe. I felt Liliputian in a land of green giants.

Compared to a midwestern forest, the woods seemed silent. There was only the rustle of wind in the foliage and the creaking of the big trees. On the forest floor lay the mossy and weathered boughs of previous giants blown down by gales. The wind, twisting around to the south, was working into the estuary. The trees moaned as if in pain. Suddenly in the distance there came a loud crack, a pause, then a *thump*! The soft ground shuddered. We had already eaten dinner and were holed up for the night, but I peered out the tent door. In the half-light I couldn't see a thing. I began to muse about the number of rotting trees in our vicinity, the irony and gore of having life ended by a toppling tree.

I was fast asleep, tired after a long day of exploring the lower Chickamin River, when a garbled racket woke me. It took a few moments for the hoarse, low-pitched voices to register through my semiconscious haze. Crows! An incredibly noisy flock of northwestern crows was in the trees overhead. I rubbed my eyes and looked at my watch: only 5 a.m.

Silently cursing the crows, I pulled on my pants and shirt, slipped on unlaced boots and piled out of the tent. Seeking some tranquility, I strolled to a rocky ledge overlooking the estuary. The bay sparkled in the morning sun, and beyond, Behm Canal was oily green, as smooth as old glass. Conditions were ideal for paddling and we were headed for Walker Cove, supposedly one of the most scenic areas in the monument and infrequently visited.

I puttered around camp for awhile waiting for Judy to awaken. When the crows left I decided we had lots of time to paddle and crawled back into my sleeping bag. Once again peace fell over our domicile.

No wind, bright sun, a tide in our favor: the weather held as we paddled toward Walker Cove. Gliding over the smooth seas, we were joined by loons, gulls, auklets, puffins and ducks in their usual abundance, not to mention new contingents of harbor seals. Because the weather was great and it was a Saturday, we thought it odd that we encountered no other watercraft.

Despite our late start—it was a ten-mile journey from the Chickamin River—we reached Walker Cove in time for lunch. Hungry though I was, I forgot about eating when we pulled ashore at the rock-strewn entrance and gaped inside. "Unbelievable!" I cried. "Amazing!" I was heavy on the superlatives, but everything I had heard about this place was true.

Seven miles long and averaging a half-mile wide, Walker Cove was the steepest saltwater canyon I had ever seen, a textbook example of a glacier's bulldozing abilities. The lofty granite walls, towering 3,000 feet above the water, are so sheer in most places that only crusty lichens can find a purchase. Even in the midday light, the cliffs were luminous, blasted bare and gray. Near the mouths of creeks and on less severe slopes, a thin fringe of flat green forest straggled up from the high tide mark. Above the treeline, at about the 4,000-foot elevation, was a series of open ridges and knuckles covered with alpine meadows and, higher yet, permanent snow. The peaks flanking us were gentler than I had expected, rounded into soft curves by the ice and wind.

While Judy did some stretching exercises to relieve a sore neck, I inspected the high country across the fjord, more from habit than because I expected to see anything. A few minutes later I interrupted Judy's physical rehabilitation. "Jude, take a look at that mountain top, near the snowline in that avalanche chute. What do you see?"

She reached for her binoculars, a compact and expensive pair of 8x20s we bought after her last cheap ones went for a swim. "Mmmm. Patches of snow," she pronounced.

"Those binoculars are wasted on you," I teased. "Look closer."

She squinted through the barrels and fiddled with the focus some more. "Are those mountain goats?" she asked. They were—a dozen creamy white figures moving against the hard glare of the snow, their shaggy coats, beards and slender, black horns quickly distinguishing them from Dall sheep, the only other all-white animal in Alaska that inhabits the same range.

Today the sun shone and the green heath was bare, but more often than not the heights these animals inhabit are wrapped in cold, rolling mist and deep snow. We watched as the goats boldly traversed the steep scree slopes. Their padded, suction-cup hooves and sturdy legs were custom designed for this type of extreme mountaineering. Climbing higher on faint game trails, the animals deliberately picked their way to safety up a final sheer ledge. Then with a burst of exuberance, they trotted over the crest out of sight.

The chasm offered few places to land. We paddled far up the fjord between the water-streaked cliffs, poking in nooks and crannies for possible breaks. Around three o'clock we came to the head of the cove and our last hope. A creek had carved a V-shaped valley through the coastal mountains to tidewater. There was a narrow strip of level, open land above the beach large enough for a couple of tents. From the looks of the flattened vegetation under the hemlocks, someone had camped here before. But that didn't bother us. The site was spotless, enclosed by three stupendous walls with a splendid view of the creek's outlet.

We spent the next quarter-hour lugging everything from the shoreline to the trees. We accomplished this process in a number of stages. First we heaved the loaded Klepper a few inches above the water, taking care not to damage the boat's rubber skin. Next we unearthed our food bags (mercifully shrinking every day), stuff sacks and waterproof bags from under the deck and shuttled them to the appointed site. Finally, when the kayak was empty, we tossed in the paddles and life jackets and each grabbed an end; it was virtually impossible to carry the boat alone.

"I'm glad we'll be spending two nights here," I puffed, trying to maneuver my end of the unwieldy Klepper without slipping on the seaweed-covered rocks.

The continued good weather allowed us to explore Walker Cove in depth. We basked under the glacial-sculptured mountains, prowled the beaches and kayaked over blue, bottomless waters that were home to salmon, porpoises and seals. We saw more grizzlies (a mama sow and her two cubs), black bears, river otters, mountain goats and numerous birds. Except for a couple of sailboats that came quickly in and out, we had the cove to ourselves.

There came a point in our wanderings when we actually began to complain about the heat, usually whenever we left the shadows of the fjord's walls. My thermometer registered seventy-two degrees Fahrenheit in the shade; I wasn't interested in what it was in the sun. After paddling over to another canyon, even steeper and more vertical than the one in which we were camped, Judy decided to cope with the heat by going for a swim. I stood on shore by the kayak, sweating in my wool pants and long-sleeved shirt. Voluntarily swimming in an Alaska fjord was not for me.

"It feels *grrreeeat!*" Judy coaxed. "You have to try it." She was twenty-five yards from shore in clear, glassy water up to her chest. Never without my thermometer, I measured the temperature, more for her enlightenment than mine.

"No way!" I shouted. "It's sixty degrees at the surface. You know me: I'm allergic to bath water colder than my blood." She persisted, a cajoling siren of the sea. Oh, why not, I thought. It did look fun. Peeling off my grimy clothes and rubber boots, I gingerly waded in up to my bellybutton. The water was on the cool side, not unbearable, though. I might even have enjoyed it had I not been surrounded by some little fishes nibbling at certain tender parts of my anatomy. When the nibbling fish became aggressive, I thrashed out of the water and reached shore before any bigger ones came along.

We left Walker Cove a day later than planned, setting up camp on Ledge Point overlooking Behm Canal. After making an early stop, we had the rest of the afternoon to loaf. Our only chores consisted of mending a torn shirt and patching a leaky rubber boot. The remaining time we spent reading, daydreaming and snacking, or gazing out across the canal at the gray-mauve mountains receding to the west.

I set the camera on a tripod and clicked off a few shots with the self-timer to document our bout of laziness and the perfect camp. In the eight seconds before the shutter dropped, I would sprint back to Judy, hug her tightly, and remind her to smile as idiotically as she could. Dressed in matching clothes right down to our khaki sun hats and olive-green boots, we were the perfect example of a "happily married couple enjoying the Great Outdoors."

We were on Behm Canal at the onset of ebb tide. The assist from the current was nice, but there was a downside: the tidal currents were in opposition to the wind, creating a closely spaced chop. We snugged up our sprayskirts for a wet ride as our little boat climbed slowly over the backs of the waves. Up . . . over . . . plunge . . . up . . . over . . . plunge; our wooden-ribbed vessel flexed as if it were a living animal. When I calculated our rate of speed, I was surprised that we were averaging two-and-a-half miles per hour, pretty respectable considering the headwind. I decided that the previous day's rest must have done us some good.

Around noon the clouds burned off and the sun came out. The breeze fluttered and died. The swells became gentle, relaxing. Rhythmically—pull with the right hand, push with the left—we dipped our paddles in unison into the sea. Swirls of flecked water eddied past the wooden blades and against the hull.

One of the advantages of paddling in the stern of a double kayak is that you can blink out without your partner being aware. I closed my eyes to shut out the bright light. We wouldn't crash into anything—the jagged shoreline was a quarter-mile to port. Shadows passed over my eyelids, indiscernible shapes. Without vision, my other senses took control: water gurgled against the bow, moist salt air caressed my face, the muscles of my upper body responded to the paddle. It was dreamy, hazy, a natural high. I could do this forever, I thought, paddle on to new horizons.

I shifted mental gears and drifted back to reality. I slowly opened my eyes and squinted from the glare. I saw Judy's back, cloaked in a yellow parka. She was wrapped in her own thoughts, her paddle resting across the deck, her hands dangling over the side. Too far away to touch her, I nudged her with the toe of my boot.

"What's that for?" she said, turning around to face me.

No one has ever accused me of being overly sentimental or affectionate, but occasionally I do reveal my tender side. "I just wanted to let you know I was still back here thinking of things. . ."

"And?"

"And one thing I haven't told you in a few days is that I'm glad we're on this trip together. . . ."

"And?"

"And we'll get to Rudyerd Bay a lot faster if I have some help paddling."

A few hours later we entered Rudyerd Bay, called in a park brochure the "Yosemite of the North." With its Yosemite-like walls, verdant forests, and a backdrop of dazzling mountains, the comparison was legitimate. Named in 1879 for an English engineer who rebuilt a nearby lighthouse after its destruction in 1703, Rudyerd Bay extends southwest fourteen miles from Canada's Coast Mountains to Behm Canal. A couple of side inlets and coves add another six miles or so to Rudyerd's total length.

Our days in Rudyerd Bay were a mixture of paddling and hiking. The kayak allowed us to explore the intimate, twisting channels of the fjord's upper reaches, an ocean trench so spectacular, so fractured, it would have to inspire awe in even the most jaded sea kayaker. From our water-level perspective it felt as if we had slipped between a crack of the earth's crust. Except for a few small tidal meadows where sylvan creeks entered the sea and drunkenly leaning hemlocks and cedars clung boldly to the slopes, we were surrounded by precipitous, bare rock walls as smooth as porcelain plates.

The topographic map fastened to the spraydeck on my lap gave me an eagle's eye view of what lay beyond. To the north, west and south was country we were already somewhat familiar with, but to the east, stretching for more than thirty miles, was a rich wilderness of serrated ridges, peaks and cirques sliced by deep, sequestered valleys and clear-running streams. Only when the mountains approached the Canadian province of British Columbia, on the other side of the long and narrow Portland Canal, did the rough and tumble terrain become less severe.

A few short footpaths constructed by the U.S. Forest Service allowed us to penetrate the mountains and the rain forest and exercise our legs. The trailhead to Nooya Lake lay directly across the fjord from one of our camps. I became edgy as soon as we landed and carried the boat ashore. Above high tide the berry bushes and skunk cabbage were rank with bear digs and droppings, and there were well-worn paths where bears had pushed through the grass. One set of fresh tracks—I couldn't be sure whether they were made by a black or grizzly—meandered up the same trail we planned to take.

Cautiously we followed the spongy path through the moss-draped trees. I was in the lead, feeling pleasantly spooky, all my senses in touch with the rain forest. I half-expected a grizzly to come bounding out of the leafy forbs and fruit-bearing shrubs. Long brown guard hairs—griz hairs—clung to low branches that had fallen across the trail. The place had a faint odor of rotting fish. I unsnapped the holster sheathing my revolver in case we needed to make a loud noise in a hurry.

We climbed steadily up the overgrown switchbacks, topping out at an elevation of 350 feet. My trepidation melted away at the sight of Nooya Lake. Nestled in a U-shaped valley, a positive indication of erosion through glaciation, the two-mile-long lake looked as perfect and pure as if it were newly created. With binoculars I searched the alpine tundra on the mountain slopes and a muskeg clearing at the lake's far end. All was perfect habitat for a variety of big animals, including bear. After the suspense of the hike, I was disappointed that we saw none.

Our final camp in Rudyerd Bay was in an enormous, rock-hewed amphitheater named Punchbowl Cove. On one side was a smooth-faced Yosemite "Half Dome" brimming with waterfalls, and the rest of the cove was a panorama of spruce-tipped ridgetops.

Thus far we had seen only a few sailboats cruising into Rudyerd Bay in the afternoons. But since no suitable anchorages exist, they all left well before nightfall. We were surprised therefore to encounter a small cabin cruiser anchored at the far end of Punchbowl Cove, about a mile from our camp. The next day we learned that the motorboat served as a floating base for a Forest Service trail crew, stationed in Misty Fjords National Monument for the summer. We bumped into the crew while hiking on a trail they were improving that led toward Punchbowl Lake. The group, younger than we, consisted of one full-time Forest Service employee and three seasonal volunteers working for room and board. Taking a break from their laborious, dirty task, they told us they had arrived in Punchbowl Cove a month earlier and that they hadn't seen many kayakers.

"You're invited to come aboard for dinner tonight," the trail boss said, wiping the mud from his pick-axe. "We'd be interested to hear more about your trip."

I was hesitant to say yes. Not that I'm totally antisocial, but we were in the wilderness to be away from people. This was the first time I'd been invited to a party under such unusual circumstances and I couldn't imagine how six of us could enjoy dinner on their tiny boat. It sounded novel, though, and we agreed to go.

"Terrific," the trail boss said. "Come over around five-ish."

We returned to the tent to get "dressed-up" for dinner. I changed into my cleanest clothes, garments I would be embar-

Judy Bradford in the fog at Punchbowl Cove, an offshoot of Rudyerd Bay.

rassed to take to a public laundromat. I recoiled, shaking my head at the odor. "Those guys really must be desperate for conversation to ask us to dinner."

"Yeah, I just hope it's not too warm on the boat," Judy said, brushing her teeth. "The fewer layers, the more unpleasant it is."

That evening we and the trail crew huddled inside the boat's cozy cabin, listening to raindrops drum on the wooden roof. Peals of laughter occasionally drowned out all other noise. Sometimes while traveling there is an instant connection among strangers. By the time dinner was served, I felt as if I had known these guys for years. The cook, a native Alaskan who grew up in a village near Ketchikan, doted over us like a Jewish mother. "Anyone who spends two weeks in the backcountry must be starving for real food," he pronounced. He was right. Fish and crab cake hors d'oeuvres were followed by chicken cacciatore and spaghetti entrees, steaming hot off the two-burner Coleman camp stove. Side dishes included mounds of boiled potatoes, hot garlic bread and fresh green beans.

"I'd better quit eating," I protested, as I grabbed a batch of homemade chocolate chip cookies passed around for dessert.

"Just one more course," the cook implored, his face creased by a mischievous grin. He stepped out of the cabin for a moment and pulled back a tarp. "Ta daaa!" A big round watermelon appeared.

"We got resupplied by floatplane a few days ago."

Late at night, when the rain stopped, we bid goodnight to our new friends, thanking them for their hospitality and the terrific meal. In the murky twilight we paddled back to our camp in the forest, the only light coming from a waxing half moon that shined through a slit in the clouds. The stillness of the cove was overwhelming in contrast to the gaiety aboard the cabin cruiser. Our solitude was emphasized. We couldn't have felt more content.

We caught the 6:37 a.m. ebb tide, slipping silently out of Punchbowl Cove before signs of life appeared on the Forest Service boat. The sky was bright and clear; only a few fat clouds remained from yesterday's torrential rain. There wasn't a shred of wind as we left Rudyerd Bay and rounded the corner onto Behm Canal. The kayak sliced through the surface, leaving a long, trailing V in its wake. We were seven miles from Winstanley Island, our rendezvous point with the floatplane. No sense rushing it, not with this weather. Our pilot wasn't due until the following day.

I set my paddle down and reflected on how special this trip to Alaska was. But then they all seemed to be. When I thought of other Alaska journeys Judy and I had shared, a kaleidoscope of vivid recollections came rushing forth. The mental imagery filled me with a warm glow. Each journey was an expanding circle that solidified our love for the wilderness and our commitment to each other. There were the wildlife, the country, the characters we'd met. I felt a sense of pride that we had planned and executed these trips ourselves.

I picked up the paddle and sliced a spoonblade into the water. The boat lurched forward. Rudyerd Bay and one more memory for my kaleidoscope passed astern.

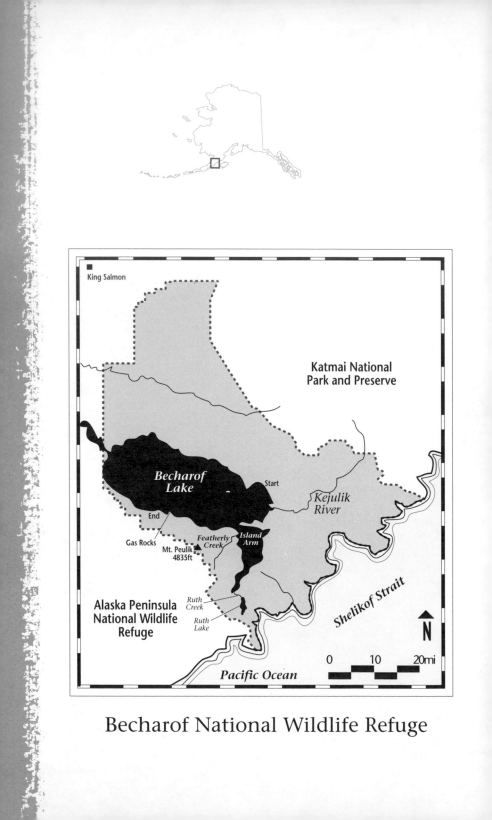

Becharof National Wildlife Refuge

THE
BROWN
BEARS
OF
BECHAROF

SPECIES: *URSUS ARCTOS*, THE Alaska brown/grizzly bear, coastal variety. *Range*: found along the coast from the Alaska Peninsula southeastward to southernmost Alaska, and on some adjacent islands. *Color*: generally some shade of brown, though may be black, pale blond or yellow. *Size*: the largest living carnivorous land mammal in the world. Large individuals may grow to between nine and ten feet, stand more than four feet at the shoulders and weigh as much as 1,500 pounds; most bears, though, are much smaller. *Senses*: hearing and smell are excellent; eyesight is good. *Food*: consumes a wide range of animals and plants, depending on areas and seasons. *Behavior*: unpredictable. Normally shy and retiring but can be aggressive. Normally, at least one fatal brown/grizzly attack on human beings occurs each year in Alaska.

Clyde Vicary, a thirty-one-year-old mail carrier from Peoria, Illinois, sat in the floatplane's crowded rear seat while I kept the pilot company up front. Clyde is a seasoned wilderness traveler and superb athlete; there are few people I would rather have been with in a tight situation outdoors. However, not only was this his first trip to Alaska, but until now he had seen only one grizzly bear: a rather aggressive individual in Canada's Jasper National Park that chased him up a tree.

Unlike Clyde, I had made ten previous journeys to Alaska's backcountry, during which I had seen well over a hundred grizzly bears. But like my friend, I was apprehensive about what lay ahead. We would soon be starting a paddling trip into Becharof National Wildlife Refuge, a vast, lonely expanse on the Alaska Peninsula, dubbed by one Alaska wildlife biologist as the "brown bear capital of the world."

An hour after leaving King Salmon, an isolated bush town 300 air miles southwest of Anchorage, we sighted our first bear during the final approach to the lake. A good-sized specimen, rippling with muscles under a ruglike brown coat, stood belly deep in lush green grass near where we planned to land. Hearing the floatplane's roar, the grizzly glanced up as the single-engine Cessna 206 streaked past. We must have passed too close. Defiantly, the bear reared up and swatted the air as if trying to knock a pesky mosquito out of the sky.

"You see that?" Denny, our pilot, yelled above the airplane's drone. "That griz is bad!" I swiveled in my seat and caught Clyde's eye. He looked a little pale. I wondered if he was thinking what I was thinking: maybe we should call this whole thing off and ask the pilot to turn the plane around.

Too late. The aircraft banked sharply and suddenly my stomach was in my mouth. We dropped a quick 500 feet. The stall-warning buzzer blared as we skimmed the water. The Cessna shuddered. Splash. Touchdown was perfect. Denny taxied to the sloping beach and cut the engine. An old hand at bush flying, he was nevertheless nervous about the weather—a fog had started to settle over the lake. He instructed us to unload without delay. Forming a human chain, we tossed the gear out of the tiny baggage compartment and lugged it through the shallow water to shore.

Denny then darted around the airplane like an excited bumblebee, pumping out the floats, checking fuel levels, examining rudder cables. Within minutes after landing, he was ready to depart. "I doubt you'll be seeing anyone else out here," he said, stepping onto the aluminum float. "If there's anything you forgot, now's your chance to let me know."

I stared at the disorganized pile of equipment at our feet. Kayak bags. Tent. Sleeping bags. Clothes. Pots and stove. Food. We had enough junk to outfit a troop of Boy Scouts. "I think we'll be all right," I shrugged. "Even if we did forget something, I don't think we'd have any room to carry it."

"Okay, then. I'm out of here. Have fun."

He climbed into the cockpit, slammed tight the door, and gunned the motor. The bright red Cessna picked up speed and after a short taxi rose easily off the lake. Circling once, Denny returned to the simple comforts of King Salmon, leaving us gazing after him, alone on our gravel bar.

The din of the motor soon faded. The silence became deafening. We moved sluggishly, still decompressing from the whiplash of modern-day travel now that our umbilical cord to civilization had been severed. The day before we were in muggy central Illinois on the way to Chicago's frenetic O'Hare Airport. Twenty-four hours later we were wearing long underwear and pile jackets in one of Alaska's wildest areas, with a hundred miles of elbow room in all directions.

Becharof National Wildlife Refuge, located in the northeastern section of the Alaska Peninsula between Katmai National Park and Preserve on the north and the Alaska Peninsula National Wildlife Refuge on the south, is one of the newest, largest and least explored units in the National Wildlife Refuge System. Established in 1980, the refuge comprises over 1.2 million acres, an area slightly larger than the state of Delaware. Within its borders lie a variety of landscapes, including tundra-covered hills and plains, lakes and wetlands, volcanic peaks and seaside cliffs.

The cliffs, bays and poorly drained lowlands of Becharof Refuge provide excellent habitat for sea birds, raptors, waterfowl and shorebirds. Millions of birds use the refuge primarily as a staging area during migrations to and from nesting grounds in the Arctic. The refuge also contains important habitat for scores of mammals. Marine species such as harbor seals, Steller's sea lions, northern fur seals, walruses and sea otters often use the Pacific coastline of the refuge, while on land thirty species are known to be present including brown (grizzly) bear, moose, caribou, wolverine, red fox and wolf.

The centerpiece of the refuge is Becharof Lake, named for a Russian navy navigator stationed at Kodiak Island in 1788. By the late eighteenth century, Russian fur traders seeking otter pelts had established settlements and camps up and down the Alaska Peninsula. Although it is likely that people were on refuge lands as early as 7000 B.C., the Peter Korsakovskii expedition in 1818 was the first well-documented case of Europeans reaching Becharof Lake. They crossed through the area in search of an old Russian settlement and any fur-bearing animals they could find.

Fifteen miles wide and thirty-seven miles long, Becharof is the second largest lake in Alaska; only Lake Iliamna to the northeast is bigger. The lake and its tributary streams provide important habitat for the Bristol Bay salmon fisheries and for hundreds of brown bear. Surprisingly, very little is known about the lake; its depth is uncertain and hydrological studies are still incomplete. My initial idea to paddle Becharof was met with some skepticism by the refuge staff. They were unaware of anyone else undertaking a self-propelled boating and camping trip into Becharof's interior, at least in modern times. With notoriously rotten weather, a lake that can erupt in whitecaps without warning, and, as one King Salmon sourdough put it, "a bear behind every bush," our planned eighty-mile kayak trip along Becharof Lake's south shore promised us an interesting vacation. The refuge manager cleared our plans when he was certain we understood the risks.

While I assembled the Klepper kayak, Clyde organized our considerable equipment. It was all lightweight backpacking-type gear, including prepackaged plastic-bagged food, but it was a puzzle how so much stuff, not to mention two six-foot-tall men, could fit inside a boat that is seventeen feet long, two feet wide, and shaped like a submarine.

The kayak was ready to go and partially loaded when I noticed movement down the beach. Out of a clump of tall grass two reddish-brown grizzly bears emerged, ambling our way. "We've got visitors," I warned Clyde, pointing to the interlopers. "Probably part of the Becharof welcoming committee."

My partner was not amused. "We've been here, what, a half-hour, and already we're shit-deep in bears! This is going to be one helluva trip."

That was the extent of our conversation, as the bears were picking up their pace. We hurriedly threw what we could into the boat and paddled offshore. The grassy tundra offered no protection.

Bobbing in the kayak, we suddenly realized that most of our food was still on shore in nylon stuff sacks. I thought Clyde had thrown it in the boat; he thought I had. As the bears sniffed the air, I pondered what it would be like going hungry for the duration of our trip. I could probably catch enough fish with my emergency line and lures to ensure survival, but Clyde, a confirmed vegetarian, would have a more difficult time. Lean and muscular without a single ounce of fat to spare, he once told me he would rather starve than eat meat. I hoped he wouldn't be put to the test.

When the bears got uncomfortably close to our gear, we contemplated how best to frighten them off. We were packing Clyde's .44 magnum revolver and my .357, but we preferred not to fire a warning shot unless there was no choice. There were other, less disruptive techniques to try first.

Our bear repellent arsenal was three-pronged. First we tried loud yelling; the bears reacted as if they were deaf. Next we waved our arms and paddles; they continued toward the bags. As a last-ditch effort we employed Plan Three. Like street-corner Hare Krishna, we banged together cooking pots and cups as if they were tambourines. The tinny clatter did the trick. The grizzlies stopped at the water's edge, looked quizzically at us, then strolled off the beach into the brush. I felt guilty scaring the animals; they belonged on this strip of beach more than we did—but my instinct for self-preservation was stronger than my guilt.

We returned for our gear and haphazardly jammed it under the deck. We were tired, it was late, and a steady rain had begun to fall. Swirling mist obscured the surrounding mountains halfway up their slopes. At least there was plenty of light left: at eight o'clock, dusk was still several hours away.

We pitched the tent on a patch of dry, lumpy tundra, the best site available among the cottongrass and tussocks. As soon as we had thrown our clothes and sleeping bags inside, we got started on dinner. We hadn't eaten since morning and were famished. Drawing water from the lake, I waited patiently for the two quarts to boil. My meal tonight (and every night) would begin with soup and a bagel and cheese, followed by a bag of reconstituted Minute Rice, freeze-dried vegetables and oriental noodles. Clyde had a more Spartan diet of uncooked grains, raw carrots and green sprouts that he had nurtured from seeds—rabbit food, I called it. He needed hot water only for tomato soup.

Soup was on when Clyde gestured to some large, dark shapes lurking in the foothills beyond camp. Moose? Caribou? Bear? I put down the cup and got out my binoculars to confirm the identification. Instantly I lost my appetite. On ridge tops, on hillsides, in meadows and alder thickets, grizzlies were everywhere! Sows with offspring wandered through grassy clearings, wary of big adult males, which sometimes kill cubs. Other bears, both solitary and paired, grazed on the tundra like contented cows. And scanning more closely, I discerned still more furry creatures curled up on the tundra taking a snooze. We each counted the number of bears within view. Clyde finished first.

"How many you got?" Clyde asked.

"Not done yet, give me another minute."

Finally, my tally completed, I looked at Clyde. He looked at me. I had sighted nineteen bears, he came up with twenty.

"No way," Clyde said. "That's too many. We probably counted bears twice. Let's do it again." Methodically scanning from left to right, our total this time was twenty-one.

It was a very long night in the tent. A rustle of fabric—"Larry, do you hear that?" A low moan—"Clyde, is that you?" Ominous shadows flickered outside the nylon walls in the subarctic half-light.

Sunrise ushered in scuddy clouds and gusty winds, typical August weather in these parts. Nasty whitecaps and swells adorned Becharof Lake. Like it or not, there would be no paddling today. We wiled away the hours reading books, hiking the beach and watching loons, cormorants, scaups and mergansers surf the waves. We saw only a few bears. The foothills were empty. Somehow the bruins had disappeared like phantoms despite their size. The only other large mammal we observed all day was a magnificent bull caribou. Sporting enormous velvety antlers, the bold animal trotted right through camp on his way to some distant herd.

During the layover, with ample time to talk, Clyde and I reminisced about the set of circumstances which had brought us together in such an unusual place. Feelings flowed freely, based on a trust built up during a number of shared backcountry trips. Still, there were many things about Clyde I didn't know. Over cups of steaming tomato soup, ever-watchful for bears, we talked.

I met Clyde while he was working at a Peoria backpacking store where I previously had worked part time. We hit it off immediately, both kindred spirits in our appreciation for wild places. Soon we were sharing canoeing, backpacking and cross-country skiing adventures a couple of weeks each year. Now, with a new job as a U.S. mail carrier, Clyde finally had the funds to travel north to Alaska, a place he had wanted to visit for a long time.

The following day we got a break. Rain and low clouds still lingered, but at least the wind had decreased to a manageable breeze. Taking down the soggy tent, we packed the boat by trial and error, stuffing things in nooks and crannies until everything was securely stowed under the deck. Clyde took the bow, I squeezed into the stern. It felt good to be on the move, heading for someplace new.

All morning and afternoon we paddled. First we passed the

braided mouth of the Kejulik River, a stream with headwaters in Katmai National Park and Preserve to the east. At the river's mouth was a broad sandbar delta that served as a magnet for all types of wildlife. In short order, we saw caribou, river otters, tundra swans, bald eagles, flocks of sandhill cranes, ducks, geese and shorebirds. We scoured the open mudflats for bears, but to our surprise saw none.

Detour or not, we couldn't resist the temptation to explore upstream. We paddled hard against the current, our progress complicated by shallow water and submerged sandbars. We saw virtually no animals along the river's banks. Perhaps it was because of the thick brush. Becharof Refuge lies in a transition zone between forest and tundra plant communities to the north and the generally treeless grass/sedge/low shrub tundra typical of the Alaska Peninsula to the south. The Kejulik watershed is unique in Becharof because of the abundance of tall, spindly cottonwoods and other trees that line the river, whereas in the rest of the refuge only patches of head-high alders are found. We probed upstream until the current became too strong, then spun the boat around and floated swiftly back to the lake.

Seven miles further on we rounded a high-ridged peninsula separating Becharof Lake from a funnel-shaped bay called the Island Arm. Dripping wet from rain, and with cold hands clutching varnished paddles, we slid through the narrow gap and left the big lake behind. Flashing through my mind was the thought of a hot meal and dry sleeping bag.

The Island Arm, with its adjacent coastal mountains and low wetlands, is considered to be among the highest-quality fish and wildlife habitats on the Alaska Peninsula. We were warned to be especially cautious here. Though only fourteen miles long, the Island Arm is the center of Becharof's brown bear activity. During an aerial survey in August of the preceding year, refuge biologists had counted ninety-three bears in this area in a single day. The biologists estimate that 300 to 400 bears concentrate here during salmon spawning season, making this one of the densest populations of brown/grizzly bears in North America.

We had planned to camp near Featherly Creek, a winding tundra stream just inside the Island Arm, but upon reaching it we changed our minds. The ground was lousy with bear sign, and no wonder. Throngs of sockeye salmon were gathered by the creek's mouth waiting to struggle upstream; hundreds more had already spawned in the shallow water and were dead or dying. Even the prodigious appetites of Becharof's bears—animals that routinely consume ninety pounds of food per day—couldn't handle such an abundance.

There was limited daylight left, and the nearest potential camp—a site that we considered "bear-safe"—was a tiny, treeless island a mile offshore. Reaching it was no problem; we were there in twenty minutes. The island was a pleasant spot, with a convenient place near the water to pitch the tent and a small hillock to climb, but when a storm swept in from the Pacific Ocean that evening, bringing with it boat-swamping whitecaps and driving rain, there were other places we would have rather been than on an acre-sized patch of grass.

The tent whipped furiously the entire night, and the next morning's weather was no better. Gale-force winds raked the Island Arm, driving streaming waves onto our island sanctuary. Our dome tent was strong, but not that strong. We tied it to the kayak for ballast, pegged out extra guy lines and drew the rain fly tight around the windows and the doorway. Numbed by the sound of flailing nylon and unable to sleep, we hunkered down the best we could. We read and talked. When this got old, there was always a quick walk outside to wake us up. Alaska Peninsula storms can last for days, up to a week. How long our internment would last was anybody's guess.

During sporadic lulls in the gale, we prowled our prison and learned a few things about Becharof Lake we might otherwise have missed. Apparently caribou and fox don't mind swimming to islands on a regular basis; their fresh spoor littered the shoreline. Also, when Clyde located an old set of grizzly tracks near camp, it became clear that our island was not the sanctuary we thought it. Recent research has revealed that Becharof's bears routinely visit islands in the Island Arm. What's more, the bears also use the islands for denning during the winter, a highly unusual behavioral trait because Alaska's grizzlies normally den on mountain slopes above a thousand feet, not on a lake only a few feet above sea level.

After three nights the storm finally abated. Like paroled prisoners, we were free to leave. After stuffing the kayak, we cleaned camp. Except for some flattened grass and foottracks in the sand, no trace of our stay remained.

A calm lake and clearing skies boosted our morale even further. Through the parting clouds we received our first glimpse of the snow-covered crown of Mount Peulik to the west. Called "Smoky Mountain" by the native Aleuts in honor of its 1814 eruption, the

4,395-foot volcanic summit is the highest point in the refuge, and, in our opinion, its most spectacular. Before I could focus my camera, though, a curtain of low, drizzly clouds rolled in and the mountain disappeared. Forgetting about pictures, we eased into a steady rhythm of paddling. Our goal was to reach the head of the Island Arm, eleven miles away, by dusk.

During the first few hours as we skirted the shoreline we counted a half-dozen bears patrolling the beach. Despite the threat they embodied, it was good to see grizzlies again. We swung wide so we could study them without intruding. The circumstances brought back vivid memories. I told Clyde about how Judy and I had floated off Margot Creek in Katmai National Park—my first paddle trip to Alaska—inconspicuously observing bears as we were doing now. It was as if I were talking about something that had happened yesterday, so clear were my recollections.

Eventually, though, we had to pull over to eat lunch. As was our custom, we conducted a quick reconnaissance of the beach to see what had been there before. It didn't take long to determine that two grizzlies had exited dripping wet from the lake minutes earlier. Their soggy tracks on the hard sand told the whole story. I never believed much in a "sixth sense" or premonitions, but a little voice in my head warned me that the bears were still around. Clyde had already moved toward the boat. A slight rattle in the bushes was all it took for us to forget about lunch and move on.

Our reprieve from the wind lasted until late afternoon. A southerly breeze grew in intensity, and before long we were in a familiar duel with roller-coaster waves and stinging rain. Fortunately, we did not have far to go. Tired, stiff and damp from sweat and spray, we were elated to slip into a protected cove opposite the mouth of Ruth Creek. Directly to the south lay the Aleutian Range. It was the closest we had been to these coastal mountains thus far. Although only 3,000 to 4,000 feet high, the rugged, snow-stippled slopes seemed much taller than they actually are. The terrain was inviting, far better in life than in the photographs I had seen on the refuge office's wall. Ruth Creek lies in the heart of a 447,000-acre designated wilderness area within the refuge, where protection of the landscape is federally assured. Seeking solace in Alaska's backcountry, I was tempted to journey no further on this trip. Whatever else we saw in Becharof couldn't be much better.

There was, however, an incongruity with the wilderness classification. A hundred yards from our newly established camp, a dilapidated wooden cabin with a caved-in roof protruded from the knee-high greenery. Poking around inside the leaning structure, we found yellowed and tattered magazines from the early 1970s, a few spent 30-06 rifle casings and the usual cabin junk such as old leather boots, empty whiskey bottles and opened tins of food. The cabin was one of about a dozen built by hunters and trappers long before the refuge was established. All are now slowly crumbling from neglect and decay. Some Alaskans contend that bush cabins should be maintained for emergency use, even in federally designated wilderness areas, and are pressuring the management agencies to repair the structures. While in certain situations that rationale may be legitimate, in most cases backcountry cabins are used less for emergencies and more often than not for hunting and fishing camps—activities that are still permitted within Becharof and most other Alaska wildlife refuges. This particular cabin was of interest to us for the memorabilia it contained, but the image of fly-in hunters shooting grizzlies and caribou from its front porch made us hope that it would never be used again.

We luxuriated in the knowledge that we didn't have to move camp for the next three days. There was no need to get up at first light. No stuffing a wet tent and damp sleeping bags. No packing the kayak. No fretting about whitecaps or wind. We could wake up when we wished. We could have leisurely breakfasts. It might even be possible to indulge in second cups of hot tea to ward off the morning chill. The layover would give us the opportunity to become intimate with Ruth Creek and its environs.

Gushing out of Ruth Lake, the second largest lake in Becharof Refuge, with a surface area of 1,000 acres, Ruth Creek's three-mile length is all high-caliber salmon habitat. Its bottom is clean sand and gravel, and its waters—shin-deep, cold and clear—are sprinkled with riffles and pools. As it was mid-August, the time of the peak of the sockeye run, we found the creek choked with breeding salmon. Silver-humped backs protruded above the water as the fishes writhed and wriggled upstream to ancestral spawning beds.

The commercial value and ecological importance of sockeye salmon make it the most important fish species in the refuge. The sockeye run in Becharof Refuge varies in size from two million to six million fish, making it the largest in the world. Biologists at the Alaska Department of Fish and Game estimate that nearly one million adult sockeye return to Becharof Lake annually. Eighty-five percent of the spawning occurs in the Island Arm. The fry (young salmon) typically spend two years in Becharof Lake, feeding on zooplankton, before migrating to sea as smolts in early May to mid-

June. They spend two to three years in the Bering Sea and northern Pacific Ocean before returning to fresh water to spawn.

Fish-eating scavengers were plentiful along the creek. From camp we observed river otters, ravens, bald eagles, gulls and more bears. Our guess was that we had about twenty-five grizzlies for neighbors. A Becharof kayak trip was something we both had wanted to do, and thus far our experiences had exceeded our expectations, but when a dozen bears appeared simultaneously within a few hundred yards of the tent, we freely admitted that what we were doing bordered on the absurd. Watching the brawny animals fish and bulldoze the tundra in search of ground squirrels, I was reminded of a television documentary on great white sharks I had seen a few years before. A pair of scuba divers, tethered to their support boat in a protective cage, were surrounded by the formidable beasts. The men resembled scrawny little dolls compared to the sharks. I mentioned the program to Clyde. "Yeah, I saw it too," he said nervously, looking left to right to keep all the bears in view. "Right now I wish I was in that metal-barred cage they used."

In spite of our close proximity, we—the bears and Clyde and I—usually managed to keep out of each other's way. During day hikes up to Ruth Lake and the foothills behind camp, we walked slowly and stopped often to scan the countryside. We saw many bears before they saw us, but, as a veteran Alaskan bear biologist once told me, "Don't fool yourself; for every bear you see, there's probably two more you've missed. Grizzlies are among the most sly and secretive of animals. That, plus their strength and unpredictability makes them so dangerous."

While hiking a ridge above Ruth Creek, a route that we had taken earlier in the day, we broke a cardinal rule we had set for ourselves in Becharof: no matter how familiar the route is, never let down our guard. Only by sheer, stupid luck did we manage to avoid walking right into a nest of bears—a sow with nursing cubs. The animals were hidden by knee-high grass and alders, and we didn't spot them until we were only a few paces away. Our savior was the wind. Because a strong breeze was blowing from them to us, carrying our scent and sound away, they never did know we were so close.

Shell-shocked from seeing so many bears, we were glad the next morning to be inside the tent, waiting out a morning rain. It felt nice just to lie in our sleeping bags, dry, snug and secure.

Secure?

When I heard a slight scuffling sound outside I didn't pay much attention—probably the river otter we had spotted earlier or another porcupine bumbling through the grass. But as the noise grew louder I grew more uneasy. Slowly, I unzipped the tent door to take a peek. Gawd! Only a few feet away loomed a brown bear three times the size of Hulk Hogan with a face more frightening than Mr. T's. When a pair of tiny squabbling cubs popped up over the bank, I felt as if I had just stepped into my worst nightmare.

I sucked in a deep breath and managed to squeak, "Buh-bear," to Clyde, who was still blissfully unaware of the danger outside. Those whispered syllables created a high-voltage chain reaction as terrifying as a tornado. The mother grizzly coughed a command to her cubs. Instantly they scampered to her side. I became lightheaded, certain the animal was going to charge. But the sow, herding her cubs before her, roared past the tent instead of through it.

Too stunned to move at first, we gathered the courage to peer out the door. The bears were already on a distant knoll and lumbering away at a steady lope. Flooded with relief, I collapsed back inside the tent.

"You all right?" Clyde asked. Glassy-eyed and grinning, I knew I must look demented, but from where I sat Clyde appeared even more bizarre. Standing outside barefoot in red-and-white-striped long underwear, with his shoulder-length red hair and beard blowing in the wind and a long-barreled .44 magnum in his hand, Clyde looked like Charlton Heston's Moses or Clint Eastwood's Dirty Harry. What really had me worried, though, was the way in which he gazed skyward as if searching for something. Bear-a-noia strikes again.

On a cool, dark morning, with clouds so low they actually scraped the ground, we left Ruth Creek and proceeded north along the east shore of the Island Arm. For two days we weaved through the archipelago, taking advantage of the bay's many isles to avoid the worst of the wind and waves. Conditions remained dreary, with continual showers and temperatures in the mid-forties, roughly the same temperature it had been throughout our trip, day or night. The hypothermic weather was not pleasant, yet neither of us was cold. With bodies encased in polypropylene underwear, pile pants and jackets, rain gear and rubber boots, and further protected from the waist down by the kayak's sprayskirt, we remained fairly comfortable even in a snow shower.

Ultimately we rounded the peninsula and reentered the main body of Becharof Lake. After having been confined to the Island Arm for more than a week, the vast sheet of green water looked to us like an inland ocean. Twenty-five miles away, toward the west, loomed the Gas Rocks, rising abruptly about 600 feet above the heath-coated dunes and knolls of the Becharof plain. These knobby tripeaked cinder cones would serve as a reliable landmark in all but the most rotten weather, which was good because in four days we were supposed to rendezvous with the floatplane on their far side.

According to the map there were no major watercourses along this final stretch, just insignificant little creeks represented by squiggly blue lines. We expected to spot a wandering brown bear or two, but nowhere near the number of grizzlies we had already seen. Just as well, I thought. Bears had occupied my mind ever since planning this trip a year earlier, and now with the end in sight, I was ready to let down my guard a little and take it slow and easy.

I never told Clyde this, but several times prior to leaving home I had been troubled by nightmares. They all had the disquieting theme of me being chased or mauled by a grizzly bear. Usually I would escape—these dreams weren't too bad—however, sometimes the bear would catch up and pin me down. Straddled by the half-ton animal, nearly suffocated by its hot, stinking breath, I would watch in slow-motion dread as the grizzly's dagger-like canines bore down onto my head. Mercifully, just before the moment of searing pain, I would always awake in a cold sweat. Strange stuff, these dreams, considering that since arriving in Becharof, with real bears everywhere, I had had no nightmares. My only explanation is that after taking the necessary precautions, such as never eating near the tent and storing food away from our camp, whatever happened was out of my hands. Perhaps my fatalistic attitude was naïve, but I felt that if I was destined to be attacked while sleeping, there was no point in worrying about it. That, plus knowing Clyde always slept with one eye open and his gun near his head, helped get me through the night.

When we cruised past the first of the blue lines on the map, it became apparent that our trip to the Gas Rocks wouldn't be as peaceful as we had anticipated. Hundreds of gulls, squawking and fighting over scraps of food, indicated that a lot of dead fish were in the vicinity. We paddled closer to investigate, to see if our assumption was correct.

When still a quarter-mile offshore, we noticed a number of animals among the low bushes bordering the lake. I kept the boat on course while Clyde exchanged his paddle for binoculars. A gasp emanated from my partner's lips. "Oh, man, you won't believe this!" "Tell me anyway," I insisted. "There's four—no, wait—make that seven griz near that creek."

I snapped up my binoculars. He was right: There were bears on the bank, on shore and in the water up to their necks. No wonder so many gulls were around.

"Let's get closer," I suggested after the initial shock. Clyde stared at me as if I were crazy. He didn't budge. "C'mon, Clyde. It's the best chance we've had yet to get bear photos, and as long as we're in the boat there won't be any risk."

By the time we were within telephoto range, all the grizzlies were at the water's edge trying to snare a salmon for supper. Because the creek was only inches deep—not nearly deep enough for salmon to swim upstream—the fish were forced to spawn in the lake bed near shore. For the bears, it was as easy as scooping goldfish out of a glass bowl. Judging from the stacks of fish carcasses that lined the shore, they had been gorging on salmon for weeks.

As we drifted slowly toward the beach, paddles pulled in and cameras clicking, a curious thing occurred: it was obvious the bears saw, heard and certainly smelled us, but they didn't act frightened or aggressive. Far from being the bloodthirsty beasts often por-trayed in the "hook-and-bullet" press, these grizzlies were posi-tively placid. Even when Clyde and I conversed in a normal tone of voice and paddled a few strokes to maintain the boat's position, the animals paid us no more attention than they would have a piece of floating driftwood. However, every neighborhood has its bully, and this block of bears was no exception.

We had gone through a couple rolls of film, when, as if on cue, all the animals began to act uneasy. One by one, they swung their long-snouted heads into the wind, sniffed, snorted and shuffled away. A moment later we learned the cause of their concern: one of the largest bears I had ever seen swaggered over the bank like a regal king.

Unlike the others, this scar-faced old boar did notice us. To him, we were trespassers, other creatures imposing on his territory. Foul-tempered and mad at the world, the bear paced back and forth while uttering a throaty warning growl. When this intimidation didn't work, he slid down the sand bank and really began to strut his stuff. Most of his tricks I had seen before. The one I hadn't, and which was definitely the bear's most effective display, involved rearing up on hind legs, manwalking to the lake's edge and dropping back down with a huff.

Clyde checked the water depth. By now, pushed landward by the breeze, we were close enough for me to replace my telephoto

An agitated grizzly bear approaches Clyde Vicary and Larry Rice, who are a short distance offshore in their kayak.

with a wide-angle camera lens. "About four feet," he reported, pulling up his kayak paddle.

"We're okay," I replied. "If that old geezer wants us he'll have to swim."

During the ensuing minutes, the grizzly continued to make more half-hearted charges into the shallows. We were safe in the deeper water, but I shuddered to think what might have happened if we had been on land instead. As we prepared to leave, the animal did something quite extraordinary. With massive head held high and blackish lips curled back, the grizzly waded into the lake—up to his knees, then to his neck. Flabbergasted, it took me a second to react. "Damn! He's swimming after us!" I sputtered. "Let's get out of here!"

With a flurry of motion, we dropped our cameras into our laps, snatched the paddles and churned the water like a Mississippi River paddlewheeler in full reverse. The amphibious grizzly stopped advancing. I wasn't surprised. From his perspective, we must have looked like easy prey that had metamorphosed into a water-spouting sea monster. Making an abrupt U-turn, he broke off the attack and returned to shore.

If we had been hiking the next few hours rather than kayaking, our nerves would have been shot. We passed ten more streams, each narrow enough to jump across, each with salmon around their outlets where they were joined by noisy gulls and satiated bears. As before, the majority of the animals were nonchalant about our presence; some grizzlies reared up to get a better look at us, but most just stared, then continued whatever they had been doing.

Only once more were we charged. Paddling a few yards offshore, we noticed a chocolate-brown grizzly glaring at us from the far end of the beach, its coarse neck and shoulder hairs bristling. Suddenly the bear barreled toward us at a full gallop. Gravel flew as it screeched to a stop at the water's edge. A display of teeth-clacking and grunting convinced us this character wasn't bluffing.

"This isn't good," Clyde said.

"Not good at all," I agreed.

We quickly retreated into the solitude of the lake.

The Gas Rocks were still five miles away when we decided to camp for the night. We chose the most open spot we could find, hoping to minimize the chance of a bear surprise. There are no trees in Becharof in which to hang food, so as always, we stored our plastic-wrapped victuals in waterproof bags and cached them in separate spots well away from the tent.

Until now the weather had been decidedly Aleutian—that is wet, windy and wild; altogether we had seen sunshine and clear skies for less than an hour. Thus we were thrilled when the thick mass of cheerless clouds split apart, revealing Mount Peulik, five miles to the south. In the planning stage of our trip we had considered climbing Mount Peulik, but seeing it now we laughed at our folly. Bathed in soft yellow light, the mountain's broad base was cloaked with a green band of alders that merged into snow- and ice-covered slopes. Above was the glistening, dome-shaped summit. Even with perfect weather, which, of course, is out of the question on the Alaska Peninsula, an ascent of Mount Peulik would require heroic efforts.

The sun transformed the countryside. Becharof Lake sparkled green to blue to gold as light beams danced across its ruffled surface. The tundra, a composite of herbs, grasses and sedges rooted in lichens and mosses, glittered with complex hues. We hastily spread out damp clothes and sleeping bags, but they hardly had time to dry before another rampart of rain-sodden clouds moved in. Our world turned familiarly gray again.

That evening was among our spookiest. Bears funnelled past camp like commuters at a corner bus stop. I was at the lake filling water bottles when I heard, "Larry! Get over here!" I ran back as fast

Clyde Vicary in a rare sunny moment as he and Larry Rice prepare to set up camp. Snow-stippled Mount Peulik, the tallest peak in Becharof, is in the background.

as I could. When I got there my jaw dropped. Clyde was in a Mexican standoff with a large, honey-colored grizzly bear. Only fifty yards separated them, a span a bear can chew up in seconds. While I rummaged through the kayak for a noise-maker—the revolvers were in the tent—Clyde slowly backed up. The bewildered grizzly took a couple of steps toward us, considered what to do next, then as I was about to blow a whistle—the first noise-maker I could find—it begrudgingly shuffled away. Clyde never went anywhere without his gun, not even to pee, from then on.

We watched the parade of animals until about ten o'clock, when it became too dark to see. In an effort to ward off intruders, before retiring, we beefed up our perimeter defenses. We blocked the tent door with the kayak and paddles and positioned gear bags along the sides. Our "walls" were ridiculous, we acknowledged—Alaska's coastal brown bears are, after all, the largest living carnivorous land mammals in the world—yet our makeshift barricade did make us feel a little more secure. "Kind of like sticking your head in the sand," I mused, as we crawled inside our makeshift fortress.

Midnight. I couldn't sleep. The excitement of the day still hadn't worn off. For distraction, I wrote in my journal. The pages soon bulged with accounts of wildlife we had seen since morning:

twenty bear, six caribou, one porcupine, two red fox, sandhill cranes, bald eagles, cormorants, loons, ducks and geese. I closed my notebook and cut the light. An inky void enveloped the tent. Minutes ticked by. I could hear my heart pounding. With eyes wide open and ears straining for the slightest sound, my neck muscles twitched like stretched rubberbands.

I nudged Clyde. "Hey, you awake?"

He pretended he wasn't, but I knew better.

"Clyde, you awake?" I poked him a little harder.

"Yeah, I am now. What is it?"

"I can't sleep."

"Oh, is that all? I thought you were going to say we have a visitor." To make sure, Clyde unzipped the tent door and peered into the blackness. Nothing peered back, as far as he knew.

Since we were both too wired to sleep, we passed the time telling stories. Figuring that the more boring the story the better—something like counting sheep—I talked about growing up in a Chicago suburb in the early sixties.

"It was life in the white bread lane. My nickname was Butch. Little League baseball was in, so were those awkward dances at the American Legion Hall. Of course, there were other things to do, like go to bar-mitzvahs and take summer vacations with the family. We were, you might say, a typical burb family."

I was just getting warmed up, ready to dive into my high school years, when Clyde begged me to stop. "I can guess the rest. Your dad's name is Ward, your mother's name is June, you have a brother Wally. I bet you even had a best friend called Lumpy." Hmmm, I had to come up with something better next time.

Instead of milk-toast childhood memories, Clyde chose to delve into the macabre; under the circumstances, not exactly what I wanted to hear. He told a tale about a horrific night he once spent in a St. Louis bus station, a grungy place adorned with winos, drug addicts, hookers, pimps, thieves and toughs—a real who's who of losers. "That was one of the most unpleasant nights in my life," he confessed. "But you know what? Tonight is worse."

We both agreed we had never looked forward to morning so much.

It took awhile, but I finally fell into a restless sleep. In the wee hours of the morning, with a shadowy light illuminating the tent, I rolled over and gazed upon a fascinating sight. My foggy brain told me it was someone praying, but when my vision cleared I realized it was Clyde. He was propped up on his elbows and knees with the

.44 magnum in his hands, staring out the tent door.

"Clyde?"

"Yeah?"

"What are you doing?"

"I heard something. Might be a griz."

"How long you been that way, I mean holding the gun?"

"Not long. Maybe about four hours."

Dawn brought with it a new outlook on life. A front was moving in. The sky was patchy blue, the air breezy and chilly. We ate a cold meal of granola and shoved off, feeling much safer in the kayak than we had at the campsite.

The lake was choppy, but not difficult. Churning away with double-bladed paddles, our course set by a foot-operated rudder, we rode gracefully over the moderate waves. We were within two miles of the Gas Rocks when a blast of cold wind hit us in the face. Stronger gusts followed, along with a steepening of waves. We pulled harder with the paddles, yet still lost headway. Surely the waves couldn't get steeper, but they did.

Wham! A gust hit us broadside, nearly tearing the paddle out of my hands.

"What the hell is going on?" Clyde yelled.

"Williwaw!" I shouted. "Tighten your sprayskirt; we're in for a rough ride." Extricating ourselves from this mess wouldn't be fun.

The open bay offered no protection, nowhere to run. There were no coves to shelter us, no islands to hide behind. We bounced through the growing whitecaps. The boat's wooden frame creaked and groaned. Clyde took the brunt of the chest-high swells in the bow. Shielded by his body I was not nearly as wet, but with spray-smeared eyeglasses, I was virtually blind. The williwaw slowed us to a treadmill crawl. Paddling at full power, the final few miles to the Gas Rocks took us four hours.

Not long after we arrived the williwaw faultered and died. Light winds blew across the lake, whereas before they were reaching velocities upward of fifty miles per hour. The irony was not lost on us. We could have avoided a lot of hard work if we had waited out the storm.

We made camp at the base of the promontory, next to a shallow cave where we were able to brew hot drinks protected from the elements. Etched in the sand at the rear of the cave were a multitude of indistinguishable animal tracks. Our eyes darted to the shadows, expecting at least a cave man or a prehistoric sloth to emerge, but we found nothing out of the ordinary.

Renourished and rewarmed, we spent the remainder of the afternoon exploring the Gas Rocks, which draw their name from the fact that they still intermittently emit steam. The Gas Rocks are a bizarre hundred or so hellish acres. A conglomerate of reddish and black rocks that have been fused together by heat and molten lava, weird formations taking the shape of goblins and minarets and hoodoos rise out of the giant cinder block. Some of the rocks have worked loose; near our tent were two truck-sized boulders that had fallen from the 600-foot-high precipice. Other boulders were fastened like big marbles to the cliff sides, needing only a little push to come tumbling down. Little is known about the Gas Rocks, other than that a major volcanic eruption created the cinder hill. At the moment, no steam was rising out of the Gas Rocks' vents, but in the lake near shore were a pair of bubbling cauldrons from a subterranean spring, showing that there was still some life in the conduits below.

Morning greeted us with boiling clouds and spitting rain. The lake was adorned with whitecaps. However, a good night's sleep and a hot breakfast worked wonders; by midafternoon we were ready to go. Our objective was to paddle around the promontory to a semisheltered cove about three miles away. We figured that would be the best location to rendezvous with the plane in two days.

Again the lake did not want to cooperate. Leaving the lee of the Gas Rocks, we were met by a headwind that tried to drive us back. Doubling our paddling cadence, we pushed and pulled, knuckles white from the strain. At 6:30 we reached quiet water. The paddle fell from my hands, released by fingers that were curved in the shape of grappling hooks.

A well-used bear trail ran parallel to the lake where we beached the boat. Dead salmon lay every few feet. The surrounding terrain was open and exposed, covered in ground-hugging vegetation that can resist Becharof's strong winds and cold summer temperatures.

While hauling our gear to shore I heard something just over the bank in a clump of dwarf birches. I ripped off my hood. There it was again, closer. The bushes started trembling.

"Bear!" I shouted.

"Where?" Clyde shouted.

"There!" I pointed to the bushes.

We rushed to the kayak, flopped in and paddled to deep water. We watched and waited for the animal to materialize. When it did, Clyde groaned. "Nice call, Rice. You only took ten years off my life."

My "bear" was a harmless porcupine.

By now the wind was really blowing. Clyde, a skilled windsurfer, estimated the gusts were hitting forty to fifty miles per hour. We had an early dinner and headed for the tent. It was too nasty outside to do anything else. I stripped down to my polypro long underwear, which by now had become a second skin. As usual, Clyde grimaced and pinched his nose until I was securely ensconced in my sleeping bag. I let out a sigh of contentment, oblivious to his histrionics. He, too, hadn't changed long johns since we arrived, but I was polite enough not to say anything.

Our last full day in Becharof began wet and gloomy. We didn't care. This was our only opportunity to examine the Ukinrek Maars (a *maar* is a form of volcanic explosion crater that releases pressure through cracks in the earth), and we weren't about to let a little weather get in the way. Consisting of two volcanic pits in the tundra northwest of Mount Peulik and a mile south of Becharof Lake, the Ukinrek Maars are one of Alaska's most recent volcanically active sites. Their 1977 eruption belched ash into the sky for several weeks.

Human beings might have explored the maars before us, but there was no evidence that they had. Everything about the area suggested the surface of the moon, a terrain more suited to astronauts than mere terrestrial hikers. The ground was wind-scoured, smothered by an unfathomable quantity of black cinders and sloping ash fields ejected during the cataclysmic eruption.

We came upon the smaller crater first. Was it 300, 400 feet across? Fifty, a hundred feet deep? Distances were impossible to measure accurately in a land without scale, but when Clyde stood across the crater from me, he seemed like a speck engulfed in nothingness. The second crater dwarfed the first by comparison, being twice the size in width and considerably deeper. Steep-walled and crumbly, its basin was half-filled with an emerald-green lake. I dared not get too close to the lip: to fall in meant a quick trip to oblivion.

The raw energy necessary to create such explosion pits must have been phenomenal. Underneath the folds of ash and lava are many square miles of once verdant tundra. As always, though, life was slowly returning. Lichens and fungi, the pioneers of the plant world, were scattered throughout the ash fields. Harebells and fireweed added welcome color with their pale blues and fiery reds. Lapland longspurs scratched the cinders for windcast seeds. A lone caribou bull, taking a shortcut to better grazing grounds, passed through the desolation. And even here, a well-worn trail of flat-footed bear tracks encircled each crater rim.

On the way back to camp, we hiked over to a cinder mound overlooking a small tundra stream, the same stream that entered the lake near camp. An unbelievable quantity of dead salmon littered the waters; hundreds more fish were stacked up like cordwood on shore. Here, too, as we had seen in the maars, there was life in the midst of death: thrashing past the rotting carcasses was a steady flow of live salmon heading inland to spawn. Here, too, the largest-looking grizzly of the trip was sitting on its haunches in midstream, so satiated it could hardly move.

We arrived at camp late in the afternoon. The air was very calm. Although it was overcast, there was no rain. I could hear the raucous cries of gulls and the far-away bugling of sandhill cranes. For the first time on this trip the mosquitoes were bad. Dousing ourselves in repellent, we took apart the boat and packed most of our gear. The tent would stay up until last. Tomorrow morning we were expecting to be plucked from Becharof for the trip back to King Salmon.

Clyde and I were ready to leave. We were physically fine, but the constant anxiety over bears the past few weeks had taken its toll. Our next year's Alaska trip, I promised, would be a radical change—we'd be paddling among walruses instead of brown bears.

Clyde mulled that one over. "Rice, sometimes I think you don't want us to grow old."

"Vicary, if we keep doing stuff like this, we'll stay forever young."

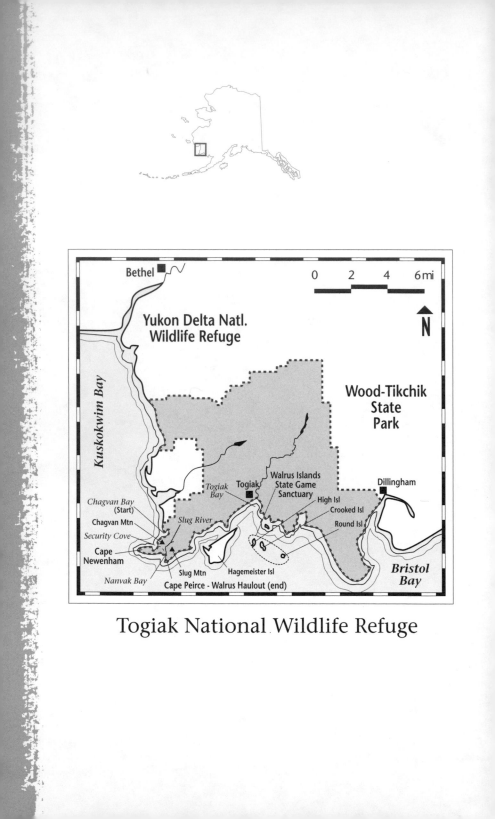

Togiak National Wildlife Refuge

In Search of Togiak's Tuskers

WE WERE THREE MILES AWAY, standing on top of a low, grassy knoll, when we spotted the animals. Through binoculars they resembled a swarm of red ants clustered at the base of the dune-lined beach. Clyde's twenty-power spotting scope made them appear even more surreal, like fat, shapeless maggots that had squirmed out of Bristol Bay. But these were no lowly creatures. They were bull walrus, thousands of them packed tusk to tusk, at one of the largest haulouts for their kind in the arctic and subarctic seas.

With a big smile, Clyde peered through the scope. "This is incredible," he said jubilantly. "They completely cover the beach."

I nudged him aside so I could take another turn at the long-barreled lens. I, too, hadn't been this excited watching wildlife since our days in Becharof among the bears. Squinting with one eye, I tried to estimate the number of walrus, but it was hopeless. "Too bad Mike stayed back at camp, eh? He's never going to believe this."

"He will tomorrow when we kayak over there," Clyde reminded me.

I stood up from the tripod, my back creaking. "*If* we get over there," I sighed. "The way things have been going on this trip, you never know." This journey to Alaska had thus far unfolded rather differently than planned and there was no reason to expect things to change now.

Ten days earlier, Clyde, Mike Peyton and I had stood on the shores of Chagvan Bay, one of several coastal bays that touch Togiak National Wildlife Refuge, a 4.3-million-acre preserve about 400 air miles southwest of Anchorage. We had been dropped off by a Dillingham-based charter pilot, whom we left with instructions to pick us up in two weeks further down the coast. On the day of our arrival, gray, cheerless clouds pressed down on us, and Chagvan Bay, connected to the Bering Sea by a narrow strait, was relatively calm. Only a few feet deep at low tide and protected from ocean waves and pounding surf, Chagvan forms the base of a food chain feeding a variety of wildlife. In the fall hundreds of thousands of ducks and geese would congregate here, attracted by thick beds of eelgrass. But now, in late July, we could see only a few thousand scaup, pintails and scoters that had arrived early on their southerly migration.

Heads bowed to the wind, we followed the sandy beach for a quarter-mile or so to the Bering Sea. Our view of the open ocean was not encouraging. Fully exposed to the prevailing southwesterly winds, whitecaps and big curling waves smashed heavily onto shore.

"We're not going to paddle in that, are we?" Mike asked. He was stroking his beard, something he did only when nervous. An ex-science teacher and Vietnam vet, now self-employed as a carpenter, Mike was an experienced wilderness traveler. This, however, was his first trip to Alaska and was about to be his maiden foray in a sea kayak. I could empathize with his mounting anxiety. My own sea kayaking experience was limited and the fear of high winds and surf was causing my gut to churn.

"No," I finally said, addressing my own doubts as well as Mike's inquiry. "That's too rough for paddling. We could, you know, but there's no need to this early in the game."

The waves grew steeper the longer we watched. The clouds unleashed a cold, dreary rain. We all looked glum, especially me since coming here had been my idea. We had not even unbagged the boats, and already we were intimidated by the elements.

Our route had looked so uncomplicated during that initial planning meeting months ago. Sitting on Mike's living room floor, the three of us had penciled in the course on the map. Starting at

Chagvan Bay, adjacent to Kuskokwim Bay, we would paddle our Kleppers approximately seventy miles to another coastal lagoon on the Bristol Bay side, the site of the walrus haulout. The crux of the journey would be rounding Cape Newenham, a large basalt promontory topped by 2,300-foot Jagged Mountain, which thrusts into the Bering Sea—ten miles of continuous cliffs with no place to land. We had convinced ourselves we had enough kayaking and canoeing experience among us to handle easily a trip of this magnitude. It wasn't very far to paddle and we all were veterans of wilderness travel. The problem was that we didn't possess a critical piece of historical information during that or subsequent meetings that might have altered our plans. Only after the trip was over did we learn that even the Eskimos of the region avoided paddling around Cape Newenham, preferring an overland portage instead.

The days passed at Chagvan Bay as we waited for the weather to improve. Although it irked us to be grounded, we had the opportunity to do a little archaeological sleuthing. Our camp was located near a site referred to as "Igloo Camp Area" on the U.S.G.S. topographic map. The name is derived from the fact that aboriginal people have populated this point of land for at least 2,000 years. At Security Cove, the next beach on our itinerary, there was evidence of human occupancy dating back 4,000 to 5,000 years.

Three different groups of Eskimos lived within the refuge centuries ago. The people residing in the vicinity of Cape Newenham harvested walrus, seals and beluga whales for their meat, blubber and oil. Walrus were also prized for ivory, used in trade and in the manufacture of tools. In addition to the marine mammals, salmon and arctic char were important parts of the Eskimo diet. They took caribou whenever possible, and harvested sea birds and waterfowl for meat, eggs and clothing. Another Eskimo group, the Togiagamiuts, who occupied lands from Chagvan Bay east, probably did not depend as completely on resources of the sea as did most coastal Eskimos. They hunted and gathered sea mammals and other marine resources, but expended considerable effort in pursuit of the caribou and brown bear that roamed Togiak's interior mountains and valleys. The hunters and their families spent winters in villages along the rivers near the coast. In the spring they traveled into the interior and spent several months hunting. In mid-summer the families would return to their villages to harvest salmon, and in the fall they would then go back into the interior to hunt and pick berries. The food thus gathered was generally sufficient to carry them through the coldest winter months, when weather conditions restricted hunting and fishing activities.

Within a half-mile from our camp we saw a number of shallow excavations, pits that had once been laced over by driftwood or whale ribs and covered with sod and skins. The crude shelters would have been cold, dark and musty, but much more practical than our high-tech tents for long-term use in winter.

We rambled past Igloo Camp to investigate the low, smooth hills. Walking was easy across the upland heath. Fierce winds, severe cold and brief summers combine to stunt plant life in much of Togiak; along the coast, not much grows taller than ten or twelve inches. Anchored in a bed of mosses and lichens was a slow-growing mat of crowberry, bearberry, alpine blueberry, dwarf birch and creeping willow. From a thousand-foot high knob we were able to discern features of the landscape we couldn't see from sea level: outcrops of rock poked through grassy tundra curves like elbows through an old sweater; further off, the coastline was a rugged assemblage of volcanic rock cliffs, offshore pinnacles and sand and gravel beaches.

Established by the Alaska Lands Act of 1980, Togiak is one of the largest units in the National Wildlife Refuge System. Though six native villages are found in the vicinity, the refuge is roadless and unpopulated, encompassing an area equivalent in size to the states of Connecticut and Rhode Island. Further protection is afforded Togiak by its neighbors: Yukon Delta National Wildlife Refuge to the north and Wood-Tikchik State Park to the east. Two hundred fifty species of resident and migratory wildlife are found on or adjacent to Togiak refuge. High-quality rivers provide necessary spawning habitat for five species of salmon and other sport fish.

Although the land supports thirty-one species of mammals, including brown and black bear, moose, caribou, red fox, river otter, wolf, lynx and wolverine, Togiak's lagoons, estuaries, wetlands and lakes are heavily used by migrating waterfowl and shorebirds. And in the Cape Peirce–Cape Newenham area, a part of the coast we hoped to see, is one of the largest concentrations of cliff-nesting seabirds on the Alaska mainland. Except for a few ground squirrels and voles, we saw no terrestrial mammals. I was perplexed and especially disheartened that we didn't come across even a single bear track, particularly since brown bear were supposedly the most common big game species in Togiak, and the streams feeding Chagvan Bay teemed with dead and spawning salmon.

"There's griz around here somewhere, count on it," I kept

telling Mike, who was eager to behold his first Alaskan grizzly, not to mention his first caribou, wolverine, et cetera. But when no bears or anything else much larger than a rodent showed from one day to the next, he began to question openly whether all my talk of Alaska wildlife were mere hyperbole.

On the fourth day the tent began to tremble long before sunrise. Rain drummed off the nylon canopy, driven by vicious winds. Staring up at the darkness, I again asked myself why I had planned a *kayak* trip here. Backpacking would have permitted us to explore more of the refuge's interior, without this nagging uncertainty about whether we would reach our destination.

When Clyde and I poked our heads out the door at first light, we knew we were in for a tedious siege. The sky was pewter gray. Even the ducks had left the bay. Normally sheltered Chagvan was wild with whitecaps. Pegged to a flat tundra bench, our tents were fully exposed to the wind. I peered through the rear window to see how Mike was faring. His cone-shaped mountain tent was set up a few yards from us, getting flattened by the crushing gusts.

"Hey, Mike!" I shouted. "You okay?"

"Oh, yeah, I'm doing just great!" came his muffled reply. "My tent's leaking and I'm about to be blown away!"

"Welcome to Alaska!" Clyde yelled.

As the wind increased in velocity we couldn't quite make out Mike's "expletive deleted" reply. But we understood it. After awhile our amusement wore off and Clyde and I sat in the tent, grim faced. With side walls turning inward, our dome tent swayed back and forth as we braced against the aluminum poles to keep them from buckling.

"This storm can't last forever," I muttered, offering brilliant insight into the situation. I wanted to crawl back into my sleeping bag and forget about this wearisome wind. Not a chance of that with Clyde for a tentmate. Every so often, usually after a hard-hitting gust, he would peer outside and announce that the weather was growing worse.

It had been awhile since we last heard from Mike. When I called out, there was no reply. "He can't hear you," Clyde said, himself barely audible over the shuddering rain fly. I unfastened the side window and held the flap open. The rain-soaked tundra was deserted!

Just then I heard Mike outside. "Hurry up. Open the door." When I did so, Mike's dripping face burst inside. "Had to move the tent," he boomed. "I dragged my stuff to that swale near the beach. Everything is a mess, but at least the wind isn't as bad over there."

Not eager to pick up stakes in the driving rain, Clyde and I stuck it out for a few more minutes—until a walloping gust slammed both the tent and us into the floor. "Want some help moving this thing?" Mike offered, appearing again as if summoned by telepathy. We did not need to be asked again. Clyde and I pulled on our boots, fastened our hoods and wriggled out on hands and knees. With all three of us holding onto the wildly flapping tent, we managed to carry and drag it to the shallow dip without becoming airborne.

That evening the rain slackened and the storm died. We gratefully ate a hot meal and discussed whether we should break camp and paddle to Security Cove. It was 7:30; the cove was eight miles away. If we hurried and the weather remained good, we could get there around midnight. After being stuck in the same spot for so long the temptation to get going was strong, but the possibility of making a surf landing in the dark convinced us to stay. We set our watch alarms for 3:30 a.m., hoping the calm would last another day.

Satisfied with our decision, Mike and I straightened up camp in preparation for our early departure. Clyde went off to watch the sunset. He woke me when he returned at midnight. "It was beautiful," he whispered as he slipped into his sleeping bag. "The sun was a bright red ball on the horizon. I think we'll have good paddling in the morning." I thanked him for his report and reminded him that morning had already arrived and we'd better get some rest.

Under cool, pale starlight we broke camp and loaded the kayaks, anxious to get underway. I was feeling better. Maybe we'd round Cape Newenham after all.

By five o'clock we were in the Kleppers—Mike and Clyde sharing my double, and I in a borrowed single—waiting for first light. Just a tinge of red was visible above the horizon. We nudged the boats against the pebbly shore. Cold and damp and not yet fully awake, I closed my eyes and tried to imagine I was somewhere else— somewhere like my bed at home, nestled against Judy's warm body.

I must have nodded off. The next thing I remember is Clyde's voice, saying, "Let's move it." I groggily pushed off and followed Clyde and Mike out to the open sea.

We didn't get far. In our eagerness to leave we had miscalculated a critical point: it is impossible to exit Chagvan Bay's narrow mouth during a flood tide (we learned later that *Chagvan* means "swift water" in Yup'ik Eskimo, referring to the tide rip); furthermore, our tide table book was useless for this stretch of coast. For an hour we tried to muscle through the incoming surge. One moment we were along shore, the next we were fifty feet away struggling to get back to land. Shrouded by the darkness, each boat was in its own disoriented sphere.

We were discouraged as we pulled ashore inside the mouth of the bay. But being delayed at the edge of Kuskokwim Bay had its benefits. Long strings of sea birds skimmed the water as they flew from feeding areas to nesting colonies, and we found Japanese glass floats among the driftwood and flotsam as we explored the beach waiting for the tide to turn. A pack of harbor seals cruised offshore to check us out. And most significantly, we saw our first Pacific walrus, *Odobenus rosmarus divergens*, the "tooth-walker," instantly distinguishable from its relative, the seal, by a pair of tusks that looked like outsized buck teeth.

The big bull exhaled jets of steam while swimming in the shallows near shore. Numerous large bumps, or tubercles, were plainly visible on his thick neck and shoulders, the skin wrinkled like the bark of an old oak. His broad muzzle, festooned with a soup-strainer mustache and many short, heavy bristles, reminded us of a lecherous old man. "That's a mug that only a mother could love," Mike laughed. "Or a barkeep," Clyde added. With his bloodshot, bleary eyes, the walrus did look as if he had guzzled one too many.

Virtually all the walrus found in this region during summer are fully grown males. Female walrus, smaller and generally with shorter tusks, inhabit the Chukchi Sea far to the north, where they give birth on the ice floes and raise their young. In late fall, carried south by the drifting ice pack through the Bering Strait, the females and young are reunited with the males. In winter almost all of the animals dwell in the seasonal icepack of the Bering Sea.

The fellow before us was undoubtedly from one of the major haulouts in Bristol Bay adjacent to Alaska's Bering Sea. The most well known of these is Round Island, a tiny knob of rock managed by the Alaska Department of Fish and Game. The other location that hosts a large percentage of summer bachelors was our destination—sixty miles west of Round Island, near Cape Peirce at the mouth of Nanvak Bay. Walrus have historically hauled out at Cape Peirce, but the site was abandoned in the nineteenth century because of commercial hunting. It wasn't until 1983, after several years of enforced protection on the Soviet and Alaska coast, that significant numbers of walrus began to reappear there. More than

12,000 bulls have been counted at Nanvak Bay, rivaling Round Island as the most significant walrus herd in the United States.

With the expanding herds, however, has come disturbing news. Although controlled hunting has allowed the Pacific walrus to flourish, scientists fear that the species, whose current world population is thought to be well over 250,000, has passed the peak of its population cycle and is beginning to eat itself out of its Alaska home. Evidence suggests that the shallow sea bottom around Round Island has been depleted of bottom-dwelling invertebrates, particularly the clams and whelks that are the animal's major food source. In order to satisfy their enormous appetites, a growing number of walrus have begun using the richer waters in the vicinity of Cape Peirce. How much longer the food will last there is subject to debate.

The walrus surfaced again. Peering at us with those streaked red eyes set among folds of cracked leathery skin, blowing puffs of steam with each hot breath, the creature might have been a visitor from the Ice Age. In fact, the Pacific walrus has inhabited the Bering-Chukchi seas for at least 100,000 years. It is presumed that the species made its way across the Eurasian north coast from the North Atlantic, where a close cousin, the Atlantic walrus, lives today.

At the slackening tide we slid the boats in the water, searching the surface for a two-ton blob of pink flesh. All we had between us and the walrus's twenty-inch tusks was a thin layer of rubber and some canvas and wood strips—far from comforting considering that walrus have been known to attack small boats. Ken Taylor, an Alaska Department of Fish and Game biologist and manager of the Walrus Island State Game Sanctuary, had written me about such an occurrence. A game technician under his supervision had been stationed on Round Island for six weeks to construct a small living shelter. On one of his kayak surveys around the island, a walrus had surfaced beneath his one-person Klepper and punctured it with both tusks. It was not a particularly aggressive action, by Taylor's account, as walrus use their tusks constantly to jab each other and to communicate dominance and intentions. Nevertheless, the kayak sank to the side floats very quickly, and because of cold water temperatures the technician was fortunate to make it to shore.

As we cruised over gentle swells, the smell, the sounds, the sights made me forget what might be lurking below. Bull kelp gave the air a not unpleasant iodine aroma. The sizzle of water passing under my hull was soothing and relaxing. The sun emerged and we paddled under a double rainbow. The drab mountain peaks on the horizon became sharply articulated in glowing red. The sea itself was rich in color and contrast, showing that clear line between the green shallows and violet depths. Pulling alongside each other, we shouted about how great it was to be on the Bering Sea rather than back home in a land of mostly corn and beans. I felt cheated when our joyful ride came to an abrupt end.

The reappearance of a low cloud bank and cat's-paws on the water betokened the onset of more foul weather. Feeling the fresh breeze on my face, Ken Taylor's words came back to me: "even on a nice day the seas around Togiak can change very quickly to the point where your life is in jeopardy." I snugged up my sprayskirt and pulled on my hood. The waves steepened and rolled over the Klepper's low peaked deck. The temperature dropped as the new pressure system barreled in. Our warm and sunny morning was rapidly turning cold, windy and wet.

"Let's stay together!" I hollered to Clyde and Mike. Their longer double-seater, with twice the manpower, was considerably faster than my single. I had to paddle hard just to stay even.

As a gust of wind caught me off guard and nearly blew the paddle out of my hands, I wished I had tied a lanyard around it to connect it to the boat, but there were a lot of things I probably should have done. We were traveling with minimal equipment. We had no radio communication or emergency locating beacons, no immersion or survival suits, no flares or rockets—only a single bilge pump between our two boats. With endless water on our right and sheer cliffs on my left, I felt a steady flow of adrenalin pushing me on. I could only imagine what Mike and Clyde were thinking, since this was their first time on the ocean in a small boat. If I were they, I'd be cursing me for planning a kayak trip to one of the stormiest seas on earth. Every few moments their boat disappeared as either they or I slid down the trough of a wave. I felt much better when they reappeared. The ocean was lonely enough when the other boat was in sight.

As we drew up on Pinnacle Rock, a jagged tower that marks the beginning of Security Cove, we were met by a cluster of seabirds that took flight upon our approach. On the ledges and in the cracks of the vertical cliffs I could see black and white downy chicks, safe in their rock nests from foxes and other predators. The murres and puffins provided us with fleeting companionship, then settled back down as we paddled past. But when Clyde and Mike tried to round the pinnacle, they were blown back. "It's no use!" they stammered as they bumped alongside my boat. "The headwind's too strong."

A few hundred yards behind us was a small beach. It wasn't entirely protected, but it was the only place for us to land unless we wanted to paddle five miles back to our previous campsite. Mike and Clyde went ahead, scouting out the shore from just behind the surf line. Suddenly they powered in with paddles churning, trying to ride the crest of a breaking wave. Their boat (my precious Klepper) rose up for a moment like a breaching whale, then as if falling off the edge of a table, nosedived straight down. The next wave pitched the boat on its side, spilling Mike into the foam. Clyde jumped into the waist-deep surf to lend a hand. When the wave receded, they dragged the heavy kayak up the beach before any more damage could be done.

I hung anxiously offshore until Mike and Clyde waved me in. I positioned the kayak's nose at the edge of the breakers, waiting for just the right wave. When it came I paddled hard and rode it in, leaning and bracing into its face with my outstretched paddle blade. I don't know which of us was most surprised when I made a perfect landing on the beach, me or my friends.

We were hungry and drained of energy. After a bite of food, we surveyed the damage. In addition to Mike's sopping clothes, the larger kayak had sustained a few broken sections in its wooden frame. Although the damage could be repaired, the mishap suggested that paddling around Cape Newenham was going to be considerably more difficult—and dangerous—than we had anticipated. Given the spate of weather we'd been having, it might even be considered a foolhardy thing to do. We weren't hard-core sea kayakers: we were three guys interested in seeing walrus and experiencing wilderness. No one, however, wanted to be the first to wimp out. We waited for the wind to settle, listlessly evaluating our options.

An hour, or maybe two, passed before the suggestion was made to tackle Pinnacle Rock again. Clyde, a former wrangler on a Wyoming ranch, spouted some cliche about falling off a horse and jumping back on. Mike and I were unconvinced, but realized we couldn't just sit for the duration.

Paddles at the ready, we sealed ourselves inside our boats at the water's edge and waited for the next big wave to lift us off. We waited, but nothing happened. The technique doesn't work too well if the tide is ebbing. Cursing our ineptitude, Mike and Clyde got out of their boat, grabbed hold of my boat and launched me into the surf. As soon as I was free, they eased the double into deeper water and shoved off.

Again we paddled past Pinnacle Rock, and again we were met by whitecapped rollers that we were unprepared to handle. The winds were from the south, the same direction we were headed—stout, gusty winds that caused tears to well in my eyes. We sloshed around at the base of the cliffs, toy boats being jerked by a string. Within the hour we were back at the starting point, glad to be free of the ricocheting waves.

The beach was a welcome port despite its having only a single campsite, a moderately flat spot above high tide backed by rolling, grass-covered hills. We huddled under a big brown tarp stretched between the tents as we ate our supper in a pouring rain. Clyde, the strict vegetarian (no dairy products, cooked or processed foods) grazed on his usual fare of miso soup, dried tofu, raisins, carrots, fresh sprouts, rolled oats, amaranth cereal and multivitamins. Mike and I are considerably more omnivorous, but on backcountry journeys we, too, usually go meatless—especially when Clyde is around. Our dinner meals this trip were a concoction of minute rice and ramen noodles mixed in with mashed potato flakes, freeze-dried vegetables, powdered milk, instant soup and lots of spices.

"You know," Mike said, digging his spoon into the lumpy swill, "this stuff isn't half-bad. Of course it's dog food compared to what I've got planned for our big slide-show feast." A consummate cook when the occasion demands, he closed his eyes and drifted off into food fantasyland.

After our chocolate bar desert, Mike and I decided we had had enough nature for one day and crawled into our respective tents, he to begin a paperback, I to catch up on three days of sketchy notes. Clyde chose to stay outside a while longer and decided to go jogging. Coming from anyone else I would have been astounded, but since it was Clyde I merely shrugged and said, "Have fun!" when he loped off down the beach.

The next morning clouds lay sullen on the hills, but it did not rain. The surf was much louder, though, caused by a high tide and the wind's clockwise shift to the west. Clyde was still asleep; I assumed Mike was also because there was no noise from his tent. I lay in my bag, irritated by the weather, frustrated at the way this trip was turning out. We were six days into our journey and had paddled only five miles. We were having some good times, but we definitely weren't getting anywhere by boat. I sighed and pulled on my pants and pile sweater. At least we could explore the surrounding land.

We ate lunch on the side of Chagvan Mountain, a double hump that rises 1,700 feet out of the coastal plain. Our lookout wasn't terribly high, but we were able to gaze over the heath-covered hills and fractured valleys; any higher and our heads would be in the clouds. Visible in the foreground was Security Cove, our most immediate goal. About ten miles overland was the mouth of Nanvak Bay, our ultimate destination. From a kayaker's perspective, neither body of water looked very appealing, with high surf peeling into their shores. More tranquil was the Slug River, rising out of the lowlands to our east and flowing into Nanvak Bay. Beyond Security Cove, sprawling west, were Jagged, Gap and Tokomarik mountains, all standing in a line on the long peninsula that ended with Cape Newenham.

"I wish we had the time to climb them," Clyde mused, studying the approach routes through binoculars. "Probably could do all three in a single day."

"Maybe *you* could," I said. "In any event, if this wind keeps up you might be able to try."

When we returned to camp later that afternoon, a break in the weather made us practically dance with joy. For about two hours the sun poked through the ragged cloud cover, long enough to dry out damp clothes and sleeping bags. Mike was ecstatic. He stripped down and waded into the frigid creek to sponge off the sea salt that was making him itch. Soon Clyde was in there too. My companions cajoled me to join them.

"I'm not dirty," I replied. "Just ask Clyde." My diplomatic tentmate only shook his head.

A little later, we debated if we should go for Security Cove or stay put. The discussion ended almost as quickly as it began when the sunny weather changed to a building gale.

At first opportunity the following morning we sneaked out of the cove. The waves were still high and a steady drizzle obscured visibility, but we felt a pressing need to move on. I launched first and paddled steadily to Pinnacle Rock, thinking Clyde and Mike would be right behind me. But when I reached the rendezvous and looked back, they were nowhere to be seen. I bobbed in the waves for a few more minutes, then pushed on for Security Cove. I concluded that they must have already rounded the point further out without me seeing them.

As I had expected, a stiff breeze belted me in the face when I turned the corner past Pinnacle Rock. The ocean's surface was roiled and foam flecked. I kept the rudder angled to starboard, trying to keep the bow into the wind and the boat well away from the confused waves rebounding off the cliffs.

I was becoming frightened in that little boat in the cold green sea. The fear produced an enormous outflow of energy. My paddle seemed to be windmilling so fast I could have been mistaken for Olympic kayaker Greg Barton sprinting for the gold in Seoul—but this race was mine alone. Every few strokes I swiveled my head, scanning the horizon for the other boat. "Where could they be?" I grumbled. The five- to six-foot rollers swallowed everything.

An hour of white-knuckled paddling took me to the center of crescent-shaped Security Cove. Behind a sandbar at the mouth of a stream I found a haven from the whitecaps and swells. I wiggled out of my boat and dragged it ashore. There was no evidence of other people on the sand, but perched on the tall grassy bank a hundred yards inland was a small, solid cabin, its austerity softened by a wild garden of fireweed, geranium and parsnip. Built before the refuge was established, the cabin served as an emergency shelter for commercial fishermen who sometimes ply these waters. As long as the hut was vacant, I figured we could avail ourselves of its sturdy walls.

I waited at the sandbar for Mike and Clyde, eager to tell them about our new campsite. About ten minutes later they arrived, driving the kayak hard against the shore.

"Where the heck were you guys?" I said good naturedly as they bumped to a halt.

"Where were *we*?" Clyde bellowed as he climbed stiffly out of the boat. "Where were *you*?!? Didn't you see us wave our paddles when you were at Pinnacle Rock?"

"No, I didn't," I replied, caught off guard by this uncharacteristic hostility. Paddle-waving was our prearranged signal that a boat needed assistance. "In fact, I never saw you guys once I left the beach."

"Hmmph!" Clyde grunted, unzipping his life jacket and throwing it in the boat. "Nice to know we can count on you, Rice," he said in disgust. As I moved forward to help them, I noted that their kayak was half-flooded. Still seated, Mike was in water up to his hips and didn't seem very amused.

While bailing and dragging the boat to higher ground, they explained that during their surf entry a big wave had swept over them before the sprayskirt was affixed. A tubful of cold water landed right in their laps. Partly flooded, they had to paddle mightily to avoid the next incoming breaker; no way were they going to reenter the surf to drain the kayak. They proceeded to the rendezvous with the intention of picking up the hand-operated bilge pump, which I was carrying, but I had already left for Security Cove. Ill-prepared, without a cook pot or anything else for bailing, they were forced to paddle the low-riding Klepper four miles to shore.

"The whole time we were dreaming up ways to get even with you for not being there," Clyde admitted, dumping the water out of his boots.

"That's right," Mike chimed in. "From now on we launch first and carry the bilge pump. If we just happen to be around when you need it, you can use it. But don't expect us to wait for you."

I was touched. Were these terrific friends, or what?

We trudged up the bank to inspect the cabin, in a quandary about whether to continue with our original plans to round Cape Newenham, still fifteen miles away. David Fisher, Togiak's refuge manager, had written me that the south side and westernmost end of Cape Newenham is nearly all vertical cliffs dropping from several hundred to over a thousand feet into the sea. "There are very few, if any, safe harbor or pull-out areas if you should run into problems going around the Cape," he warned. "Pick your day to do this and be flexible on your time table to allow for weather delays. Weather around the Cape Newenham area is sporadic, generally with rough seas on one side or the other. I would think that rounding the Cape would be extremely hazardous for a kayak."

To emphasize his point, Fisher mentioned the travails of two parties, each using eighteen-foot aluminum boats and twenty-five horsepower outboards, who had made the trip during the spring and fall of the previous year. The first party consisted of native subsistence hunters who spent four days at Chagvan Bay waiting to head south around Cape Newenham. "Luckily for them," Fisher noted, "they were able to eat waterfowl for the unplanned extra days." The other party comprised two men traveling from Whitehorse, Canada, down the Yukon River, then south along the coast to the Alaska Peninsula. "They had to wait five days before heading south," Fisher added. "They had not planned for the delay since their last supply stop, and had it not been for our field camp at Nanvak Bay, would have been hunting for food. You are a better judge of the seaworthiness of your kayak and how it performs in rough seas than I am. Enough said. You be the judge."

When formulating the trip we had left ourselves an escape route if things got too rough on the Bering Sea: we could portage from Security Cove to the head of Nanvak Bay. This option was never seriously considered, however, because sea kayaks, especially heavy Kleppers, are meant to be paddled, not carried upside-down like canoes; and although it was only a 300-foot elevation rise and a four-mile hike across open tundra, the portage was certain to be a multiday, back-breaking affair.

We mulled this over as we carried our gear up the bank, but our first priority was changing into dry clothes. The cabin was in fine shape, heavily reinforced against storms with steel cable guylines, and equipped with a couple of tables and chairs. In the corner was a barrel stove, which Mike, the traditional woodsman among us, proceeded to kindle with driftwood from the beach. In short order the damp, chilly interior was almost like a Turkish bath. Wet clothes and boots hung from the rafters, producing a cloud of steam near the ceiling as moisture was forced out. We pranced around naked, cracking jokes about each other's pale, prune-wrinkled bodies while laughing about our misadventure on the Bering Sea. But after the joviality came sobriety. The ocean had been toying with us. We had to be more careful.

The warmth of the cabin began to loosen our tight muscles, including our tongues. Totally relaxed, we talked about our objectives for the days ahead, about future plans, future trips, about things a million miles away at home.

Clyde mentioned that he wanted to stop at the central post office in Anchorage upon our return. Still employed as a mail carrier, he had been trying to get transferred to Alaska since our trip to Becharof and figured he'd stand a better chance if he made his appeal in person. I knew how much Clyde wanted to move—I couldn't blame him for not wanting to live in an apartment in a factory town—but for purely selfish reasons, a part of me hoped he didn't get the transfer. I knew once he got to Alaska, with millions of acres of wilderness within a few hours' drive, I wouldn't see him unless I went up there myself.

Mike also spoke often about emigrating from Illinois, but unlike Clyde, he didn't feel the urgency to make the big escape. One reason was that he already lived miles from the city and a fair piece from the nearest small town. His house, which he had designed and built himself, was situated on a river bluff surrounded by a mixture of lightly settled woods and farm fields. His country home was his refuge, which made residing in central Illinois acceptable, even enjoyable, despite his criticisms of the summer heat, mild winters and scarcity of wild land. The other reason was that his school-teacher/naturalist wife was happy where she was, surrounded by friends, wildlife, her flower gardens and an unpolluted sky. Mike's homestead kept his life centered, as my rural residence and Judy's companionship did for me.

When Mike cracked the door to cool the cabin down, the sight of the portage route framed outside immediately refocused our attention on the problems at hand. After dinner we poured over the Togiak maps, measured miles and checked the weather. Finally the painful decision was made: Cape Newenham was scrubbed; we would portage to Nanvak Bay.

That evening we began the ordeal by carrying the solo boat and a seventy-pound gear bag halfway across the wide hummocky pass. Surrounded by low featureless hills that oozed water into the valley, the sedge and grass tundra was mostly boot-sucking mire. Mike and I lugged the kayak; Clyde had the bag. The Klepper was awkward to carry, whether on our shoulders or in the crook of our arms. Clyde's duffel lacked shoulder straps and had to be hefted like a sack of coal. We returned to the cabin a little past midnight, shucked our boots and crawled into sleeping bags on the plywood floor.

Wind whistled between cracks in the walls, waking me up. I rolled over and hit the light button on my watch. Eight o'clock! We had slept late, fooled by the cabin's dark interior.

Right after breakfast we began the next portion of the portage. Mike and I started off carrying the double kayak. Clyde shouldered a pair of gear bags with a combined weight of about 120 pounds.

"How's he do it?" Mike asked, as our bionic friend cruised past us as if we were standing still. "I thought I was in pretty decent shape until I started doing trips with him."

"You are, for an old man," I teased him. A few years older than I, the next spring Mike would turn forty.

We started out strong, carrying in fifteen-minute shifts and resting for five, but soon it was the other way around. Our conversation changed from pleasant chatter to teeth-clenched barbs directed at the uneven footing and burdensome boat. Not one to shy away from hard physical exertion, Mike, the former jock, flatly stated that the portage was more strenuous than anything he'd ever done.

Mike wasn't alone in his pain. I was sweating buckets through my rain suit. My shoulders ached, and I was favoring my right knee, having undergone arthroscopic surgery for a torn cartilage only a month before. I could have used my lame leg as an excuse to ease up, but if I did, Mike would never let me forget it once we got home.

During the last segment of the portage we changed our tactics.

We harnessed ourselves into tow ropes and dragged the boat like huskies pulling a sled. With so much friction against the rubber hull, however, our best efforts were repaid by tortuously slow progress. When we collapsed beside Clyde at the halfway point, we were pleased to learn that the bionic man was also beginning to show signs of wear. "I don't think I'll go for a run tonight," he casually mentioned.

We started the final march to the divide early the next morning. We secured the cabin door, packed up our remaining possessions and trooped up to where we had left the boats. From here we would follow a pencil-thin stream down to Nanvak Bay, where we planned to spend the night.

Except for salmon and trout that had managed to work their way up the stream and a few sandhill cranes and ptarmigan in the upland heath, we saw no animal life during the trek, nor did we stop often to look. Toiling nonstop, we had everything on the west shore of Nanvak Bay by 7 p.m., except for the solo kayak, which remained a mile up the pass. We chose to leave it there until the following day, unable to stomach another minute of boat hauling. It had taken us three trips—twenty miles of trudging—to transport our gear from Security Cove. I was tired, hungry and unusually filthy. I was glad that the portage was over, glad that our search for walrus could begin.

First there was the matter of choosing a campsite. Disinclined to pack up and paddle to more promising spots down the bay (especially since we were minus a boat), we made do with a hard mud tidal flat lightly covered with green scum. I strolled among the most recent flotsam line left by the receding tide. "We'd better be ready for a quick getaway tonight," I suggested. "A rise of half-a-foot from the last tide will flood this site."

Since our departure might be in haste, we pitched only the larger dome tent. Stuff that wasn't needed at night we stored in waterproof bags, which in turn we loaded into the kayak. If we did get flooded, at least we'd be able to reach safety.

As we sat around the stove waiting for water to boil, we began to observe things we had been too busy to notice before. Dead salmon were strung out on the mudflat, raising an awful stench when there was a lull in the wind. Some of the spawned-out fish came from the tiny creek we had followed down, but the bulk undoubtedly were washed out of the Slug River, a mile to the east across the bay. The carcasses should have attracted a variety of hungry animals, yet gulls were the only creatures picking over the fish.

While roaming the mudflat we had not seen a single bear track. Odd, very odd. A place such as this, especially during the salmon spawn, should have been thick with griz sign.

I remained puzzled by the absence of bears until after our trip, when I acquired a copy of Togiak's *Final Comprehensive Conservation Plan/Environmental Impact Statement and Wilderness Review,* published in 1986.[1] Contained within the 514-page tome were references that helped explain why we weren't seeing any bears or other large land mammals.

In the past, according to the U.S. Fish and Wildlife Service document, illegal harvests of grizzly bears, moose and caribou may have contributed to their present low population levels in the refuge. Caribou, once abundant in Togiak, had disappeared by 1900. Today there are seldom more than fifty caribou on the refuge at any given time, although there is an abundance of suitable habitat. Togiak's moose and brown bear populations are also far less than the range can support. Fewer than thirty-five moose are estimated to be within the refuge; and brown bear, the most common big game species in Togiak, probably number no more than 300 to 400 animals. With their low reproductive rates, bears especially cannot tolerate excessive hunting pressure. To illustrate the point, in the spring of 1985, sixteen brown bear were harvested in a single Togiak river valley, prompting the Alaska Department of Fish and Game to instigate an emergency closure.

The report concludes on a sour note: "Continued hunting pressure today continues to keep the populations from expanding— illegal harvests are probably the most important limiting factor for big game populations in Togiak Refuge. If excessive or illegal harvests continue in the future, it will interfere with the Service's goals of maintaining wildlife populations, and restoring big game populations to their historic levels." Disappointed by this dearth of large mammals, we consoled ourselves that at least we had walrus to look forward to.

After dinner, Clyde and I volunteered to do a little scouting before the next day's paddle. Because Nanvak Bay is shallow and laced with sandbars at low tide, we needed to know which side offered the best route. A grass-covered dune a mile away offered the lookout we needed. It was during this scouting expedition that Clyde and I spotted the thousands of tuskers on the beach.

A hard, driving rain greeted us in the morning. Whitecaps raced across Nanvak Bay, and the tent was once again buffeted by the full fury of the wind. We huddled inside, weary and dirty and cramped. While tossing down a rushed breakfast of cold granola and raisins, we argued about what to do next. The most obvious task was to break camp immediately; the tide was flooding and our spot could be inundated. We also had to retrieve the kayak left behind in the uplands. A troubled silence ensued. Finally, Clyde offered to go for the boat if Mike and I would dismantle camp. We protested, saying that the two of us had barely been able to drag the kayak over the hummocks. How was he going to sled it by himself?

"Don't worry, I'll manage," Clyde said tersely, throwing on his foul-weather gear. "Meet me at the edge of the bay. I'll be there as soon as I can." Without another word, he unzipped the tent door and took off jogging, a lonely figure among the dark and misty tundra valley.

"Well, he did it again," Mike said as we piled out of the tent into the monsoon.

"What's that?" I groused, in no mood for riddles.

"You know, made us look like a couple of weenies."

Not wanting to shirk our responsibilities, we broke camp in record speed. Another incentive was the tide: it *was* going to flood our site. We carried the Klepper and gear to the edge of the water, then paddled over to a strip of high ground on the other side of the swollen stream. We finished our chores just as Clyde appeared on the horizon about a quarter-mile away. Mike and I were shocked to see him back so soon. We hollered and waved while running up to help him.

"What took you so long?" Mike gasped, as he slapped Clyde on the back.

"Yeah, we were getting worried about you," I added. "You were gone a whole hour."

Clyde only grunted as he dropped the tow rope and sat in the wet grass.

Leaving him to rest, Mike and I shouldered the boat. By the time we got to the shore, I felt like I was carrying a concrete ship.

"How's he do it?" Mike asked when we threw the dead weight to the ground. This had become a standard refrain between us mortals.

"You got me. Maybe there's more to this vegetarian stuff than we realize."

We loaded the kayaks in a hurry as the rain hammered down. By now we knew where everything went, so we didn't waste a second. In my case, the tapered bow and stern drybags were wedged under the canvas deck; camera bags, water bottles, tent poles and ground pad were jammed alongside the gunwales; and squeezed between the rudder pedals and seat was a large storage bag that fit under my bent knees. Every time I bent over to stuff something, I felt another wet spot against my skin. So much for my brand-new, lifetime-guaranteed waterproof parka and pants. I mentally dictated the letter I was going to write when I got home, telling the well-known manufacturer of mountain wear where he could stuff his raincoat.

We slipped into the cockpits, clipped on our sprayskirts and eased into Nanvak Bay. Our route took us past the Slug River, where the night before we had seen thousands of ducks and geese milling around its mouth. I glanced over to the braided channel hoping to see a bear or caribou or wolf on the sandbars, but even if they were over there in the open, I wouldn't have known. The deluge had become so intense that I was forced to squint, and all around me was a gray blur. Fortunately the waves were small because of the sheltering terrain and shallow water; nevertheless, I managed to complete my soaking when occasional chest-high breakers washed over the boat.

With the wind in our faces, we struggled to make headway toward the south, hopscotching from point to point, trying to take advantage of any lee shore. In one quiet cove we ran into a flock of waterfowl. Suddenly the air was electrified with tight, twisting bunches of ducks. Pintails, eiders and scaup whistled wave-top-high off my bow, coming so close in the confusion that I thought we would collide. We veered away so as not to frighten the rafts of geese that remained. The Canadas, brant, emperors and white-fronted chose to stick tight rather than take flight in the gale. The only creatures that seemed impervious to the weather and us were the harbor seals. Staring at us with their black eyes set in gray, melon-shaped heads, the sleek, streamlined animals popped up a few yards from our boats, then submerged when we approached.

Strangely enough, one of the most interesting sights was not the live animals, but those that were dead. Staggered along the narrow sand beach were at least a dozen walrus the color of dried scabs. We stopped to examine the carcasses. The bloated, gaseous bodies presented a ghastly sight. None of the walrus had tusks—just empty sockets from where the overgrown canines had been cut out. The rest of the body had not been touched. We couldn't be certain how these individuals had died, but it was clear that not all of them had succumbed to natural causes.

At one time native Alaskans living along the Bering Sea based their lifestyle on walrus. The meat was used for food, the skins for fashioning boats and towlines for dog sleds, and the intestines for making raincoats. Although many natives still follow these ancient traditions of utilizing the entire animal, the primary value of walrus today comes from its ivory, which is the preferred medium for artistic carving. Shaped into all sorts of decorative figures and implements, the finished pieces sell for premium prices. Consequently, it is not uncommon for natives to concentrate more on the ivory of harvested walrus and less on the meat.

Because only native Alaskans are permitted to take walrus in the United States under historic rights, other means to acquire walrus ivory have surfaced. Hundreds of walrus along the Bering Sea coast are shot illegally each year by ivory marketeers, their tusks removed and the bodies left to rot. Since at least one animal is lost for each animal retrieved, many wash ashore days or weeks later. Some pilots of small planes make a practice of scouring the coast for these beached walrus. When they find them, they land nearby and chop the valuable tusks out. The U.S. Fish and Wildlife Service, the agency in charge of Pacific walrus management, requires that a permit be obtained to possess any part of a walrus because the species falls under the 1972 Marine Mammals Protection Act. Flouting the law, tusk traders are willing to take the risk of serious penalties in exchange for exorbitant profits. Illegal walrus hunting has even occurred recently in Togiak Refuge.

Leaving the grisly sight, we wasted no time paddling the last half-mile over thick beds of eelgrass with less than a foot of water under our hulls. We had to rush to prevent the rapidly ebbing tide from dumping us on a broad mudbar far from where we wanted to land. At the base of a low, grassy dune some distance from the mouth of Nanvak Bay was an excellent campsite, soft and flat, protected on three sides from winds. We were anticipating a hot meal, but this evening dinner could wait. A quarter-mile away was our long-sought goal. The hunt was almost over. We armed ourselves with cameras and binoculars and hiked over the sandy swells to see Togiak's tuskers up close.

We were excited as we plunged through the soggy, knee-high grass. Nearing the haulout, we crouched low, not daring even a whisper. The thought of scaring the walrus was inconceivable, unacceptable. Studies in both Alaska and the U.S.S.R. have shown that walrus will abandon traditional haulout sites if they suffer frequent harassment.

In the final few yards I snaked ahead on my belly. Slowly, cautiously, I crept to the crest of the dune and peered over the ridge. My jaw dropped. "Oh, no!" I moaned. "The beach is empty!" All that remained of the great herd was one lone walrus, and it was dead. A glaucous-winged gull was perched on its grotesque head.

Mike slumped over. Clyde looked stunned. I stared in disbelief at the lifeless beach. We returned to the inlet and set up camp, utterly dejected, but trying to be optimistic. Five days remained before our pick-up at the north end of Nanvak Bay. Surely the walrus would return by then.

Later that evening we learned that we had missed the spectacle by less than one day. This news came from Kelly and Paul, summer volunteers for the U.S. Fish and Wildlife Service, who were stationed at a seasonal field camp near the haulout to monitor the herd. At their one-room cabin a half-mile from our camp, they informed us that about 9,000 individuals had been counted the previous afternoon, the highest number recorded this season. "It's too bad the herd left last night," Kelly said, still amused at having three kayakers suddenly drop in unannounced. "I think we were headed for a record-breaker." Tall and lanky with a whimsical red beard, he sifted through a book of census data and showed us an entry for July 27 of the previous year. On that day the walrus population at Nanvak Bay rose to over 12,000. "I was here then," he said smiling. "It was awesome."

The volunteers—both recent college graduates who were provided room and board—told us that the Nanvak Bay area has become a well-known reestablished walrus haulout over the past three to five years. "It's the only major haulout that's at least partly on national wildlife refuge uplands," Paul said with a trace of pride. Pulling out a map, he pointed to three other comparable haulout areas in Alaska that are either exclusively on state uplands and tide-submerged lands or are on privately owned uplands.

Both Kelly and Paul explained that, through various tagging methods, it has been determined that after loafing on a beach for a few days, the big males leave to feed, going up to 150 miles offshore for about three to ten days. As long as they're not disturbed, they generally come back to the same haulout.

Until recently, the method by which the walrus obtained their food was a mystery. It was always assumed that the animals used their long tusks—actually vastly elongated upper canine teeth—to dig for bottom-dwelling invertebrates found on the relatively shallow and rich Bering-Chukchi Platform. But close examination of tusks, whiskers and snouts has revealed that a walrus doesn't dig with its tusks at all. Instead, it grazes along the sea bottom like a vacuum cleaner, using its narrow mouth and piston-like tongue to suck up clams, whelks, snails, crabs, shrimp and worms.

Biding our time until the walruses returned, we mapped out several days' worth of hikes. The first of these took us across the plateau-like highlands to an area of bare cliffs rising sheer from the sea. For several miles, the only breaks in the rampart were where the incessant action of wind and waves have sculpted out caves, pinnacles and arches near the base. We came to a halt at a precipice overlooking a black, brooding rock a quarter-mile offshore in Bristol Bay. Named "Walrus Island" by the Russians in 1826, Shaiak Island rarely hosts walrus anymore, but does abound with nesting marine birds. Through the spotting scope it appeared as if every square foot of the half-mile-long island was occupied. The sea around the island was equally congested with rafted birds. There were black-legged kittiwakes and common murres and pelagic and double-crested cormorants, horned and tufted puffins, parakeet auklets and pigeon guillemots. I was overwhelmed by this profusion of life. The island hummed with activity as a steady flow of seabirds launched into the wind; an equal number dropped down on the guano-streaked ledges, flapping once or twice to get their balance before settling in.

Birds of prey were also attracted to the area. Bullet-shaped peregrine falcons became a regular sight as they rocketed across the treeless mainland or skimmed the seaside crags. For diversion they engaged in mock aerial dogfights with the dark, glossy ravens that also roamed the skies. Peering over the edge of a cliff, we discovered the aerie of another winged predator. On a narrow shelf a hundred feet below us and several hundred feet above the crashing waves was a massive bald eagle stick nest with two nearly full-grown eaglets inside. Their parents patrolled nearby, toying with the wind, performing lazy loops and rolls. They toyed with us also, soaring fearlessly past our lookout on vibrating wings, their cold, yellow eyes locked on our own.

Wandering the Cape Peirce headland, recognized as one of the most outstanding scenic complexes in the state, it quickly became apparent that terrestrial mammals were as scarce as birds were abundant. The vegetation along the Togiak coast provides little in the way of forage or protection. Winds blow ceaselessly, trimming the plants at ground level. Scattered patches of willow and alder and lush grass grow only in sheltered pockets. We did see voles, ground squirrels, marmots and a number of inquisitive red foxes, some brazen enough to trot to within a few feet of us to pose for photographs. We crossed an old griz track or two, but despite all our scanning of the open countryside, none of the bruins was observed. However, as Clyde found out, that didn't mean no bears were around.

I was on a high piece of ground opposite Shaiak Island, taking photographs of puffins and murres on the cliffs below, when I noticed Clyde a mile or so off, climbing toward me from a distant beach. He was easy to spot against the empty green heath, clad in his red Gore-Tex parka and moving with a brisk stride. I locked my binoculars on him, wondering what he had been up to. He was holding a pair of long, curved objects. Odd-shaped pieces of driftwood, I thought, or maybe whale ribs. Curious, I huddled behind a boulder out of the wind, waiting for him to arrive.

I must have dozed off, because the first thing I saw upon opening my eyes was a pair of huge walrus tusks, over two feet long, blood-streaked and pointed like fangs. "Take a look at these babies," Clyde said triumphantly, waving the jumbo teeth in my face. "They must weigh six or seven pounds apiece, and geez, do they stink!" He dropped the tusks on the ground and wiped his hands on the mossy turf. "I don't know how I'm going to get rid of this smell."

The tusks were in mint condition, unlike others we had found on shore, which were chipped, dull and a fraction of the size. I was mildly shocked when Clyde explained how he had acquired them. "I was hiking the far beach, looking for glass floats, when I saw this dead walrus. It was a big bull, partly bloated and pretty ripe. I worked like crazy pounding the tusks off with a rock. There was fresh griz sign all around—I'm certain a bear had been munching on the carcass just before I got there." Clyde took a deep breath before continuing. He looked pale, as if he were going to be sick. "It was really gross whacking at the head. I almost gagged on the smell. But something came over me when I saw those tusks—I had to have them. Pretty weird, huh?"

I nodded my head, thinking, "Yeah, Clyde, *very* weird." His clothes had absorbed the foul odor, a strange perfume for a strict vegetarian who had once told me he would never kiss a woman who ate meat.

Using the excuse to fetch my camera, I moved away to cleaner air and snapped a few portraits of my friend with his trophies. Scrubbed and polished, they would look great in his living room as Togiak mementos, but there was the matter of getting them home.

Not only did the tusks stink, they were illegal. Federal law allows only native Alaskans the right to harvest walrus. There is, however, a provision that enables non-natives to possess beach-found ivory upon registering it with the U.S. Fish and Wildlife Service. Clyde planned to complete the necessary red tape in Anchorage, assuming the airport personnel in Dillingham allowed his unique cargo on board the plane.

As interesting as the saber teeth were, walrus body parts were not what we had come to see. We had noticed a few walrus swimming beneath the cliffs or lolling in the waves, but they were a far cry from the thousands that had been here before. Our time was running out and I was trying to reconcile myself to the fact that I would not observe the multitude more closely. Then, as suddenly and mysteriously as they had disappeared, the behemoths started to return from their feeding sojourns. At first it was just a trickle— a few of the bulls, gliding along with the easy majesty of blimps, moved steadily toward the beach as larger groups began to mass offshore. Then the trickle became a stream and the stream became a flood. The ocean's surface, previously empty except for rafts of seabirds, was now alive with big-toothed, bobbing heads.

We stayed up until past midnight watching the big bulls maneuver tirelessly in the surf. Their numbers swelled as the night progressed. A few walrus made half-hearted lurches toward land, letting the waves wash them ashore, but each time they touched the beach an invisible force pulled them back. The reason for their vacillation was fundamental: slowly evolving to a complete aquatic existence like whales, walrus are more at home in the sea than on the land they left millions of years ago.

We were up early the next morning, and while drinking hot cocoa and tea, we discussed the fitful night we had just spent. "This walrus thing is starting to frazzle me," Mike said, running his fingers through his thick, graying hair. "All night I heard this strange grunting and bellowing. At first I thought I was dreaming, then I realized it had to be them. But didn't Kelly say walrus have never been known to haul out near here?"

Clyde and I glanced at each other and grinned. We, too, had suffered insomnia because of the animal racket. At one point, when the roaring was loudest, we had wondered whether the walrus were right outside our tent door. Now, however, with the wind blowing hard offshore, we couldn't hear any rumbling. Even the sound of the surf was being carried away from our ears.

We put down our breakfast and crept up the sand dune nearest

Clyde Vicary modeling a pair of walrus tusks he pulled from a dead bull walrus on the beach.

to camp. Before reaching the ridge, I clicked on my big 300mm lens. "Ready?" I whispered nervously, feeling like I was about to charge a machine gun nest on Iwo Jima or Normandy. Clyde nodded. Mike gave me a thumb's up sign. Crawling on our bellies, we elbowed up the final few feet of loose sand. I could have cheered, but I gulped it down. Spread along the water's edge on the other side of the swell were over a hundred walrus within camera range. My hands trembled, reminiscent of the time I got "buck fever" during my first deer hunt with bow and arrow. I put down my camera and watched. This wasn't the immense herd we had come to see, but no one was about to complain.

I had always wondered how biologists are able to sneak up on sleeping walrus to attach radio transmitters and colored bands to their tusks. Now I knew. By moving stealthily—the eyesight of a walrus is poor, but it is able to pick out sudden movement—we managed to crawl from sand mound to sand mound without frightening the tuskers. When we stopped behind some tufts of bluejoint grass with only our heads poking up, only twenty yards separated us from the herd. We were close enough to count the whiskers in their chins.

"This is great," Mike said softly at my side. He and Clyde were propped up on their elbows, looking quite satisfied. And why not? The air was tinged with salt spray. The temperature was cool and comfortable. No bugs. Long lines of seabirds flew directly overhead, and harbor seals moved with the current offshore. Even Cape Newenham, our dreaded nemesis when we pondered rounding it, cooperated by providing the perfect background when viewed through my telephoto lens.

Every time the light changed or the animals altered positions, new photo opportunities arose that we couldn't resist. The walrus (from the Swedish *hvalross*, which means "whale horse") were adorably ugly. Their bodies lack form and are incredibly fat. Their thick, wrinkled skin is full of warts and is the color of red wine. Their faces are raw, spongy and stupid, and their flippers absurdly short. Most of the bulls had a pair of full-sized porcelain white tusks, but some had only a single tusk or merely a peg of a stump. The animals might have broken the specialized tooth while plucking shellfish off the sea floor, or perhaps it had been lost during a joust with another bull.

I couldn't help anthropomorphizing. They reminded me of a bunch of street toughs with time on their hands and no females in sight. Not the most delicate of creatures, the bulls slurped, grunted, farted and roared while slobbering a frothy spittle over themselves and their neighbors. Most just wanted to be left alone to snooze and catch a few rays, but arguments did ensue, leading the unruly bachelors to duke it out. It seemed that anything could send a walrus into a rage. When one of the bulls dug a shallow hole with his flippers, tossing wet sand on his back to avoid being sunburned, those nearby lashed out with their tusks at the troublemaker. Tusks are used often in mutual display—usually those with the largest canines dominate the others. We never saw blood being spilled, but plenty of long, slashing scars attested to the ferocity of the scuffles.

At the main haulout, the walrus numbers continued to build throughout the day and into the evening. In single-file procession, they inched up the beach toward the dunes, a formidable task for a two-ton mammal equipped with paddle-shaped flippers instead of legs. Those that lagged behind remained in the surf waiting their turn to get in line. When something would startle the rear contingent at the fringe of the beach, a rippling panic swept through the herd, causing a stampede back into the water. A few minutes later, the tuskers regrouped in the shallows, gathering momentum for another attempt to reach the hauling ground. A tortoise could have made the journey faster. Stopping repeatedly to rest and look around, the walrus writhed ahead at a top speed of a foot every minute.

Before retiring that night, we stationed ourselves on a grassy knoll and counted at least a thousand of the tuskers in various stages of progress toward the promised land. Some had made it all the way to the base of the dunes a hundred yards inland; most were still creeping along at their agonizing pace. With so many bodies packed together defecating and pissing onto the sand, the beach smelled as rank as any pig lot. Instead of turning up my nose, I inhaled deeply of the earthy aroma. Combined with the dim light and the otherworldly scene below, the smell helped set the mood of the place.

Our final morning at the site was overcast and blustery. We broke camp and readied the kayaks for the return trip up Nanvak Bay. Because low-flying aircraft can cause a walrus herd to stampede, we had been instructed by the refuge staff to arrange for the pick-up at least three miles from the hauling ground. Since there was no need to reach our next campsite until evening, we left the boats and hiked across the dunes for one last look at the tuskers. Even from a distance, the clamor was noticeably louder than be-

Clyde Vicary watching over the walrus haulout at Nanvak Bay.

fore. The steady guttural din suggested that many more walrus had heaved onto the beach during the night. And they had. The size of the herd appeared doubled and more walrus were surging onto the beach, dragging their supine bodies out of the sea. Never before had I seen so many big mammals squeezed together in so small a space.

A few hours passed, our last with the herd. The tide was dropping. If we wanted to avoid a long carry across a mudflat, we would have to leave soon. Reluctantly, we put away our cameras and slid down the dune.

Walking back to the boats, the finality of the trip began to creep into our conversation. Even though we were still miles from nowhere, part of us was already gearing up for home and civilization. The trip had not gone quite as planned and had provided some difficult moments, but any group of people could enjoy easy times. It's getting through tough times that cements the bond of friendship and often makes the experience more memorable.

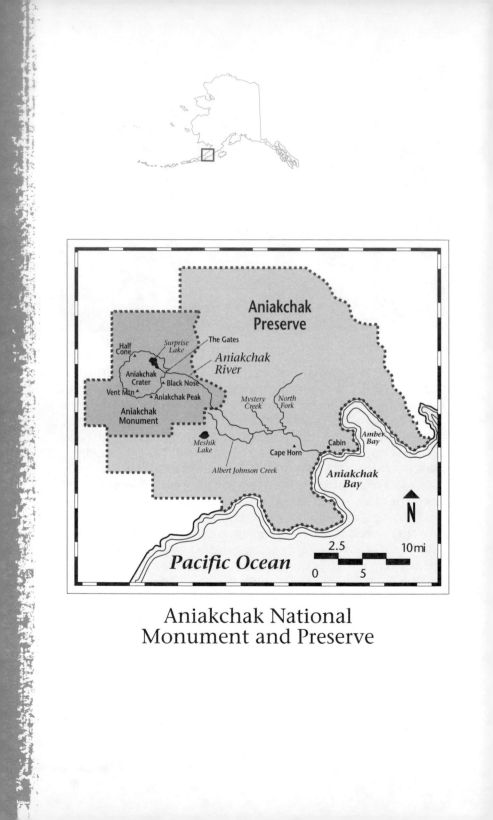

Aniakchak National
Monument and Preserve

ANIAKCHAK: FROM CALDERA TO SEA

AT SUNUP OUR GROUP OF five had a brief christening ceremony. The inflatable rafts—identical blue eleven-footers—were named *Father Hubbard* and *Hail Mary*, and the monikers were inscribed on their tubular sides with a black felt-tip pen.

After breaking camp, we paddled the floating bathtubs across Surprise Lake and entered the headwaters of the Aniakchak River. Mike and I, in *Hail Mary*, took one last look at the great caldera we were leaving and instantly were funneled downstream. In a few minutes we were at the threshold of the Gates, a precipitous, 2,000-foot-deep rift in the caldera rim. According to Father Hubbard, the Jesuit geologist called the "Glacier Priest," the Gates of Aniakchak before us were a "prelude to Hell." If that were true, we had just spent four days in purgatory and were ready for some paradise.

As the river narrowed, the water flowed faster. "Slow up! Back-paddle!" I shouted to Mike, who was in the stern of the small, spongy craft, steering hard to maintain control. "I can see the tops of the rapids below."

The closer we came to the whitewater, the greater the temptation was to run the rapids, but common sense prevailed. Water velocity in the Gates is extremely swift, and numerous large, sharp volcanic boulders choke the compressed channel. Taking the rafts through would jeopardize our journey at the very start. We angled to the right bank immediately above the portal, spun into an eddy and yanked the boat ashore. A moment later Taura, Marion and Clyde joined us in the *Father Hubbard*.

The portage went better than we had anticipated. In two hours we were done, having hauled the rafts and 350 pounds of gear a half-mile over a faint, rocky game trail that dropped steeply into the river. We were retracing history: this was the same trail Father Hubbard had used when he first entered the caldera. One difference was that Hubbard had followed a grizzly bear into the Gates, while we met griz on the way out.

A hundred yards past the breach, standing in the middle of the river fishing, were a couple of blonde bears. They were probably the same individuals Mike and I had seen while scouting the rapids the previous day. Round and woolly like huge and purposeful teddy bears, the animals watched us with interest and showed no apparent aggression. However, for someone who has never been in grizzly country, the first sight of *Ursus arctos* is guaranteed to evoke lasting memories.

"What are we going to do, about the bears I mean?" Taura asked, studying the beasts as we loaded the gear back into the rafts.

"Paddle past them, I guess," Clyde replied. He finished lashing down the bags and looked down the river. "When they see us coming, they'll run away."

"And then they may not," I whispered to Taura as I grabbed my camera and walked down the bank, positioning myself atop a large boulder at the first set of rapids. "Hey, Clyde," I hollered. "I'd like to get some action pics. You mind going first?" He assented, not about to eat his words. Mike held onto *Father Hubbard* while Taura and Marion straddled the bulbous bow tube and secured their feet under the inflated cross thwart. Clyde centered himself atop the enlarged rear chamber where he could see over their heads.

"Ready?" Mike asked.

Marion and Taura nodded. "Okay, let 'er go!" Clyde said.

Mike shoved the boat into the current. The raft hung motionless for a second, then shot downstream. Just before entering the rapids, Clyde stood up defiantly and gave the camera a raised fist salute. I whooped and waved in reply as they plunged into the drop, got wet and raced past. We were through the Gates, had griz in sight and were on our way to the ocean. Having Hell behind us was nice.

Mike Peyton guiding the Hail Mary *down the Aniakchak River. The "Gates" of the Aniakchak Caldera, through which the river passes, is in the background.*

The last day of July had been overcast and breezy when our group arrived in King Salmon on the morning flight from Anchorage. This was my third time here, and I already knew that no one notices when a Grumman Goose is loaded with rafts, paddles, life jackets and enough survival gear to last two weeks. Bush planes in King Salmon come and go all the time, except when the weather is as thick as it was now, postponing our departure for Aniakchak Caldera until the clouds lifted. After making a few radio calls to scattered airstrips and scrutinizing the flat gray scud, the pilot expressed his doubts about our leaving that day, but warned us not to stray too far. "Sometimes we get a break when it seems hopeless. Hang loose. Go get yourselves a cup of coffee."

Feeling fidgety, Clyde and I left the air taxi office, leaving Mike, Taura and Marion to inform us of any departure updates. Across the gravel street was one of those ubiquitous ministrip malls. The new wooden building housed some gift shops, which we weren't interested in, and the Aniakchak National Monument and Preserve office, which we did want to visit. The Park Service ranger who oversees the monument had met us at the airport and suggested we come over to review our trip plans.

Though the walk was short, it was nice to be alone with Clyde for awhile. I hadn't seen him in three or four months and we had a lot of catching up to do. Although I had known that his leaving Illinois would be inevitable, I was nonetheless surprised when he had announced in April that his post office transfer to Anchorage had come through. Clyde had been ecstatic. He bought a four-wheel-drive compact pickup truck. What he couldn't stuff inside, he sold or gave away. It was as if he were purging himself forever of the Midwest, ready to start a new life.

From our talk, it was obvious how much Clyde was enjoying Alaska. "It's unbelievable how much there is to do in the Anchorage area," he gushed. "Bike trails, running trails, cross-country skiing all over the place. Great hiking in the mountains right outside the city. And wildlife! I can be in griz habitat in half an hour and see beluga whales in Cook Inlet while I'm jogging."

He didn't come right out and say it, but I knew he was also enthusiastic about Marion, our newest group member. As recently as a month ago, our Aniakchak band had consisted of just three Togiak veterans—Mike, Clyde and me. Judy couldn't go because she had started a new job, and a friend of Mike's had to cancel after buying his airplane tickets. The open seat was filled when Taura enlisted. Taura, Mike's stepdaughter, was eager to go on this, her first wilderness trip—so eager that she was prepared to spend virtually all of her life savings of about $1,500.

Only two weeks before our departure, Clyde had called. He had asked Mike and me if we minded having another person join our Aniakchak party. He had met Marion, an outdoorsy Anchorage schoolteacher, on a sea kayaking trip a few weeks earlier. A group of five was larger than I really preferred, but we did have room in the rafts and the chartered airplane could handle the extra passenger. "Sure, Clyde," I said after we had discussed all the angles. "Marion sounds great. I'm looking forward to meeting her. But I do hope you warned her about what it's like traveling with us!"

By the time we reached the park office, I was totally jealous of Clyde's new environment, but I tried to maintain a sense of humor and even made him feel good by giving him the news that it had been ninety-eight degrees when I left Peoria. With some embarrassment, I acknowledged that I had finally broken down and installed central air-conditioning in our house.

When we met Natural Resource Specialist David Manski I was in for more reminiscing—of a time nearly a quarter-century before when I was in high school. Aniakchak's chief ranger and I, it turned out, had grown up in the same Chicago northside suburb, we had gone to the same high school and we had earned degrees in closely related fields at the University of Arizona. We couldn't understand how our paths had been so close yet never crossed. "Probably because I'm so much younger," Manski joked. "You graduated Niles West in '68; I'm from the class of '69."

I could tell Clyde was growing weary listening to us gossip as if we were at a twenty-year reunion; one nasal Chicago accent is bad enough, two in tight quarters is insufferable. When we finally got down to business Manski listened to our plans, with which he was already quite familiar because during the preceding months he had supplied me with reams of reference material about the relatively new park.

Above everything else, I had learned that wilderness is a reality in Aniakchak. No modern structure stands within its 600,000-acre expanse. No human road or track can be seen within or even approaching its boundaries. Access to the interior is only by aircraft or arduous overland backpacking, or from the Pacific Coast by boats that must travel fifty miles or more through difficult waters. A park service pamphlet warned that "weather is a frequent and even life-threatening challenge to the unwary or unprepared; the need for self-reliance and self-sufficiency in Aniakchak is extremely high."

"The place is going to blow you away," Manski said, chuckling at his own pun. "All of the monument and preserve is high-quality wilderness, but the caldera offers a scenic experience unavailable elsewhere in Alaska or the lower forty-eight." As proof, he pointed to a gallery of color photographs on the wall taken from within the caldera. The scenes, some quite spectacular, depicted black, charred volcanic terrain. "That's where you're going. Nice, huh? The caldera is the most awesome place I've ever been in."

When our conversation moved on to the river, Manski rummaged through a pile of photos on his desk. He held up two pictures, one of an inflatable raft negotiating a stretch of nasty whitewater, the other of a wide river valley. Manski had run the Aniakchak River with some other park rangers two summers before and had obviously been impressed. Though neither very wide nor very long, the Aniakchak is the largest river on the Alaska Peninsula flowing into the Pacific Ocean. As it rushes through the Gates, the river drops turbulently at an average of seventy feet per mile for its initial thirteen miles (forty feet per mile is regarded as extremely fast water). The remaining eighteen miles of the river wind sedately southeastward through green, rolling ash fields to Aniakchak Bay.

Aptly enough, the Aniakchak and all its tributaries were designated as a component of the National Wild and Scenic Rivers System in 1980. Far from being overused, less than ten parties had run the river at the time of our visit, the last to do so being Manski's group.

Manski was in the midst of giving us some last-minute advice on areas of high bear densities when Mike burst in to tell us the Goose was ready to fly. "You guys are really fortunate," Manksi said as we threw our things together. "It's not uncommon for parties to wait three or four days before getting flown into the caldera. Hope your pick-up works as well."

We thanked Manski again for his help and said a hurried goodbye. As I ran to the airstrip I couldn't help thinking about my former schoolmate and the odds of us bumping into each other in this tiny Alaskan bush town. With his help, we were well fortified with background information about this rarely visited and little-known destination.

Aniakchak National Monument and Preserve lies in the center of the Alaska Peninsula, about 400 miles southwest of Anchorage, between the Bering Sea and the Pacific Ocean. At the heart of the park lies the thirty-mile-square, 2,500-foot-deep Aniakchak Caldera, one of the world's largest. Frequently wrapped in clouds and belted by storms, the ash-filled bowl remained hidden to all but native inhabitants until 1922, when a party of government geologists noticed that the area's taller peaks formed a strange circular configuration on the map they were making. The discovery of the giant caldera helped explain why so many valleys as much as thirty miles away were entirely blanketed by volcanic ejecta. When the geologists reported their findings, they suggested that Aniakchak was worthy of preservation in a national monument. However, it wasn't until 1980 that the caldera and the land around it were officially protected.

It is believed that Aniakchak Caldera was created 3,500 years ago when the summit of a once-lofty, 7,000-foot mountain collapsed in a single massive eruption. On a global scale, the explosion would have ranked as one of the largest in recent geological times. An estimated 15.4 cubic miles of ejecta were cast across the Alaska Peninsula, more than three times the amount thrown out by Krakatoa in 1883, an East Indies explosion heard 3,000 miles away and whose released ash turned sunsets unusually red around the world for two years. Since Aniakchak's initial formation, several lesser volcanic events have occurred that have resulted in varied features on the caldera floor, including small, collapsed explosion pits and ash and lava flows of different ages. Because these features are of rather recent origin, Aniakchak may be classified as a "resurgent" caldron.

On May 1, 1931, the resurgent caldron boiled over. Flames were thrown 7,000 feet in the air and ash shot up into a mushroom cloud 30,000 feet high. Detonations from the blast were heard 200 miles away. At a salmon cannery forty-five miles to the south, ash fall during the height of the eruption was reported to be a pound per hour for each square foot of land. A smear of floating pumice five miles in diameter was observed in Bristol Bay.

By a stroke of luck, the cataclysmic event was documented "before and after" by Father Hubbard. His findings provide an important benchmark by which to judge the rate at which vegetation and wildlife will return to the devastated caldera. A year before the eruption, Hubbard's party had found Aniakchak Caldera to be a "plant, fish, and animal world" enclosed by towering walls. When Hubbard returned in June 1931, his mountain garden was devoid of life. He described the climb up the caldera as "going through a valley of death in which not a blade of grass or a flower or a bunch of moss broke through the thick covering of deposited ash."[1] The interior of the abyss was even more of a nightmare: "black floor, black walls, black water, deep black holes, and black vents." Surprise Lake, in the northeastern part of the caldera, was choked with ash. New, perfectly circular ash craters dimpled the floor. Fresh cinder cones sprouted out from the ground. And although the volcano had cooled, the soil, still hot, registered as much as 1,000 degrees Fahrenheit at a depth of twelve inches. In his usual theatrical way, the Glacier Priest donned vestments each morning and set up an altar in the center of the caldera. He held mass surrounded by columns of superheated vapor spiraling a thousand feet into the air, "using the stately columns of ascending smoke" for altar candles.

Hubbard's films, books and *National Geographic* articles gave Aniakchak international recognition, but forty more years passed before anyone returned to seriously investigate it. Although Aniakchak is quiet now—no major eruptions have occurred since that of 1931—very few people have seen the caldera and fewer still have walked upon its floor. Park records show that only one or two parties visit Aniakchak each year.

The low-level flight through overcast and drizzle was fairly standard stuff by now: a rumpled, off-green tundra below; families of swans on nearly every pond and small lake; scattered bands of caribou moving restlessly, grazing as they went; and something new, a lone gray wolf that gazed up at us, then took off loping across the broken ground.

About an hour after leaving King Salmon, we finally saw the caldera ahead (at least the map showed it to be a caldera). Through the rain-spattered Plexiglass, it looked like any other flat-topped mountain of the Aleutian Range, until the ground changed as we flew closer. Instead of a carpet of lichens, mosses and creeping shrubs, the land became a bare ashy skin. When the 1946-vintage Goose began its long ascent to clear the caldera rim, I couldn't help feeling our luck was running stronger than usual. The scuddy clouds ended a few miles before the approaching walls. Ahead was blue sky and dazzling sunshine.

The Goose's twin engines whined as we climbed from a few hundred feet to three thousand on the altimeter. Cliffs striped with shafts of snow and dark cinders streaked past the silver nose. The five of us pressed our faces against the windows, gawking at the rapidly changing scenery. Suddenly the Goose bellied over the caldera wall and skimmed over the lip. The next instant, when I looked straight below me, I felt a surge of vertigo. Beneath me was a sheer drop of several thousand feet to the black crater floor. When the plane banked, I saw through the port window a pool of turquoise water, the color a startling contrast to the burnt surroundings. The pilot turned to me, pointed to the gem and mouthed the words, "Surprise Lake."

I smiled to myself. Once again I was following in the steps of Father Hubbard. In 1932, on a return visit to Aniakchak after the eruption, his party, including dogs and supplies, was the first to be landed by airplane on the two-and-a-half-mile-long lake.

The amphibious plane circled once, slipped sideways and dropped inside the closed world. As we skidded atop the water a few gulls flew off and a bald eagle flapped heavily away. It felt sacrilegious to shatter the tranquility of the caldera, but I consoled myself that the intrusion would be brief and would not leave any scars. With the big overhead engines idling, we taxied over to a spot on the lake's southern shore that Manski had recommended as a campsite. We unloaded the aircraft quickly. When the Goose flew off, we were totally alone, deep in isolation, completely overwhelmed. Though the steam and columns of smoke that Hubbard had described were gone, the caldera was still the somber heart of a mountain the likes of which we had never seen.

Gradually the shock began to wear off. The fiercely burning sun spurred us into action. We changed from foul-weather gear to shorts, T-shirts and running shoes. "I can't believe it," I said, remarking on all the exposed flesh. "Absolutely no black flies or mosquitoes to make life miserable."

We carried our gear about a hundred feet from shore, to a gully where a small bunch of waist-high alders and willows (the largest shrubs around) offered a modicum of cover for the tents. Taura's smaller mountain tent we set up between the two VE-24 domes. "Make sure that all the guylines are staked down tightly," Clyde told her. "According to Manski, it can really get crazy in here." Since we planned to be at this camp for four to five days, we took the additional precautions of using heavy rocks and the sixty-pound folded rafts as deadmen anchor points.

Although we were tired, it was too fine a day to waste even a second of it resting. We broke off into groups to explore the terrain around our campsite. Clyde and Marion prowled along the shore, searching for the warm mineral springs that feed the lake and make lighter chalky puffs around its edges. Mike, Taura and I set our sights on climbing the two cinder cones at the northwest end of the lake. The tallest was only about 400 feet high, but it promised to offer a panoramic view of the ruptured crater floor.

From camp the cone had looked like a conical pile of coal where no plants could possibly grow, but as we climbed its steep slope we found many small, unidentified flowers blooming on the rocky surface. When we reached the pointed summit, rather than looking at the small details we tried to take in infinity. We were surrounded on all sides by a near-perfect circle of unclimbable ash-covered walls, a brown and gray skeletal rim dominated by the snow-frosted mass of 4,400-foot Mount Aniakchak. There were only two ways for us to exit this six-mile-wide pit: one was Birthday Pass on the western rim of the caldera that leads to Port Heiden on Bristol Bay via a difficult fifteen-mile hike through alder jungles and tundra meadows; the other was the one we were taking, the more direct route by water through the Gates.

We slid and stumbled down the long incline, and by following undulating sweeps of ash continued to the west. Scattered across the pockmarked floor were the charred debris and scarred formations of past volcanic activity. Ancient lava flows spread out from plugged vents in twisted streams of rock, reminding me of scabs not yet healed. Offering the only bit of sparkle in the otherwise stark landscape was the pale green lake. Fed by snowmelt and mineral springs, Surprise Lake is the source of the Aniakchak River, which exits the caldera through the Gates. Without this gash in the caldera wall, Aniakchak would ultimately turn into an Alaskan "crater lake" similar to the slightly smaller, well-known caldera that holds Crater Lake in Oregon.

A rusty-red rivulet, inches deep, caught our attention. The source of the runoff, a bubbling spring, welled up right out of the caldera floor and eventually emptied into the lake. The water was warm to the touch. Matching rusty-red algae floated in pools and covered the shoreline rocks. In a few eroded swales were fingers of vegetation. Sedges, horsetail, grasses, marsh marigold and pioneering forbs grew out of the ash adjacent to the moist banks.

The thin mantle of life created enough of an oasis to attract the animal life of the caldera. Running ahead of us, probing the soft mud, were semipalmated plovers, small shorebirds with a single black band around the throat. A flock of snow buntings took off at our approach, flashing their characteristic snow-white wings. Gleaning seeds from the wildflowers were Lapland longspurs and water pipits, sparrow-like birds the same ashy gray color as the ground.

When Hubbard first visited the caldera, he found huge bear tracks one to two feet deep around Surprise Lake. By contrast, we observed very little griz spoor, but that didn't mean we weren't watchful.

The white-bleached scats of red fox were common. The small carnivores apparently find enough mammals to eke out an existence here, because when I tore the droppings apart, I found a high percentage of small mammal remains, especially the mandibles and teeth of voles and possibly lemmings. Also plentiful were the fresh tracks of caribou. As we wound up the runnel, their hoofprints led us to a deep gully where a pair of big bulls were feeding. They were so preoccupied that they didn't see us until we were close. When they galloped off to the center of the basin, their white neck bibs and the white dust spurts from their hooves were backlit by the low rays of the setting sun.

We climbed a flat plateau made by a ragged lava flow that spilled across the plain like milk froth boiled over from a saucerpan—yet the color of a dead, cool fire. The surface consisted of razor-sharp rocks and grotesquely melted boulders of black obsidian that had been wind-scoured to a shiny glaze. The higher perspective offered us a better view of the billowing clouds that continually spilled over the southern rim down toward Surprise Lake. These were Aniakchak's extraordinary "cloud niagras" I had read about in Hubbard's books, a phenomenon he described as "a

Inside the Aniakchak Caldera; "cloud niagras" can be seen on the caldera rim.

huge wash-tub filled with soapsuds running over and down its sides."[2] As cold air from the Bering Sea collides with the warmer air of the North Pacific, a fleecy torrent is often brewed which rides the downdrafts over the crater's lip like a river plunging over a precipice. What made the niagras even more interesting was that the clouds never hit the bottom, dissipating instead about two-thirds down the wall. We stood amazed, unable to take our eyes off this oddity, mesmerized by the strangeness of it all.

A heavy fog blanketed the caldera floor in the morning. It was six o'clock, still and calm, with minimal visibility. While everyone was still asleep, I threw on my rain jacket and pants and went walking. I couldn't see much, but it was pleasant to be outside.

I was watching clear water lap on the rocks when a flock of mew gulls rushed out of nowhere, so close that I heard the whoosh of their wings. Squawking loudly, their next pass was even closer to my head. The birds harassed me all the way back to camp.

By mid-morning the fog had burned off and the temperature rose dramatically. First we stripped off our raingear, then our pile jackets, then finally our long underwear. Decked out in shorts and T-shirts, we were ready for a long day of hiking. Everyone picked a destination that interested him or her most. I took off to climb Vent Mountain, a steep secondary cone that rises 2,200 feet above the crater floor. Five miles in circumference, it is the most prominent feature inside the caldera, a volcano within a volcano.

A short distance from camp the terrain became mostly level with only a slight elevation gain. The floor of the caldera was pavement hard, probably an old sagging lava field, and walking was easy, but by the time I was halfway up the cone's north face, I had sweated through my T-shirt and my feet were burning up. When I came upon a trickle of ice-cold water running through patches of snow that had survived since winter, I filled up my plastic bottle and poured the contents over my head. Goosebumps pricked my skin as the shock ran down my neck and over my back.

I climbed in short bursts up the sliding shale, a freshening wind helping to blow me uphill as I neared the crest. Later, when I reached the cone's 3,350-foot summit, I was intrigued by the sight of a smaller, dry crater at the top. Vent Mountain had blown its lid during a previous eruption, resulting in a 400-foot-deep, concentric pit about a quarter-mile wide. Looking to the south over the pit, I could see the faint blue horizon of the Pacific Ocean, where we would be in a week or so. In the foreground, roistering through the

Gates under the rueful stare of Black Nose, 3,800 feet high and capped with deep snow, was the river that would take us there. To the west lay Birthday Pass, a possible but not preferable route out of here. And far to the northeast were lofty mountains rimmed with glaciers. Could they be part of the high Aleutian peaks in Katmai National Park? I checked my map. They were—150 miles away! I thought fondly of the trip Judy and I had made to that area some years before.

I was sitting on the knife-edged crest, wrapped in reminiscences, when a clatter of loose rocks startled me. I spun around. Marion, dressed in shorts and a halter top, waved from further down the rim and came over to join me. The others, she said, were searching for the site of the 1931 eruption on the valley floor. There was nowhere to go atop Vent Mountain except around it or back down, so we circled the lip, careful to watch our step. A misstep to one side or the other would have resulted in a long, painful fall. Seeing the others starting their climb on the west side of Vent Mountain, we began our descent to meet them.

The first thousand feet or so of drop was easy: going down the loose pumice absorbed a lot of energy and we could run with loping strides, sliding and sinking with each step. The final thousand feet, however, was down a very steep snow chute. Marion, an accomplished downhill skier, was able to carve turns into the wet, packed snow by angling the soles of her hiking boots and shifting her body weight. I was unable to duplicate her finesse and followed oafishly as best I could. She waited up for me with only a few hundred yards left to go, suggesting I should glissade—slide on my butt—down the remaining run.

"No thanks," I said. "You *do* see that pile of boulders at the bottom, don't you?"

"Sure," Marion replied casually. "But don't worry, you'll stop way before then." With that, she pushed off and schussed down the slope.

After only a few steps I slipped and landed on my butt, and by no decision of my own, I was glissading after all. Instantly I picked up speed, careening out of control. My bare hands and arms scraped into the corn snow without slowing me down. As brakes my feet were useless; if I dug them in I would do a full-body somersault and likely break my neck. My glissade lasted about as long as a trip down a water slide in an amusement park, and I ground to a halt a few yards from the rockpile.

For a moment, as I lay catching my breath, I saw nothing

stirring. Then on a ridge opposite there appeared, one by one, a long string of grayish-brown figures walking dreamily in single file, their white hocks standing out clearly as they emerged from the bare ground. By the time I had wiped the snow out of my eyes, the caribou had continued on their way, vanishing behind some clumps of cinder.

It got windy during the night, the kind of wind that flaps and shakes the tent, that gnaws away at your peace of mind. We battened down the rain flies, tightened the guylines and tried to sleep.

When we next stepped outside, it was as if we had passed through a doorway to the center of the earth. The top of the caldera was lost in the clouds. The gray lid and gray walls heightened our sense of isolation. After a late breakfast, Mike and I left for the Gates to scout the chasm and the whitewater we soon would be facing. The walking was easy along the lake: the mile-wide field of obsidian and pumice was as firm as asphalt underfoot. The wind, however, was another matter, gusting out of the Gates into our faces. We had enjoyed our days of blue skies and sunshine, and now it was time for normal Aniakchak weather.

"I'm glad we all got on top of Vent Mountain when we did," Mike said. "Take a look over there." I wiped the rain off my glasses with a dry cloth and followed his gaze to the center of the caldera. Even the base of the Vent had vanished in the white shroud.

When we reached the far end of the ash field we were thankful to have on our tall rubber boots. Moistened by melting snow or ice below ground level, the surface was a squishy mire, host to some of the lushest vegetation in the caldera. We waded a creek near the mouth of the lake, its riffling shallows milky and opaque. This rill was followed by another and another, both as clear as the first was murky.

We bent into the wind and entered the Gates. The river pouring out of Surprise Lake narrows here and quickens its pace. Between steep walls the foaming current flowed around and over a slew of sharp-edged volcanic boulders that had tumbled down the mountainsides. An unavoidable Class III drop in mid-stream normally wouldn't have posed a problem for our small, responsive paddle rafts, but the boulders made things hazardous. Manski had told us of one party that had braved the rapids: their raft was trashed and one of the rafters had to be helicoptered out. We studied the tricky rock garden for some time, trying to decide whether or not it was doable. Manski's party had tried lining the rafts from shore, but they tore a hole through one boat and swamped the other. With all this in mind, I knew we would carry, yet it was fun to fantasize about making it through the Gates in one quick, decisive spurt.

It was still early, and the rain we were expecting had not yet materialized. "As long as we've come this far," I proposed, "how about if we hike on through the Gates?" I almost had to shout in Mike's ear so he could hear me above the din of the rapids and the wind.

The wind was a definite force in this connecting river canyon. Because of a venturi effect its velocity was accelerated, similar to what happens when one's thumb clamps over the end of a trickling garden hose and a jet of water results. I began to dread the thought of portaging the rafts through the chasm with this kind of air current.

The game trail wound up and down the tilting talus slope. In the lead, Mike stopped, looked down at the rocks and picked one up. Ever the science teacher, he pointed out quarter-sized scalloped fossils imbedded in the chunks of sedimentary sandstone. "I don't know what genus they belong to," he said, "but they're definitely marine clams and snails, probably laid down in the Age of Reptiles about 135 million years ago." He noticed my glazed stare. "For the benefit of all you toads who flunked paleontology," he continued in his best professorial voice, "in plain English this means that a very long time ago the land we're standing on was covered by the ocean."

Fascinating stuff, this, but I was more interested in the fresh dung and partly eaten sockeye salmon a few feet ahead on the faint path. "Excuse me," I said, as I kneeled down to study the scat.

"Griz?" Mike asked.

"Griz," I said. "And it's quite a bit fresher than that fossil you found."

The bear sign added to the wildness of the gorge. The cold wind, the whitewater, the clatter of falling rocks reminded me of the snout of a tidewater glacier. But when we reached the downstream end of the Gates, we were in another world, one totally apart from the desolation inside the crater. The country outside the ring of walls was vivid green with a variety of vegetation, a jolting contrast to the caldera's gray barrenness. Emphasizing the difference still more was a large, furry grizzly, probably the same one who had dirtied the trail.

The tawny yellow bear shrugged, stood up and looked our way. Mike was elated—his first Alaska grizzly; he was also concerned when *Ursus arctos* didn't run off. Knowledgeable in such matters, I assured him that we were safe as long as we didn't surprise or threaten it. We climbed a scree slope above the bear and peeked cautiously around a pile of stones. About a hundred yards away the bruin resumed angling for salmon and trout, both of which have been known to spawn in Surprise Lake. However, when Mike spotted a second grizzly on the scree slope coming our way, I was the first to say, "It's time to leave."

Upon reentering the caldera, we were nearly knocked off our feet. The wind, already strong, was packing even more of a wallop as it whipped through the Gates. The rain we had been expecting finally began to fall. We were chilled and damp when we reached camp, but what a cheery sight it was to see our partners huddled under a tarp, brewing enough tea to go around.

I rolled out of my sleeping bag at 8 a.m., finally caught up with yesterday's journal entry. The distinctive three-part whistled song of a golden-crowned sparrow hung lazily in the air. I looked outside. It was foggy again, but with little wind. A lone eagle sat by itself on a sandpit about two hundred yards off; a few diving ducks—goldeneye and scaup—swam peacefully in the shallows near shore. Mike, reading a paperback, asked me to check the temperature.

"What do you think it is?" I asked, a game he and I play often, with him winning most of the time.

"Fifty degrees," he said.

"Ha! It's fifty-one," I sneered.

This was another day to hike and climb or do whatever our mood called for. I strolled off by myself after breakfast, wanting to see more of this geological wonderland. First stop was Half Cone, pressed against the northwestern wall. At one time Half Cone may have been the size of Vent Mountain, but when it blew it left an indentation on the caldera's side as large as a football field, a multicolored layering of sedimentary and volcanic rocks stained by oxidation and acidic emissions. Fantastically shaped congealed magma—called *bombs*—that had been blown out of the cone and bounced down the mountainside were scattered around the area like disfigured building blocks. Growing amidst the wreckage was a tapestry of blue flowering lupines, enough color and softness to fill my wide-angle lens.

I next visited the crater that geologists believe was the site of the 1931 eruption at Aniakchak. Some of the highest ground temperatures in the caldera have been recorded here. While exploring the area a few days earlier, Clyde, Mike and Taura had located a small fumarole where steam wafted from sulphur-blemished rocks that were warm to the touch. Despite the knowledge that others had arrived before me, I still had the sensation of being the first ever to set foot here as I climbed to the top of the massive mound. With Aniakchak's crumbly walls half-hidden in the swirling, parting, closing clouds, and the yawning gape of the doughnut-shaped hole below, I imagined myself a space voyager; this pitted landscape was as naked and lifeless as the surface of some distant planet. Then I looked closer and realized how wrong I was. At the bottom of the crater, growing in areas bare of old snow and puddles of ice, a mass of lichens embroidered the rubble with flecks of black, orange and green. The primitive plants marked the beginning of the slow and complex process of succession that, unless thwarted by another eruption, will eventually result in the garden spot Hubbard first found in 1930.

A cold breath of wind ushered in a rampart of fog that quickly covered the caldera floor. Marble-sized raindrops pelted the ground. I was adrift in white gauze, alone among the misty crags. The croaks of ravens suddenly rang out from the gloomy ceiling. The birds sounded frightened, and I thought I knew why. Unable to see, they were probably disoriented and in danger of flying into the sheer walls. Their guttural calls and the wind were the only sounds. I ate my last bit of trail mix, gathered my daypack and moved on.

The thing about sleeping outdoors is that you feel a part of the night. But I'd rather be a part of some nights than others—and this was obviously going to be one of the others. A vicious wind came up, howling and threatening to launch our tents, and us, into the lake. At dawn, Surprise Lake was a maelstrom of whitecaps and frothy spray. Great clouds of ash swirled around the caldera. The fine volcanic dust covered everything and seeped inside the tents. We were fortunate that our camp was in a small cove that shielded us from the worst of the storm. In June and July 1973, a camper had his camp destroyed twice during a six-week period and his boat blown away. More recently, Manski's tent—the same model we were using—was knocked down and some of the poles broken during a violent caldera windstorm.

We had been hoping to start our raft trip that day. Instead, we were faced with the elemental problems of keeping dry and fed. When Mike and I went out to get some food we found the "Aniakchak diner" a mess. We had stupidly left Clyde's big brown tarp, the one we had put to good use so many nights in Becharof and

Togiak, outside after dinner the night before. Stretched between the rock walls, it was in tatters. Everything we had left outside in the kitchen area was buried in black sand. We found the cooking pots some distance away, blown into a ravine. The stove was choked with dust and would have to be dismantled and cleaned. Disgusted with our carelessness, we put the site in order, then fought the wind back to our tent.

Later, bored from reading and lounging around, Taura and I went for a short hike on the ridges behind camp. The wind blew across the open caldera with the breath of an arctic dragon. In the worst of the exposed areas we had to crawl on the ground to make any headway. All the boot tracks we had left in the ashy basin were swept away, leaving a clean slate for the next caldera visitors.

Later the wind finally called it quits. No flapping tent, no waves breaking on shore. I could actually hear myself think again. We had a quick conference, calling back and forth from inside the tents. It was unanimous: we agreed to wake early, inflate the rafts and get out of the caldera if we could.

We broke camp while the tents were still heavy with dew. The lake crossing and the portage through the Gates were behind us—we were ready for the next leg of our trip, from the caldera to the sea.

The river was two to three feet deep for the most part, more than adequate for the *Hail Mary* and *Father Hubbard*. Occasionally it branched off into braided channels that called for quick decision making. We usually chose the correct route, but once we ended up charging into a swift-moving, shallow corridor barely wider than the five-foot-six-inch-wide raft. Overhanging alders scraped the boat as we passed, and hundreds of silvery salmon squirted out from under the raft, their backs slicing through the water. Twice I clubbed the fish with my paddle by mistake, but it didn't slow them down in the least.

It was inevitable under such circumstances that we would encounter bears. The comparatively mild climate of the Alaska Peninsula, the long period of food availability and the quantity and quality of food, particularly salmon, helped account not only for the large size of the grizzlies we saw, but for their abundance as well.

Father Hubbard was well behind us when Mike and I spotted a grizzly standing at a bend in the river directly in our path. We backpaddled mightily, but we couldn't stop—the current was too fast. The bear stood up to stare at us, then galloped away across the gravel bar. There were several other times that day when we surprised grizzlies fishing the shallows or loafing next to shore. Like the bears of Becharof, they certainly weren't the skittish type. A few went so far as to approach us deliberately. Though they may have been merely curious, we were always glad to reach deeper water and slip past without a confrontation.

A few miles from the Gates the whitewater became more fun, nothing dangerous, but with enough twists, turns and plunges to make it exciting. While I shoveled water and pulled the raft through the rollers, Mike kept the boat on course, trying to avoid a collision with the low cliffs or a barely submerged boulder. A couple of big, ice-cold curlers sloshed over the air tubes, soaking us from the chest down, but we were comfortable in our polypropylene longjohns covered with wind jackets and rainpants. Neoprene booties kept our feet warm.

The rafts played leap-frog on the narrow river: we would hit an eddy they would miss; they would catch one and we'd go barrelling past. We easily could have covered twice the distance, but we stopped often. The valley was quintessential Alaska wilderness: low, tundra-covered mountains and deep divides. Along the river was a mixture of high banks, scrubby alders and willows and open floodplain bottoms. We saw many new birds: magpies, long-tailed jaegers, arctic terns, bank swallows, northern shrikes, Wilson's and yellow warblers, rough-legged hawks, falcons and shorebirds and ducks. On the ridges off to the side of the river roamed bands of caribou, grazing as they went as if it were their role in life to keep the tundra mowed. Closer to the river, a red fox bounded through the grass, sniffing out mice. Of course, there was bear sign everywhere we stopped.

We set up camp about six miles from the caldera. From the tent door I could see the caldera's walls and the steel-jawed Gates through which we had come. The high peaks surrounding the caldera were distinguishable by the large amount of snow covering them; no other mountains in sight from this location were so well marked.

At sunset I had an outstanding view of the surrounding country from a small hill about 1,200 feet above camp. As a layer of clouds snaked up the valley—wispy curtains that covered the mountaintop—I hurriedly poked around the flat-topped peak before all visibility was gone. Three caribou appeared in front of me. Surprisingly approachable, the animals trotted off a few yards and stopped, torn between wariness and curiosity about the strange but apparently harmless shape in their midst. When they figured out what I was, or wasn't, they wheeled and bounded off. The caribou had every reason to be anxious. The abundance of bear sign on the ridge was spooky, especially with the fog closing in. When I heard a heavy thud I didn't stick around to see if it were another caribou or a loose rock falling off the other side. I took off running. There are some things in the wilderness that are better left unknown.

It was midnight and we were all still awake, too hyper to sleep even after another day of whitewater rafting. For the last hour we had been discussing bear attack stories we had heard or read—a woman partially eaten in the Brooks Range who miraculously survived; a man outside of Fairbanks needing nine-and-a-half hours of surgery and 2,000 stitches to repair the damage inflicted by a grizzly; a husband and wife camped in the Kenai who were attacked and mauled during the night. The list was long and gruesome.

After we had said good night, I fished out my spiralbound notebook from the tent side pocket. I wanted to collect my thoughts so that years from now I could recall what had happened on this day. It isn't often that one observes twenty-eight grizzly bears between sunup and sunset.

All morning we had bounced through haystacks and over small falls, through standing waves that slapped us chest-high. When we reached the outlet of Hidden Creek, about ten miles out of the caldera, the Aniakchak became even sportier. The river squeezed between jagged volcanic rock walls where precise maneuvering was necessary. One by one we greased past mammoth-sized boulders, only to have to backpaddle immediately and side draw to avoid collision with the next one. The raft handled well, despite the buckets of water that splashed aboard. Since the boat wasn't the more expensive self-bailing kind, I, as bowman, got stuck with the thankless job of bailing in addition to my roles as photographer, navigator and the first line of defense against rocks. I let Mike take the credit for guiding the *Hail Mary* through the difficult runs.

It was something of a letdown that afternoon when the mountains grew further apart and the valley flattened out. The whitewater fizzled to an end, replaced by a fast current with no real rapids. We didn't know then that the real action of the trip had yet to begin. Before pitching camp we had had numerous bear sightings. The first two entries in my journal, more or less, were typical of the more memorable encounters:

Mike and I were in the raft when we spotted a griz on a gravel bar downstream. The river was shallow, but the tug of the current drew us unavoidably closer. We were practically aground when the bear dropped the fish it was munching and loped toward us like a half-ton frisky puppy.

"Paddle! Paddle!" I shouted, feeling the rocks scrape the raft bottom.

"Damn it! We're stuck!" Mike stammered.

Hearing us, the bear skidded to a stop maybe twenty yards away, then, more cautiously, continued edging closer up the bank of the river. Seconds went by.

"What do you want to do?" Mike asked, the urgency of the situation reflected in a high pitched voice I had never heard before.

"I don't know," I stuttered. The sphincter tightening tension was too much.

Holding my paddle in my hands, ready to use it as a threatening club, I waved my arms and howled as if I were leading a bayonet charge. Mike jumped up and down like a Masai herdsman at a ceremonial dance and almost knocked me out of the boat. Whatever we did it worked: the griz woofed, turned and shuffled off.

Hail Mary's crew was on shore, when a grizzly suddenly materialized out of the low shrubbery across the river. The river was only forty feet wide, not much of an obstacle for an animal known to swim thirty miles.

We froze. Mike quietly started to move toward the shotgun, which was stored in a waterproof case. Before he could reach it, the bear, its hackles raised, made a bluff charge at us. Instinctively (I was getting good at this), I threw up my arms and yelled my guts out while Mike grappled with the shotgun case. We were lucky again. The grizzly abruptly ended the encounter by swiftly veering away and crashing into the brush.

Our search for a secure place to camp was tiring. The area we had originally marked on the map as our first choice was covered with a devilish growth of waist-high alders; we preferred a more open site, something on the order of a baseball stadium parking lot. We kept paddling, thinking we'd come across a tundra bank, but the land continued to be flat and brushy, with the nearest rise a half-mile away.

The river started to braid into three or four slender channels. Fortunately, the water was still deep enough. We bumped and ground on a few gravel bars, but always managed to spin off without having to get out and push. I shuddered to think how rough this float trip would have been if there had been a foot less water.

When the brush started to thin, we resumed our search for campsites, a search complicated by the fact that everyplace we stopped was lousy with bear sign (the river was teeming with fish). Beaching the rafts at a shallow side channel, we practically had to walk over the backs of thrashing salmon to get to shore. We noticed that a couple of the fish, struggling to reach deeper water, had had perfect mouth-shaped bites taken out of their humps that could have only been made by a bear.

We finally settled on a campsite as bad as all the rest. By "bad" I mean that minutes after landing we had eight grizzlies within view at the same time; by "bad" I mean that during dinner two griz haughtily strolled into camp; by "bad" I mean just before we went to bed another bear trundled down the creek behind us and got uncomfortably close before it turned away.

I closed my notebook and clicked off the headlamp. Fatigue from a full day was winning out over my anxiety. Before zipping up my bag, I held my breath, listening for the slightest sound. I heard nothing from the other tents; Clyde, Marion and Taura must have finished their Scrabble game and gone to sleep. Beside me, Mike was softly snoring, oblivious to whatever might be prowling outside. Satisfied, I jammed in my ear protectors, pulled down my hat and sealed myself in the fiber-filled cocoon. It had been a strange and haunting day, but stranger things were still to come.

Several long and restless hours later I lifted the stocking hat off my eyes. Mike was sitting up, peering outside the tent.

"Well, finally decided to wake up, eh?" he said cheerfully. "You sure thrashed around a lot last night. Have a few bad dreams?"

Without waiting for my reply, he zipped up the door and crawled back into his bag. "Might as well go back to sleep, though. We've got pea-soup fog and drizzle this morning. No sense paddling if we can't see anything."

An hour or so later, Clyde appeared at our front door, wearing only his candy-striped long underwear and rubber boots. Beads of water were dripping down his beard and long hair. "G'morning," he said, glancing over his shoulder as he spoke. "Better get up. We got a big griz moving into camp."

Mike and I crawled outside into the light rain. Even through my smeared eyeglasses I could see the chocolate-brown grizzly staring at us from fifty yards away. A fat salmon dangled limply from its mouth as it shuffled from one forefoot to another.

"What's the problem?" Mike said, sounding disappointed. "I thought you said the bear was close." Clyde and I glanced at each other and rolled our eyes. Was this the same guy who not too long ago had seen his first grizzly?

We stood in the rain wondering what both we and the bear were going to do next. Marion and Taura followed the proceedings from inside their tents. Either I said something or Mike coughed, I can't remember which. In any case, that little bit of human acoustics was all it took: the grizzly dropped the fish and melted back into the fog.

Given that it was getting late and the weather had improved only slightly, we decided to make this a rest day. When the clouds lifted some in the afternoon I positioned myself on a small knoll behind the tents and scanned the landscape with binoculars. The patchwork valley of low brush, open tundra benches and gravel bars was a natural for wildlife. I saw more bears and caribou, as well as red foxes, bald eagles, sandhill cranes, tundra swans, northern harriers and a pair of short-eared owls. Afterward, Mike gave me some fishing lessons. I felt somewhat hypocritical for breaking my self-imposed rule never to fish in grizzly country unless it was an emergency and to respect fish as part of the wilderness ecosystem I did not want to disturb, but I cast my lure in a nearby creek anyway. Either Mike was a good teacher or I was blessed with beginner's luck. Within a half-hour I caught three Dolly Varden, one a twenty-incher.

That evening I had my first fish dinner in the Alaska backcountry, prepared to perfection by chef Michael over a single-burner Coleman camp stove. At first Clyde sat at the edge of the group as we tore into the thick, pan-fried fillets, then, to the surprise of us all, he forked up a small piece of the firm, pink flesh and chewed it down. Clyde eating meat was something I wasn't prepared for. Apparently living in Anchorage had made bigger changes in him than I had thought.

We were up at nine, on the water at noon. The weather was a carry-over from the day before—cool and misty with low, thick gray clouds. A steady wind blew in from the Pacific, requiring us to paddle constantly to make headway.

The river completely changed character in this lower stretch, widening into a braided series of lazy oxbows, yet still deep enough that we rarely became grounded. No longer concerned about the next rapid, Mike and I paddled ahead, leaving the other raft to go at its own pace.

Around lunchtime we pulled over near the mouth of Mystery Creek, a shallow tributary coming down from the hills to the north. We stretched out on the air tubes and waited for the others. In a few minutes they rounded a curve and bumped alongside. Mike and I listened with interest as Taura described *Father Hubbard*'s recent close shave.

"Did you see those bears?!?" she asked breathlessly. "You didn't? Well, there were these two grizzlies on shore staring at us. We were in shallow water when the larger one charged. If Clyde hadn't yelled and beat the water with his paddle, I don't know what would have happened." Clyde, the hero, smiled and shrugged. "Anyway," Taura continued, "the bear stopped at the edge of the sandbar, really close. That gave us time to get out of there."

After lunch Clyde drew Mike and me aside. He asked if we would stay closer from now on. I think I knew why: We had Mike's shotgun. Clyde had his .44 Magnum revolver but no ammunition. In an uncharacteristic display of forgetfulness, he had left all his bullets in Anchorage.

Around five o'clock we passed the brush-choked mouth of Aniakchak's North Fork, an unrunnable rocky river with headwaters ten miles away at the base of wrinkled Elephant Mountain. A pair of caribou rattled up the cobblestones at our approach, stopping briefly in mid-channel to check us out. Just beyond the tributary we floated toward an enormous animal with only its rump showing amidst the alders. Its coat was a warm, deep russet. I heard Clyde, in the other raft, whisper, "moose," which is what I guessed it was too. Without paddling, the current took us along the deepwater bank. The rafts scraped against an overhanging branch. The beast spun around. Only then did we discover that our "moose" was actually a behemoth grizzly bear. We were safe enough in the boats, provided the bear didn't take a big leap. As we drifted past I talked quietly to the animal, trying somehow to bridge the abyss between our species. Though alert and curious, the griz had no interest in communicating.

It was eight o'clock when we found a tundra clearing atop a high cutbank. Inland was an alder savanna, part open and part jungle. More foul weather rolled in during the evening. Landmarks we had been focusing on all day were slowly covered by the drooping clouds. At this point, however, we needed to see only one.

Cape Horn, an angular black massif standing alone above the coastal plain, signalled that the end of our journey was near.

We ate our morning meal under Clyde's salvaged tarp. A thick alder hedge shielded our backs from the wind-driven rain. Even without Cape Horn to guide us we could tell that only a few miles remained between us and the ocean: the smell of saltwater was in the air; the tides were affecting the river. However, Aniakchak Bay would have to wait. We weren't going to wage war with the gale if we didn't have to. We were right on schedule despite the delay. Ample time remained to explore the coastline.

We talked and sipped hot drinks for awhile before retreating into the saturated tents. It was the perfect kind of day to slip into your sleeping bag and read a good paperback. I was halfway through *Trinity* by Leon Uris, a novel about Ireland in the 1800s. Besides being an engaging story, the book was helping me prepare for an upcoming trip Judy and I were taking after I returned from Alaska. She had planned a two-week bicycle tour of counties Cork and Kerry in the Republic of Ireland, a "civilized" adventure that I was looking forward to.

The final miles of the Aniakchak took us through scenic low hills, green as an Iowa summer pasture. The river became broader as it neared the ocean, but still carried enough water for us to squeak by. With the threat of bears diminished, Mike and I pulled slightly ahead of *Father Hubbard*. We were forced to paddle steadily to keep the raft in line with the current and buck the upstream wind.

At mid-afternoon we reached the mouth of the river, a wide, flat sandbar in the process of being flooded by the tide. "Where do we go from here?" Mike asked.

I studied the topographic map on my lap. The river emptied into northernmost Aniakchak Bay, an eight-mile wide, crescent-shaped bight that was open to the North Pacific. "We go straight out past that rocky islet to avoid some shoals, then double back to shore. The cabin won't be far away."

We exited the mouth and eased into the ocean. Although the wind was down, it was difficult to power the fat, unwieldy raft through the undulating swells.

"Remember the last time we were on the ocean?" I asked, the thought making me break into a wide grin.

"Do I?" Mike bellowed. "After Togiak I swore I'd never make another sea-going trip with you, but here I am!"

As we rounded the offshore pinnacle, a flock of cormorants took to the air, circling over our boat to investigate this new bulbous blue marine creature. A few gulls hovered over us, squawking loudly. Unrelenting, the birds followed us as we pushed toward a low ridge with a wide sandy beach in the foreground. A breaking roller carried *Hail Mary* in the final few feet. When I jumped ashore, I felt a sense of wonder that I was in this spot. It seemed that I had been brought there by magic. Coming from the inside of a volcano to the ocean, perhaps I had been.

More heavily loaded, *Father Hubbard* had a hard time making progress against the waves. Clyde steered her to land about a hundred yards from the cabin. With everyone pulling on the haul lines, we dragged the raft above the surf. We hugged each other, congratulating ourselves on a job well done. We had not covered much distance since the caldera, but we had traveled far.

According to plan, we used the cabin as a base for the next four days while waiting for the airplane pick-up from King Salmon. Now owned by the National Park Service and open to the public, the structure had originally been built by the Alaska Packers Association as a bunkhouse for workers at their fish trap site at the mouth of the Aniakchak River. The fishing operation began in 1917 and apparently was used seasonally until the 1940s.

The one-room cabin was weathered by time and neglect—boards and windows were missing, the interior needed cleaning and there were leaks in the peaked roof—but it did offer a convenient place for cooking and sitting out storms. We swept the floor and organized the furniture: a couple of wooden boxes, a moldy cot, two metal chairs and a door we used for a table. Up in the rafters, where our food was hung, were a couple of blue plastic buckets. On a bench were tattered old copies of *Time* and *Psychology Today*. Tacked to the wall was a faded yellow note from the National Park Service requesting that users of the cabin help keep it clean and sign in. Rather than sleep inside the cabin, we opted to pitch our tents in the tall grass off to the side. A small, sandy swell provided some protection from the steady onshore breeze.

The ensuing days formed part three of our Aniakchak trilogy. The hiking was superb. The shoreline was a combination of wide, black volcanic sand beaches, grass- and shrub-covered dunes and sheer eroded cliffs beneath which were large piles containing huge, rounded boulders. At low tide we probed the rocky tidal pools, each pool a miniature ecosystem crawling with small blue mussels, thumbnail-sized snails, gray barnacles and tiny fishes. Mike spent hours perched over the clear basins; from a distance he looked like a stilt-legged heron hunting for prey.

Such a diversity of habitat attracted a diversity of animal species. Seabirds rafted offshore in company with sea otters and harbor seals; even a great whale spouted far out in the bay, causing a rash of excitement among our group. Probing among the layers of kelp and seaweed washed up on the beach were dense flocks of sandpipers and other shorebirds. We saw beaver, red foxes, sandhill cranes and caribou further inland, while near the outlets of streams feeding into the bay were grizzlies drawn to the heavy salmon runs.

On our final evening in Aniakchak's backcountry, I hiked by myself onto the row of cliffs that extend into Aniakchak Bay. From that vantage point I could see the snow-covered rim of the caldera nearly thirty miles away. Gazing north, with my back to the Pacific, I imagined I was embracing all of Alaska. I could see the North Slope of the Brooks Range, where Judy, Charlie and I had struggled with cold, wet feet while trekking through some of the wildest country in North America. I could see the Klepper kayak bouncing over Sunday Rapids on the Killik River. I could see the icy slopes of Mount McKinley in late winter. I could see the fat, irascible walrus at Togiak's Navnak Bay. And I could see the ponderous ice walls at Glacier Bay.

As I headed back to camp, taking special pleasure in my recollections, Charles Darwin's lament came to mind. "It is the fate of most voyagers," Darwin wrote during his journey around the world on the *Beagle*, "no sooner to discover what is most interesting in any locality than they are hurried from it." Tomorrow I would reach the end of this Alaska journey, but I was certain that more discoveries lay ahead.

PREPARATIONS

GETTING THERE

The highway system and scheduled commercial transport (airlines, railway, ferry) can all get you to the edge of the Alaska wilderness. In many instances, however, charter air taxi or bush aircraft will be required for at least part of your journey.

Air taxi operators should be contacted several months before departure to determine rates and make reservations. Inquire about access points, water levels, hazards, etc. Chances are someone is familiar with your destination and will be able to offer firsthand knowledge of the area. This knowledge should be valued as an addition to the research you have already done. Your letter should indicate your serious interest in travel and explain your competence. Many companies have told me they don't even respond to queries about travel plans that seem haphazard or ill-conceived.

If you keep group size to a minimum, a smaller (and less expensive) aircraft can be used and only a single shuttle will be necessary. For larger groups (four or more people) or where destinations involve rough open water landings or Aleutian-type weather, twin-engine, amphibious aircraft may be necessary.

To start the search for air taxi operators, contact the federal or state agency in charge of the area you want to visit (usually this will be the National Park Service, U.S. Fish and Wildlife Service, or National Forest Service). You may also want to consult the *Alaska Vacation Planner,* provided by the Alaska Division of Tourism. This free publication includes a list of the scheduled intrastate airlines and many of the air charters in Alaska.

When to Go

Alaska is so vast that meteorological data for one part of the state are virtually useless for another. However, it is safe to say that the best months for wilderness travel are from June through mid-September, when temperatures are at their warmest, the days are longest, and wildlife is most abundant.

Rivers and lakes start to freeze in November and don't thaw until around mid-April. In northern latitudes freeze-up may be as early as October and waters may not be open until June. Plan carefully and make telephone calls to local residents, air taxi operators or federal and state agency sources for current information to determine if your chartered floatplane will be able to make it in.

The best period for winter travel in Alaska's interior and far north is March to mid-April. Snow is usually at its deepest, temperatures are moderating, wildlife is returning, and there are long hours of daylight.

What to Bring

This subject is covered in many guidebooks on backpacking, canoeing, sea kayaking and wilderness camping. Look at several of these if you are not already experienced in wilderness travel. Basically you should keep things simple and take everything you need. Except in rare instances, you will not be able to purchase outdoor equipment outside the major transportation centers. Personally field-test all equipment before you leave home. After you wave goodbye to the floatplane and a cold windswept rain descends is not the time to discover that your raincoat leaks and your tent wasn't designed to handle high winds.

Requirements for traveling in Alaska are only marginally different than those for traveling elsewhere in northern or mountainous regions. However, some special considerations are discussed below.

Clothing

Be prepared for all types of weather, from warm and dry days to cool and wet. You may encounter rain, sleet, hail or snow at any time during summer, and lowland temperatures occasionally drop below freezing at night. Strong winds are frequent. Buy the best rain and wind gear you can afford. Underneath, several layers of clothing are better thermal insulators than one bulky garment; start out daily prepared for the worst and shed outer layers if desirable. Stick with one of the many synthetics or wool. Down and cotton will lose their insulating properties when wet and take forever to dry.

TENTS

Many tents that would otherwise be adequate for backpacking are unsuitable for use in open tundra or above treeline. I personally recommend the North Face VE-24, a geodesic-dome style, or their newer model, the VE-25 with attached vestibule. This tent comfortably sleeps two, and if absolutely necessary, three large adults. When weight is a consideration, a lighter backpacking tent may be considered, but stay with a well-known "bombproof" brand and make certain you know how to pitch it before you leave home.

FOOTWEAR

Perhaps no other item you'll be wearing is as important as what goes on your feet. After a bout with trenchfoot while wearing leather hiking boots in the Arctic National Wildlife Refuge, my footwear of choice for Alaska has been pull-on, fifteen-and-one-half-inches high, top-lace insulated rubber boots with steel shanks, the kind duck hunters and farmers use in the upper Midwest. The brand I use, Northerner, is extremely comfortable and provides enough ankle-support even when I'm toting a seventy-pound pack over rough, hummocky terrain. They cost about the same as a moderately priced pair of tennis shoes. For campwear and dry-ground hiking I also take running shoes or L.L. Bean "Maine hunting shoes." However, certain terrain (mountain hiking, for example) demands the use of lug-soled hiking boots. Except in situations where crampons will be needed for snow and ice travel, medium-weight boots are quite satisfactory. Carry several pairs of quality wool socks and liners no matter what footwear you use.

INSECT PROTECTION

The Alaska mosquito, although not as ferocious as the grizzly, is certainly more annoying. Mosquitoes, blackflies and "no-see-ums" are at their zenith in late June, July and early August. The interior areas of the state have a higher concentration of these pests than coastal areas. Headnets are not used that often, but when you need one, this inexpensive item can be a lifesaver. Since they weigh almost nothing, I usually take two just in case. Carry an ample supply of insect repellent (the more DEET the better—in terms of mosquito protection), and make certain your clothing can be sealed at wrists and ankles. Be sure to have a screened tent that can keep out the smallest of bugs.

Cook Stoves

Open campfires are discouraged, not only because they aren't compatible with the philosophy of minimum impact travel, but because backpacking stoves are far more practical and convenient in an area where the treeline is erratic. Any of the well-known cook stoves is adequate. I have used the MSR Model XGK, Coleman Peak 1 and Svea 123, all with excellent results. It might be a good idea to take a spare in the event your stove dies when you are far above treeline and your dinners consist of stone-hard minute rice and macaroni. Parties larger than three should definitely carry more than one stove.

Stove Fuel

Commercial airline regulations prohibit the transportation of any flammable liquids or bottled gas. In most instances, air taxi operators will have camp fuel available if prior notice is given.

Camp Lights

In interior and northern Alaska, a flashlight is unnecessary from May to mid-August. That said, take one anyway.

Watercraft

Folding boats that can be easily transported aboard small aircraft are most practical for those destinations inaccessible by road, chartered tour boat or the ferry system. I've used Klepper folding kayaks for years and have never had a problem with them. Two models are available, the fifteen-foot long single-seater Aerius I, and the seventeen-foot two-seater Aerius II. Other kayak manufacturers to consider are Nautiraid, Feathercraft and Folbot.

For river running when maneuverability is critical or if frequent portages are necessary (conditions that don't favor straight-tracking, unwieldy kayaks), I strongly recommend Ally Pak*Canoes, Norwegian-manufactured folding canoes available in four lengths. They are tough, light, whitewater and wilderness touring boats constructed of a rubber-vinyl skin that slips over an aluminum frame. If big whitewater is expected, many river runners opt for inflatable rafts, although they are slow and cumbersome in head-winds.

Addresses:

Hans Klepper Corp.
35 Union Square West
New York, NY 10003

Feathercraft
4-1244 Cartwright St.
Vancouver, BC, Canada V6H 3R8

Folbot, Inc.
P.O. Box 70877
Charleston, SC 29415

Ecomarine Ocean Kayak Centre
1668 Duranleau St.
Vancouver, BC, Canada V6H 3S4
(distributors of Nautiraid and other sea kayak equipment)

Ally Pak*Canoes
P.O. Box 700
Enfield, NH 03748

Northwest River Supplies, Inc.
P.O. Box 9186
Moscow, ID, 83843
(supplier of rafts and other river-running equipment)

GENERAL

Trip Length—Allow ample time for cross-country travel. Hiking or boating routes may look deceptively short, but because of diffi-cult terrain and inclement weather, more time than originally expected should be allowed. The vagaries of weather can also prevent scheduled departures and pick-ups. Be flexible. Pack a few extra days' worth of food and fuel for an emergency.

Maps—Topographic maps at a scale of 1:63,360 (one inch to the mile) or 1:250,000 (one inch equals 4 miles) are available for the entire state. They can be purchased from the U.S. Geological Survey office in Anchorage or ordered from U.S. Geological Survey, Denver Federal Center, Box 25286, Denver, CO 80225. An index to topographical mapping, which shows the extent of map coverage in Alaska, is available without charge.

Camping—Camping is generally permitted anywhere in Alaska's national parks, refuges or forests, although there may be restrictions around certain visitor and wildlife use areas. Check with the site managers for details.

Drinking Water—Locating potable fresh water is rarely a problem in Alaska; streams, creeks, rivulets and lakes abound. I have never treated water in the backcountry, but giardia has been reported in Alaska's wilderness. If you have any doubt about your source, use chemicals, filters or boiling.

Hiking/Backpacking/Mountaineering—Few trails exist other than those made by animals. There are no signposts or foot bridges. Backcountry travelers often will have to improvise routes; a heavy downpour of rain or melting glaciers can turn an ankle-deep stream into a hip-deep torrent in a few hours. River crossings can be one of the most dangerous activities of your trip. Cross-country travel in the lowlands varies enormously, but usually involves tundra, bogs, tall grass, tussocks, river and stream crossings, gravel bars, willow-alder thickets and, especially in southeast Alaska, dense rain forest. Hiking above treeline on alpine tundra can be very rewarding, but of course you have to get there.

Fitness—Being in good physical condition is essential for all hikers and paddlers. Don't wait until a month before your trip to start an exercise program; better to be in pain at home from sore muscles than on your wilderness vacation.

HAZARDS

Wildlife—The Alaska Department of Fish and Game states that the probability of being injured by a bear in Alaska is only about one-fiftieth that of being injured in an automobile on Alaskan highways. Nevertheless, both grizzly and black bear can be extremely dangerous if provoked or startled.

To avoid a bear encounter, Parks Canada offers these guidelines: don't hike alone in grizzly country; watch for bear signs such as fresh tracks, digging and droppings; stay in the open and avoid berry patches and carcass remains; be especially alert when traveling into wind; carry a noisemaker (bells or stone-filled cans), but remember that it may not be effective in dense bush or near running water; don't take your dog into the backcountry—the sight and smell of a dog often infuriates a bear and may bring on an attack; and *never* go near a bear cub—the mother may be nearby.

When camping, don't encourage bears by leaving food or garbage around. Cook and cache food away from your tent. Avoid carrying odiferous foods such as bacon or sardines. And don't camp on obvious bear trails or near high-use areas like salmon streams, although at times you may not have any other choice.

In some areas, backcountry campers are required to take special measures to minimize conflicts with grizzly bears. For example, Denali National Park and Preserve now mandates that overnight hikers must store their food in bearproof plastic pipe containers furnished by the park.

Despite your best precautions, however, there may be a time when you are faced by a hostile bear. What to do? Do not run! Grizzly bears might instinctively chase after you, and, since they have been clocked at speeds of forty miles per hour, can easily run you down. If you're in a wooded area, speak softly and back up slowly toward a tree. As you do, slowly remove your pack and set it on the ground to distract the bear, then climb high up the tree (while adult grizzlies usually are reluctant to climb, they can stretch eight to ten feet up a tree). If you're in tundra or above treeline, remain still and speak in low tones to indicate to the animal that you mean no harm. If the animal continues toward you and assumes a threatening posture (you'll recognize it when you see it), it may be helpful to scream, shout, wave your arms, clang pots together or use a bear-scaring device (e.g., firecrackers, air horn) if available.

If you are attacked by a grizzly most experts recommend "playing dead." Drop to the ground face down, move your legs up to your chest and clasp your hands over the back of your neck. Your pack, if you are wearing one, will help shield your body. This technique has been successful, but not always.

The National Park Service, the U.S. Forest Service and the Alaska Department of Fish and Game each publish very informative, free brochures explaining how to avoid bear problems and the legalities and recommendations concerning the use of firearms. For a detailed treatise on the subject, read *Bear Attacks—Their Causes and Avoidance,* by Stephen Herrero, from Nick Lyons Books, Winchester Press, 220 Old New Brunswick Rd., Piscataway, NJ 08854.

Besides bears, the only other animal to be wary of is the moose. Bull moose in rut and cows with calves can sometimes be short-tempered with intruders. Stay alert and keep your distance to avoid conflicts.

River Crossings—One of the most serious obstacles lowland hikers will face are rivers and streams. Many watercourses are sluggish and can be waded even though waist-deep, or are easily fordable on the flats where they split into several branches. Some crossings, though, can be life-threatening, especially those with glacial origins, because they are murky, numbingly cold and swift. A hiking staff, ice axe or ski pole is a necessity when crossing rivers of unknown depth or where a strong current is present. Also, attempt crossings early in the morning when glacial run-off is minimal.

Don't cross rocky streams or rivers barefoot. Carry lightweight running shoes or neoprene booties to protect the feet and keep regular boots and socks dry. Face upstream and angle across the current. Loosen the shoulder straps on your backpack and completely unfasten the hip belt so that you can quickly get it off if you fall or go under.

Hypothermia and First Aid—Hypothermia is a condition in which the loss of body heat causes the slowing of all bodily functions. If the process is allowed to continue, death may result. Hypothermia can occur even when temperatures are above freezing with wind, and through loss of liquids through perspiration, exhaustion and damp clothing. Watch for the telltale signs (uncontrolled shivering, clumsiness, slurred speech and loss of judgment are early symptoms) in yourself and your partners, and know how to treat it. There are several excellent wilderness medicine books that delve into this and other health-related topics. Read them and sign up for basic and advanced first-aid courses offered by the Red Cross. In many wilderness areas of Alaska, outside help or rescue will be unavailable for days.

Williwaws—Along exposed reaches of large lakes and coastlines, strong winds, known as *williwaws*, occur rapidly and without warning and can turn a quiet crossing into a grueling, life-threatening struggle to reach shore. Alaskan waters are extremely cold, and safe immersion time is short. Even the best swimmers should wear life jackets at all times when on the water.

Impact

Alaska's boreal and tundra environment is fragile. Make as little impact as possible and treat the wilderness and its inhabitants with care and awareness. Trampled plants take much longer to recover here than in temperate climates. Camp scraps and litter thrown on the ground may never decay, and buried garbage will surface from frost heaves or be dug up by animals. Pack out everything that cannot be completely burned, and be careful about where you burn. Plan your menu accordingly so that you don't have to supplement your rations with fish or fresh meat unless it is an emergency.

With increasing numbers of people entering the Alaska wilderness each year, and with development creeping in on all sides, it is imperative that we tread lightly. To this end, the words of pioneering ecologist and conservationist Aldo Leopold are perhaps more important today than when he penned them in *A Sand County Almanac*, forty years ago:

> Land is an organism. When we see land as a community to which we belong, we may begin to use it with love and respect. There is no other way for land to survive the impact of mechanized man.[1]

Useful Addresses

Tourist Information

Alaska Division of Tourism
Department of Commerce and Economic Development
Pouch E
Juneau, AK 99811

Alaska Marine Highway System
Pouch R
Juneau, AK 99811

Alaska Railroad
Pouch 7-2111
Anchorage, AK 99510

National Parklands in Alaska
For general information and brochures, write to:

Alaska Regional Office
National Park Service
540 West 5th Ave.
Anchorage, AK 99501
907/271-4243

Selected specific areas

Aniakchak National Monument and Preserve
P.O. Box 7
King Salmon, AK 99613

Denali National Park and Preserve
P.O. Box 9
McKinley Park, AK 99755

Gates of the Arctic National Park and Preserve
P.O. Box 74680
Fairbanks, AK 99707

Glacier Bay National Park and Preserve
Box 1089
Juneau, AK 99802
or Bartlett Cove
Gustavus, AK 99826

Katmai National Park and Preserve
P.O. Box 7
King Salmon, AK 99613

Wrangell-St. Elias National Park and Preserve
P.O. Box 29
Glennallen, AK 99588

National Wildlife Refuges in Alaska
For general information and brochures, write to:

Alaska Regional Office
U.S. Fish and Wildlife Service
1011 E. Tudor
Anchorage, AK 99503
907/786-3542

Selected specific areas

Alaska Maritime National Wildlife Refuge
202 Pioneer Ave.
Homer, AK 99603
or Alaska Maritime National Wildlife Refuge
Aleutian Islands Unit
Box 5251
FPO Seattle, WA 98791

Alaska Peninsula National Wildlife Refuge
P.O. Box 277
King Salmon, AK 99613

Arctic National Wildlife Refuge
Federal Building and Courthouse
Box 20, 101-12th St.
Fairbanks, AK 99701

Becharof National Wildlife Refuge
P.O. Box 277
King Salmon, AK 99613

Izembek National Wildlife Refuge
Pouch 2
Cold Bay, AK 99571

Togiak National Wildlife Refuge
P.O. Box 10201
Dillingham, AK 99576

National Forests in Alaska
For general information and brochures, write to:

Chugach National Forest
201 E. 9th Ave., Suite 206
Anchorage, AK 99503-3686

Tongass National Forest
Forest Service Information Center
Centennial Hall
101 Egan Dr.
Juneau, AK 99801

Selected specific areas

Misty Fjords National Monument
Tongass National Forest
3031 Tongass Ave.
Ketchikan, AK 99901

Russell Fjord Wilderness Area
Tongass National Forest, Chatham Area
204 Siginaka Way
Sitka, AK 99835
or

Yakutat Ranger District
Tongass National Forest
P.O. Box 327
Yakutat, AK 99869

Alaska Department of Fish and Game
For general information and brochures, write to:

Alaska Department of Fish and Game
1255 West Eighth St.
Box 3-2000
Juneau, AK 99802

NOTES

INTRODUCTION

[1] Adolph Murie, *Mammals of Mount McKinley National Park, Alaska* (Anchorage: Alaska National Parks and Monuments Association, 1962, 1974), p. 2.

CHAPTER 1: AMONG THE KINGS OF KATMAI

[1] Walt Whitman, *Specimen Days* (1882).

CHAPTER 2: OF ROCKS, ICE AND GLACIER BAY

[1] William D. Boehm, *Glacier Bay* (Anchorage: Alaska Geographic Society, 1975), p. 48. Reprinted by permission.

CHAPTER 3: IN THE SHADOW OF DENALI

[1] Aldo Leopold, *A Sand County Almanac* (New York: Oxford University Press, Inc., 1949).

[2] Adolph Murie, *The Wolves of Mount McKinley* (Washington, D.C.: U.S. Government Printing Office, 1944).

Chapter 4: Arctic Refuge: Beyond the Brooks Range

1 Lois Crisler, *Arctic Wild* (New York: Harper, 1973).
2 Robert Marshall, *Alaska Wilderness: Exploring the Central Brooks Range*, 2nd ed. (Berkeley, Calif.: University of California Press, 1970), p. 30.

Chapter 5: Kayak Down the Killik

1 Robert Marshall, *Alaska Wilderness: Exploring the Central Brooks Range*, 2nd ed. (Berkeley, Calif.: University of California Press, 1970).

Chapter 9: In Search of Togiak's Tuskers

1 *Togiak National Wildlife Refuge Final Comprehensive Conservation Plan/Environmental Impact Statement and Wilderness Review* (Anchorage: U.S. Fish and Wildlife Service, 1986).

Chapter 10: Aniakchak: From Caldera to Sea

1 Rev. Bernard Rosecrans Hubbard, *Cradle of the Storms* (New York: Dodd, Mead and Co., 1935).
2 ———, *Mush, You Malemutes* (New York: The America Press, 1943).

Preparations

1 Aldo Leopold, *A Sand County Almanac* (New York: Oxford University Press, Inc., 1949).

BIBLIOGRAPHY

This list includes many, but by no means all, of the existing English-language publications about Alaska's wilderness, fauna and flora, history and exploration.

BOOKS

Several of these books are out of print, and may only be available through secondhand book stores, libraries and mail-order catalogs; some of the older titles have recently been republished in paperback.

Bohn, Dave. *Glacier Bay: The Land and the Silence.* San Francisco: Sierra Club Books, 1967.

Brower, Kenneth. *The Starship and the Canoe.* New York: Holt, Rinehart & Winston, 1978.

Brown, Dale, and the Editors of Time–Life Books. *Wild Alaska.* New York: Time–Life Books, 1972 (1973, 1976, 1982, 1985).

Cooper, David. *Brooks Range Passage.* Seattle, Wash.: The Mountaineers, 1982.

Crisler, Lois. *Arctic Wild.* New York: Harper, 1958, 1964, 1973.

Davidson, Art. *Minus 148 Degrees: The Winter Ascent of Mt. McKinley.* Seattle, Wash.: Cloudcap, 1987.

Goetzmann, William H., and Kay Sloan. *Looking Far North: The Harriman Expedition to Alaska. 1899.* New York: Viking, 1982.

Griggs, Robert F. *The Valley of Ten Thousand Smokes.* Washington, D.C.: The National Geographic Society, 1922.

Heller, Christine. *Wild Flowers of Alaska.* Portland, Ore.: Graphic Arts Center, 1966.

Hubbard, Rev. Bernard Rosecrans. *Cradle of the Storms.* New York: Dodd, Mead and Co., 1935.

———. *Mush, You Malemutes.* New York: The America Press, 1932, 1938, 1943.

Marshall, Robert. *Alaska Wilderness: Exploring the Central Brooks Range.* Berkeley, Calif.: University of California Press, 1956. (2nd ed. 1970).

McGinniss, Joe. *Going to Extremes.* New York: Alfred A. Knopf, 1980.

McPhee, John. *Coming Into the Country.* New York: Farrar, Straus and Giroux, 1976.

Moseby, Jack, and David Dapkus. *Alaska Paddling Guide.* Anchorage: J&R Enterprises, 1982, 1983.

Muir, John. *Travels in Alaska.* Boston: Houghton Mifflin Co., 1915 (1971, 1978, 1979, 1988).

Murie, Adolph. *A Naturalist in Alaska.* New York: The Devin–Adair Co., 1961, 1963.

———. *The Wolves of Mount McKinley.* Washington, D.C.: U.S. Government Printing Office, 1944, 1985.

Murie, Margaret. *Two in the Far North.* New York: Knopf, 1962, 1972, 1978.

National Geographic Society. *Alaska's Magnificent Parklands.* Washington, D.C.: The National Geographic Society, 1984.

Norton, Boyd. *Alaska Wilderness Frontier.* New York: Reader's Digest Press, 1977.

Orth, Donald J. *Dictionary of Alaska Place Names.* Washington, D.C.: U.S. Government Printing Office, 1967.

Rennicke, Jeff. *Bears of Alaska in Life and Legend.* Boulder, Colo.: Roberts Rinehart, Inc., in cooperation with the Alaska Natural History Association, 1967.

Rowell, Galen. *Alaska: Images of the Country.* San Francisco: Sierra Club Books, 1981, 1985, 1986.

Sheldon, Charles. *Wilderness of Denali.* New York: Charles Scribner's Sons, 1930.

Simmerman, Nancy. *Alaska's Parklands*. Seattle, Wash.: The Mountaineers, 1983.

Snyder, Howard H. *The Hall of the Mountain King*. New York: Charles Scribner's Sons, 1973.

Stuck, Hudson. *The Ascent of Denali: A Narrative of the First Complete Ascent of the Highest Peak in North America*. Prescott, Ariz.: Wolfe Pub. Co., 1988.

Viereck, Leslie, and Elbert L. Little, Jr. *Alaska Trees and Shrubs*. Washington, D.C.: Forest Service, U.S. Department of Agriculture, 1972.

Watkins, T.H. *Vanishing Arctic: Alaska's National Wildlife Refuge*. New York: Aperture Foundation, Inc., 1988.

Wayburn, Peggy. *Adventuring in Alaska*. San Francisco: Sierra Club Books, 1988.

Weber, Sepp. *Wild Rivers of Alaska*. Anchorage: Alaska Northwest Publishing Co., 1976.

Wolfe, Art, and Art Davidson. *Alakshak: The Great Country*. San Francisco: Sierra Club Books, 1989.

PERIODICALS

These are just a few of the periodicals that frequently contain articles about Alaska and general information on wilderness travel.

Alaska. 808 E St., Suite 200, Anchorage, AK 99501 (monthly)

Alaska Geographic. The Alaska Geographic Society, Box 93370, Anchorage, AK 99509 (quarterly)

Backpacker. 33 E. Minor St., Emmaus, PA 18090 (bimonthly)

Canoe. P.O. Box 3146, Kirkland, WA 98083 (bimonthly)

Outside. 1165 North Clark St., Chicago, IL 60610 (monthly)

Sea Kayaker. 1670 Duranleau St., Vancouver, BC V6H 3S4, Canada (quarterly)

Sierra. The Sierra Club, 730 Polk St., San Francisco, CA 94109 (bimonthly)

Wilderness. The Wilderness Society, 1400 Eye St., N.W., Washington, D.C. 20005 (quarterly)